Dostoevsky's Conception Of Man:
Its Impact on Philosophical Anthropology

by

Peter Mcguire Wolf

ISBN: 1-58112-006-0

DISSERTATION.COM

1997

BLANK

The Pennsylvania State University

The Graduate School

Special Individualized Interdisciplinary Doctoral Majors

DOSTOEVSKY'S CONCEPTION OF MAN:
ITS IMPACT ON PHILOSOPHICAL ANTHROPOLOGY

A Thesis in

Literature and Philosophy

by

Peter McGuire Wolf

Submitted in Partial Fulfillment
of the Requirements
for the Degree of

Doctor of Philosophy

August 1997

We approve the thesis of Peter McGuire Wolf.

Date of Signature

Joseph J. Kockelmans Distinguished Professor Emeritus of Philosophy Director, Special Individualized Interdisciplinary Doctoral Majors Thesis Adviser Chair of Committee	4/23/97
Linda J. Ivanits Associate Professor of Russian and Comparative Literature	5/2/97
Thomas O. Beebee Associate Professor of Comparative Literature and German	5/2/97
Monique Yaari Associate Professor of French	May 6, 1997

ABSTRACT

Dostoevsky's novels have contributed to a conception of man that reverberates in the conclusions of prominent twentieth-century philosophical anthropologists. Max Scheler, Martin Heidegger, Jean-Paul Sartre, Maurice Merleau-Ponty, and Albert Camus, among others, have explicitly admitted that the works of Dostoevsky had a certain influence on the manner in which they learned to conceive of the nature of man and the world in which humans live. The aim in this dissertation is to ask: what is there in the novels of Dostoevsky concerning the nature of man, of which certain philosophers could claim that in their philosophical conceptions of man they were positively influenced by him?

The main thesis is substantiated in a careful analysis of four novels by Dostoevsky: _Notes from the House of the Dead_ [_Zapiski iz mertvogo doma_], _Notes from the Underground_ [_Zapiski iz podpol'ia_], _Crime and Punishment_ [_Prestuplenie i nakazanie_], and _The Brothers Karamazov_ [_Brat'ia Karamazovy_]. These novels were chosen partly because a study of Dostoevsky's entire _oeuvre_ lies far outside the domain that can be covered in a doctoral dissertation. Moreover, I have come to the conclusion that these novels, more than others, concretely show in what sense the leading characters appear to have made themselves be what they had freely chosen to be under the circumstances in which they had to live, and that they were fully aware of the responsibility they had to bear for the implications and consequences of what they had thus decided. Based upon a close reading, four interpretive chapters employ the most significant literary criticism from English, Russian, and French scholarship.

Dostoevsky's philosophical conception of man is compared and contrasted with the conception that Scheler and Heidegger hold, i.e., that freedom is man's essence. Sartre's atheistic humanism and Camus' thoughtful interpretation of man are likewise considered.

Chapter one contains three sections: section one presents a historical survey of the philosophical positions taken on the nature of man. Section two addresses the question: What can an artwork teach us concerning the philosophical conception of man? A provisional conclusion establishes that artworks are indeed capable of providing insights concerning the truth of man. Chapter one concludes with a survey of the literature addressing some of the critical responses which have focused on the (usually) implicit philosophical conception of man in the works of Dostoevsky. This survey indicates that a philosophy of man is present in Dostoevsky's literary work.

Specific investigation reveals several observations that confirm Dostoevsky's image of man:

1) The first observation concerns man and his freedom which is not to be understood in connection with choice; rather freedom is constitutive for the essence of man. Dostoevsky depicts how his central characters go about achieving their humanity and reveals the consequences of their choices. Raskolnikov, for example, attempts to surpass his humanity with his "Napoleonic Idea." As though in negative relief, the portrayal of man attempting to surpass his humanity (Raskolnikov, Ivan Karamazov, Orlov) sketches just how fundamental is this link between man and his freedom. Likewise, the attempt to shirk one's humanity as with the Underground Man only serves to highlight the thesis

that freedom is constitutive for the being of man. Hence, man must achieve his own humanity.

2) The second observation concerns the centrality of crime in Dostoevsky's work and its relation to freedom. Dostoevsky's depiction of the "dead House" of a Siberian prison provides a "philosophy of crime" and an understanding of how freedom is vital to the criminal. The prison is a threshold where human unfreedom is highlighted in order to better "show" man. Likewise, the crisis situation such as the criminal act depicts the moment where man splits from his freedom, and is a threshold which reveals man's primary relation to freedom. Ivanov has commented on how central murder is to the later novels. Dostoevsky strategically exploits these episodes in order to better show off the problem of human freedom. Man's freedom implies a resolve to be authentic as well as a resolve to be unauthentic; the latter is a necessary condition of all evil in men. Man becomes the greatest threat to his own freedom, both individually, and collectively. The former is illustrated in the Underground Man and his self-defeating rhetoric. The latter is made clear in Ivan Karamazov's dystopic "poema." The Grand Inquisitor makes all too clear how willing humanity is to sell-out on its most precious asset, i.e., the freedom to be human and the possibility to actualize and make concrete the kind of humanity one chooses.

3) As _Crime_ makes clear, man suffers his freedom. Whether victim or criminal, man is accountable not only for his action

but his being. A close reading of the text reveals how Raskolnikov's crime cannot be disengaged from his literary presentation. He is a "criminal hero." Of all the novels, _Dead House_ best paints a tableau of the hellish prison walls which indicate to the prisoner that the problem of freedom is inescapable. That freedom and the consciousness of freedom are a source of suffering as real as any physical pain the Underground Man makes clear. Imprisoned by acute consciousness, the Underground Man reveals through a number of metaphors that the "antheap," "desiring according to tables," and the "Crystal Palace" are promises of happiness to be won with the cessation of human suffering at the cost of human freedom. Finally, the manner in which Ivan Karamazov suffers his freedom is poetically integrated into his rebellion against the creation where children must suffer. His _poema_, the "Legend of the Grand Inquisitor, crystallizes the realization that human suffering has dimensions which exceed the terrestrial.

4) A final observation: Dostoevsky does not attempt to shirk the consequences of human freedom nor to reason them away. The result of portraying man's freedom in this manner is that human freedom constitutes the ground of evil and the denial of God. The consequence of real freedom is real evil and apostasy. Dostoevsky was aware of this and yet, he did not seek to avoid the problem of human evil. He defends man's freedom in a total manner. Dostoevsky's thought concerning man and his freedom is "totalistic." It constitutes a radical approach. Ivan Karamazov, Raskolnikov, the Underground Man, and a "terrible monster" such as Orlov present all-encompassing pictures of man.

For example, the Underground Man remarks that man must hew a road wherever it may lead. There is no fixed purpose for human existence, and like the prisoners in the Dead House who toil breaking up old boats and pounding alabaster on the banks of the Irtysh, man must create his own meaning. This is a consequence of total freedom. Man cannot look outside himself to find a "boss" to allocate him meaningful projects. Such presentation of total freedom is made possible by the artistic description of a world without God. Moreover, the "artistic system" allows this total picture of human freedom which the medium of philosophy and the sciences cannot render.

Dostoevsky's works do not force one view of human freedom to be taken over the other. He provides no definitive image of man. The presentation of freedom in this manner is a defense of man, a speaking on behalf of man against dissolution into the rhetoric that theology and science bring. It is worth observing that Dostoevsky wrote these novels at a time when the "sciences of man" were beginning to emerge. His artwork defends man against a dissolution into the acid bath of psychology, sociology, and economy, all of which sought to account for man's being in terms of their own rhetoric.

Jean-Paul Sartre has written that existentialism begins with Ivan Karamazov's "all is permitted." While it is true that this conception of maximal freedom is distinctive to the existentialist conception of man, Sartre's saying does not comprehend the full extent of Dostoevsky's saying about man. The following conclusions are consonant with Dostoevsky's work: that freedom is constitutive for the being (or the mode of being; essence) of man; that his freedom is an inalienable duty; that one must become oneself; that man strives not only to overcome himself and to exceed his freedom, but in so doing invariably loses his freedom; and that man can exceed himself only in the sense that he realizes an ideal human possibility. This is the revelation of Zosima. In order to overcome himself, man must surrender in humility before men. The Dostoevskian man reveals not only the absence of human nature but also the enormous power which man possesses for achieving his ideal human possibility. To a certain extent, interpreters have overlooked these ideas while emphasizing certain others. These revelations about man are not particular and detailed but are the essential, underlying ideas which will prevail upon any philosophical anthropologist who would attempt to think about man in a foundational way. It is for this reason that Dostoevsky's works will continue to make a significant contribution to any thoughtful discussion about man and his freedom.

ACKNOWLEDGMENTS

I dedicate this work to two "heroes of my time": Joseph Kockelmans and George Dolnikowski. Without these mentors, my life would be sorely impoverished.

I acknowledge the intellectual input of my philosophy instructors in Leuven, Belgium, whose ideas still guide me and in particular, Jos DeCorte, Jan Van der Veken, Rudolph Bernet. Pierre Kerzsberg's brilliant course on Schelling inspired me to see the links with Dostoevsky and German Idealism. Alexander Bulanov introduced me to important Dostoevsky literature in Volgograd and put me in contact with Dostoevsky scholars in St. Petersburg, Russia, in the Summer of 1993.

Linda Ivanits taught me how to read Russian texts and introduced me to the most prominent Dostoevsky literature. She was also an unflagging adviser on my Dostoevsky chapters. Monique Yaari, in addition to being on my committee, introduced me to a study of André Gide and the French humanists. She encouraged me in my study of Sartre and Camus. Thomas Beebee taught me respect for the mystery of literary translation in perhaps the finest seminar I have participated in during the Spring of 1994. Monique Oyallon enriched me through our discussions of Dostoevsky and Stavrogin. Monsignor Philip Saylor has earned my respect not only for his pastoral care, but also for his diligent reading of early drafts of my dissertation.

Heidi Marx contributed to my idea building through discussion and fellowship. Zhenya Cherkasova and Ilya deserve thanks for many late night discussions about Dostoevsky, Heidegger and Russia.

A very special thanks is due to Shirley Rader whose enthusiasm for typing and editing this dissertation aided me in the successful completion of my work.

My gratitude and love for my parents, Herbert and Nancy Wolf, is total.

Finally, I would like to thank my very best friends, the Faulds family for treating me so well. David Faulds has taught me the true sense of friendship and Kim and Natalie have given me a vision of life that is pure and strong.

TABLE OF CONTENTS

NOTE ON TRANSLITERATION

The Library of Congress system of transliteration will be used in the bibliography, footnotes, and bracketed material within the text. A modified Library of Congress system will be used for the text, and accordingly, names ending in "ii" will show the "y" ending (i.e., Dostoevsky rather than Dostoevskii); and soft-sign markers in names are dropped (hence Raskolnikov, rather than Raskol'nikov).

INTRODUCTION

There is a conception of man and human freedom in Dostoevsky's work which has had a central influence on twentieth-century philosophical anthropology. Friedrich Nietzsche, Max Scheler, Martin Heidegger, Jean-Paul Sartre, Maurice Merleau-Ponty, and Albert Camus, among others, have explicitly admitted that the works of Dostoevsky had a certain influence on the manner in which they learned to conceive of the nature of man and the world in which humans live. Our aim in this dissertation is to ask: what is there in the novels of Dostoevsky concerning the nature of man, of which certain philosophers could claim that in their philosophical conceptions of man they were positively influenced by him?

We shall try to substantiate our main thesis by turning to a careful analysis of four novels by Dostoevsky: _Notes From the House of the Dead_ [_Zapiski iz mertvogo doma_], _Notes From the Underground_ [_Zapiski iz podpol'ia_], _Crime and Punishment_ [_Prestuplenie i nakazanie_], and _The Brothers Karamazov_ [_Brat'ia Karamazovy_]. These novels were chosen partly because a careful study of Dostoevsky's entire _oeuvre_ lies far outside the domain that can be covered in a doctoral dissertation. Moreover, I have come to the conclusion that these novels, more than others, concretely show in what sense the leading characters appear to have made themselves be what they had freely chosen to be under the circumstances in which they had to live, and that they were fully aware of the responsibility they had to bear for the implications and consequences of what they had thus decided. Before turning to the Dostoevsky novels, and their conception of the free human, we must address the questions: What do we mean by philosophical anthropology? and, what can a philosopher learn from an artwork?

CHAPTER 1

ARTWORKS AND THE PHILOSOPHY OF MAN

The following chapter is composed of three sections. In section one, I will explain that the concern for the essence of man has always been and remains a fundamental part of every philosophy. The view that human freedom is constitutive of the essence of man is emphasized by many thinkers, but in a very distinctive way in the philosophical work of Scheler, Heidegger, Merleau-Ponty, and in that of many other phenomenologists and "existentialists."

Section two concerns the relationship between literature and philosophy in their quest for truth. To what extent can artworks be said to contribute to the manifestation of truth? The approach of hermeneutic-phenomenology which considers the ontological perspective on the artwork guides this inquiry. In section three, "A Survey of Some Philosophical Issues Raised by Dostoevsky's Literary Work," I hope to explain that Dostoevsky's work has actually influenced leading philosophers of the late nineteenth and early twentieth centuries, particularly with respect to their conceptions of man.

<u>Notes on Philosophical Anthropology</u>

The term "anthropology" arose in the eighteenth century, while the expression "philosophical anthropology" is most likely a twentieth-century creation. However, the philosophical inquiry which seeks after the essential meaning of being human is as old as philosophy. Even though every major philosopher has questioned the essential significance of man, the subject matter was not thematized as a philosophical discipline until the 1920s.[1]

In the pages that follow I shall remind the reader of the most salient points in the history of the philosophy of man, with the aim of locating Dostoevsky's thoughts about man within this large tradition and of showing its importance and creative novelty within this rich philosophical heritage.

Antiquity

Philosophy from the very start has been concerned with questions about the essence of man, about what it means to be human, about man's place in the cosmos, about his leading prerogatives, his freedom, his dignity, and his destiny. This concern is obvious in the philosophies of the pre-Socratics, Plato, and Aristotle. It is equally manifest in the philosophies of Augustine and many other medieval philosophers.

In antiquity man was always seen as having a privileged part in the cosmos as a link with the divine. Greek religion at this time centered upon a mythic cosmology and ritual enactment of sacred mysteries. A well-ordered priestcraft attended to a number of temples and altars devoted to a number of gods. Oracular interpretation such as Sophocles and Plato described gave man a medium through which to interpret sacred will. Philosophy grew up alongside the Greek religion, and through the use of reasoned argument provided an alternative or complementary naturalistic account or "*logos*" into the "*phusis*" or nature of things. The origin of philosophy in ancient Greece highlights a conviction that the world is well-ordered [*kosmios kosmos*] and that such order is knowable by humans. Man's place in the cosmos is that he is the being capable of making meaningful statements concerning the order of the cosmos, and for giving, likewise, an honest account [ho logos] of his life. The essential Greek insight amounts to the wonder of wonders that man can say truthful things about the world and his place in it.

The Western philosophical tradition takes as its birthplace the Greek region known as Ionia, what is now the Mediterranean coast of Turkey with the sixth century B.C. as its birthdate. It finds its written origin in the fragments of the Pre-Socratics of the Ionian School, which included Thales (c. 624-546 B.C.), Heraclitus (c. 540-475 B.C.), and Parmenides (c. 530-544 B.C.). At the center of Pre-Socratic inquiry was the attempt to articulate a unified discourse concerning the underlying principle of "all that is." There was an attempt to find an underlying ground to account for all that manifests itself as nature.

From speculation concerning the intelligible ground of nature, philosophers turned their inquiry toward the nature of man.[2] From its origin in the fragments of the Pre-Socratics to its culmination in the teaching of Socrates which was recorded by Plato and corrected and refined by Aristotle, the origin of Western philosophy thematizes man's quest for understanding his place in the cosmos. In the Western Tradition which notes its inauguration in the ancient Greek desire for truth, the meaning of being human is given a concrete definition as zooion logon echon: a living thing that has reason, or a living thing that has language. It is an animal that thinks and speaks.

Socratic humanism as it is borne out in the Platonic dialogues places philosophy or dialectic at the center of the human inquiry. The dialectic provided Socrates (470-399 B.C.) with a means of weeding-out mere conjecture and opinion [doxa] from a true account of a state of affairs [logos]. In contraposition to the Sophists, Socrates' teaching was not dogmatic, but an open-ended and ironic quest for the truth concerning man's place in the cosmos and his function as a moral agent. In his ethics he held the conviction that no man can do wrong willingly (knowingly). This is the doctrine known as "ethical rationalism." Socratic humanism places a premium upon education and honesty and introduces a basically optimistic view of man's potential for truth.

Socrates' disciple, Plato (427-347 B.C.), advanced the teachings of his master into a more systematic and global account of the universe. Plato introduces a psychology or doctrine concerning the human soul which relies upon a theory of reincarnation. The human being is for Plato a body and a soul. In The Phaedrus, Plato accounts for the soul's origin, its tripartite function, and its potential for illumination and ascent to divinity.

Plato's philosophical consideration of man advances Socrates' humanism and at the same time refines a theory of education whereby man optimizes his potential for divine intelligence. In Plato, man's happiness is connected with the divine Good.

In Aristotle, the human being may be approached in several ways, in philosophy of nature, in "psychology," and above all in ethics and political philosophy. In The Nichomachean Ethics, Aristotle systematically explores the potential virtue of man's actions and possibility of finding the middle (mean) between two extremes of human moral disposition. Human happiness is directly connected with a transcendent God. He mentions "ho theos," God, and not the divine order nor the gods. His treatise on human psychology entitled De Anima greatly influenced ensuing thinkers who sought to understand the human mind. With regard to man's physical body, Aristotle reasoned that its functioning is much like that of other animals, apart from the function of its reason. Man is again defined as an animal that thinks [zoon ekhein logon]. Aristotle's Politics treats man as a social animal. Aristotle's contributions to the understanding of man's ethical, psychological, biological, and political character undergird the approach that thinking takes toward man in the ensuing millennia in the West.

The Christian Era

Three primordial streams flow into the understanding of man from classical antiquity. As seen above, there is the Greek Miracle or the birth of philosophy, which puts forward the conception of man as a being capable of speaking of the truth of his being in the cosmos which Socrates exemplified. The second stream is the Roman conception of the "civis" or citizen as subject to the laws and legislation of the all-powerful Roman Empire. Finally, there is the influence of the ancient stream of near-eastern Judaism brought into contact with the West through the teaching of the early Christian church. This Judaeo-Christian thought conceives of the human as a person, created from dust and the inspiration of an all-knowing and all-loving Father-God who created the world ex nihilo. As such the Western tradition is to a great measure the result of the influence of these three ancient streams. Its conception of being human continues to exert a power over Western man.

In the middle ages there were two fundamental approaches to the philosophical comprehension of man which derived from antiquity: the rational-naturalistic approach of Socrates, Plato and Aristotle, and the illuminative approach of Augustine. Most anthropologies written between the fourth century A.D. and the fourteenth century emphasize, to a greater or lesser extent, either a "rational" account of man's place in the universe, or an "illuminative" approach. The illuminative approach was derived from a mystical Neoplatonic element that infused Platonic metaphysical terminology into the writings of Christian theologians. Augustine (354-430) incorporated insights derived from the Neoplatonist, Plotinus (205-270), in order to account for the triune Godhead [*trinitas*] and its life in man [*vestigium trinitatis*].

Augustine inaugurates a "modern" way of knowing (anticipating Descartes' "*cogito, ergo sum*") that is primordially anthropological.[3] The human being comes to understand the truth of objects in the world in a manner that is analogous to seeing objects in the world. Man possesses intellectual sight.[4] In order to account for the manner in which a fallible mind lays hold of immutable truth, Augustine refers to a process of illumination. The illumination theory resembles Plato's theory of reminiscence [*anamnesis*]; however, Augustine no longer depends upon a theory of the soul's reincarnation in order to provide a basis for what it understands as truth. Corporeal objects come to be seen in the light which shines from the sun. The light of the sun makes possible the perception of for example a tree. There are forms, idea, reasons and rules which allow knowledge of external objects to be recognized as true. Like the light of the sun, these rules are never seen in themselves. They are not innate in the soul, and are not perceived through sense perception. "They are "irradiated into" the soul, "participated" by created beings, and "illuminated" for the mind's perception by a divine light."[5]

As a Father of the Church, Augustine's thinking operated within the center of revealed truth and theology. Even so, in many ways he was a precursor of modern philosophy.[6] He defined man as the image of God, hence indicating that man points to God for his completion and truth. God is a great magnetic center in which all truth coheres. In a contrary manner, that which seeks to move away from God, loses its truth and its being. The human will which aligns itself with God's will participates in moral goodness; on the other hand, moral evil is a privation of what an act ought to be. The movement toward true freedom is a movement toward God, and any freedom that does not move toward God is a "false" freedom. All of these applications stem from Augustine's metaphysical conception of evil as a privation of being.

In the Christian era man has always been seen as the center of God's creation. This is clear in Augustine and in anyone influenced by him. Man is also conceived as consisting of a material body which is mortal, and an immortal soul that is destined to be united with God in a life to come. An example of a Christian philosopher influenced by Augustine is Thomas Aquinas (1225-1274). Although he emphasizes Aristotle's rational- naturalistic account, Aquinas' philosophical account of man also bears an Augustinian stamp. Man is a creature, but also a creature in the image of God. The rational approach goes a long way in accounting for man as a creature of nature, but faith also seeks an account of man's specific relation to God.

The Renaissance

Two or three monumental historical events commence the modern age: Christopher Columbus' discovery of the New World in 1492; the protestant reformation spearheaded by Martin Luther; and the proliferation of the Faust Legend. These events led to a new way of conceiving man and his place on earth. The articulation of this new way of seeing things is central to the thinking of the Renaissance. During the Renaissance a renewed interest in man's place in the cosmos placed reflection on man at a premium. For example, in the Florentine Academy, an Italian humanist, Pico della Mirandola (1463-1494) attempted to return to the Greek thinking about man in an attempt to harmonize the thought of Plato and Aristotle. Man's place in the world is a "microcosmos" combining three spheres: immaterial angels; incorruptible heavenly bodies; and corruptible earthly bodies. Man is unfinished, and thus free to complete himself: "Other creatures were completed by God, but he left human beings incomplete and instead lent us a part of his own creative power. With it we complete ourselves."[7] God has granted to man a degree of freedom such that man is capable of choosing a degree of life from the lowest unto the highest. In his treatise On the Dignity of Man [Oratio de Hominis Dignitatis], Pico relates the words that God spoke in creating man:

> We have given to thee, Adam, no fixed seat, no form of thy very own, no gift particularly thine, that thou mayest feel as thine own, have as thine own, possess as thine own the seat, the form, the gifts which thou thyself shalt desire.[8]

Man's dignity consists in his nature being open and free. Man is capable of being that which he chooses to be. Further, since man is the center of the universe, he unites the cosmos with his knowledge.

Pico's man-centered view of the cosmos did not prevail. War, famine, pestilence intervened to show man's darker side. Within a century, skepticism concerning man's higher nature emerged. Michel de Montaigne (1533-1592) lived nearly one century after Pico. He wrote Les Essais at the end of the French Renaissance period. Lacking in his work is the optimism of the Italian humanist. Man is prone to error in knowledge, and the very possibility of certainty is repugnant to Montaigne: "Il n'y a que les fous qui aient imperturbablement des certitudes ('De l'institution des enfants')." The very title of his work Les Essais suggests that he is attempting to test and try knowledge rather than to definitively state it. Montaigne's preface indicates that the subject matter of his inquiry is himself, but himself as an inconstant, fluctuating being, prone to error.

The Modern Era

In the modern era most thinkers were still believing Christians; yet as philosophers they attempted to account for reality in terms of reason. The basic conceptions concerning man's freedom, his material body and his soul were framed in such a way that they were maintained on the basis of reason alone. The consequence of this way of thinking was a stress on the method of obtaining an unshakeable starting point with which to secure one's rational certainty. In the seventeenth century the origin of a "modern" conception of man commences with the Rationalists (Descartes, Pascal, Spinoza, Leibniz, and Wolff on the continent), and in particular with the philosophy of René Descartes (1596-1650). In contrast to Montaigne, the Cartesian philosophy begins with a quest for absolute, mathematical certainty. The French philosopher believed that if he could establish an indubitable method for establishing knowledge he might arrive at the universal "mathesis" which underlies all that can be known in the universe. The idea of man's existence as a "thinking thing" provides Descartes with the indubitable starting point for certain knowledge. His philosophy is entirely anthropocentric, as it begins with innate ideas in man's reason [ego cogito] as the foundation for deductions concerning God and the world. Descartes' conception of human being is that man is composed of two independent substances: mind (or soul); and body. The human being is on the one hand, a "thinking thing" and on the other hand a material body that can be conceived of as a very sophisticated machine.

At the beginning of his Ethics, Spinoza (1632-1677) advanced the idea of an infinite Substance that is the cause of itself [causa sui] which can also be called God. Spinoza introduces a pantheistic system of thought wherein the world is interpreted either as nature or as God [Deus sive Natura] depending upon the perspective taken. Accordingly, man too, is substantially indistinguishable in essence from God. Spinoza's philosophical conception of Substance is so all-encompassing that man cannot appear with his own unique, finite essence.[9]

After Descartes and Spinoza, the third continental "Rationalist" is Gottfried Wilhelm Leibniz (1646-1716). Underlying his thought is the idea of "universal harmony," an idea which figures centrally in The Theodicy: Essays on the Goodness of God, the Freedom of Man and the Origin of Evil, a work which attempts to account for apparent evil in God's harmonious universe. The central problem which faced Leibniz was how to account for evil and suffering in the world that God has made. Leibniz accounted for the pre-established harmony and rationality of the universe and man's place in his work entitled, The Monadology. The "monad" is a force-substance which underlies all that is. It is not a physical entity, but is metaphysical having no parts, extension, nor figure:

> In order to bring an infinite number of monads together in an overarching unity, Leibniz concludes, as did Spinoza, that the whole universe is in every part, and every part is in the whole universe, or, in terms of monads, the whole universe is in every monad, and every monad is in the whole universe.[10]

With his "monadology," Leibniz arrived at a thoroughly rational account of the universe. Like Spinoza, he was unable to avoid pantheism, and as a result man's place in the world could no longer be strictly distinguished from God.

In the middle of the eighteenth century at the spearhead of the French Enlightenment one finds _L'Encyclopédie_ co-edited by Denis Diderot and Jean d'Alembert. This project was not intended as subversion of ancient ways of thinking but rather a reordering of human knowledge. Robert Wernick writes: "They never pretended to have invented the new way of thinking, they were only systematizing it, publicizing it, letting it loose to spread its rays of enlightenment and disperse the clouds of ancient superstition."[11] To consult the very prominent Tree of Knowledge at the frontispiece of volume one is to find a systematic topography of human understanding. In this diagram _science de Dieu_ (theology), _science de l'homme_ (human science), and _science de la nature_ (natural science) are clearly subordinated to reason. This ordering of knowledge indirectly resulted in a heretical conclusion. Robert Darnton writes, "The premises sounded pious, but the conclusions smacked of heresy because it seemed to subordinate theology to reason. . . ."[12] The Encyclopedists or '_les philosophes_' initiated a way of seeing human knowledge which in turn redefined the objects of this knowledge. By classifying and ordering knowledge in such a manner that scientific, self-evidence assumed priority over revealed truths, the knowledge of human science found itself upon the same platform as the science of God. This does not mean that Diderot was an atheist, but it highlights the fact that a "science of man" is central to the work of the Enlightenment. Philosophy inaugurates a description of the human being in a novel position with regard to God.

Another modern contribution to man's self-understanding was advanced by the Scotsman, David Hume (1711-1776), in his work, A Treatise of Human Nature (1739-1740). Hume ". . . tried to make his study of man as empirical as possible, and so labelled his 'philosophy' of man a 'science' of man . . . ."[13] In direct contradiction to Descartes, Spinoza, and Leibniz, he advanced the idea that perception underlies any and all human knowledge. The epistemology which relies exclusively upon perception furnishes the central dogma of Empiricism. The Empiricist school flourished in Great Britain and Scotland during the seventeenth and eighteenth centuries under the influence of Hobbes, Locke, Berkeley, and Hume.

Both Cartesian Rationalism and Humean Empiricism reached an impasse for human thinking. Rationalism inescapably emerged into a doctrine of pantheism, since man, God and universe are essentially and ultimately indistinguishable. On the other hand, Empiricism, while attempting to combat the results of Rationalist philosophy, fell into the impasse of total skepticism. In particular, Hume's opus, Philosophical Essays Concerning Human Understanding (1748), resulted in a doctrine of skepticism which undermines any human attempt to establish certain knowledge.

Hume's doctrine rejects the possibility of the mind possessing any ideas which do not first originate in sensate impression. The existence of the "self" is highly dubitable since it is never perceived as a sensate impression:

> When I turn my reflection on myself, I never can perceive this self without some one or more perceptions; nor can I ever perceive anything but the perceptions. 'Tis the

> composition of these, therefore, which forms the self [italics in original].[14]

Personal identity for the Scottish empiricist is a "feeling" which accompanies the connection or coupling together of discrete sensate impressions.

Hume convincingly showed that the effort to secure an account for what-is in terms of reason is futile and doomed to skepticism. This skepticism alarmed Immanuel Kant (1724-1804), who attempted to salvage a possibility for human knowing in the face of empiricist skepticism. His philosophy is best understood as an effort to overcome this skepticism. In so doing he had to relegate God and soul to the status of transcendental ideas which refer to entities we can think but never understand. This was the principal task of his first critique, The Critique of Pure Reason (1781). In his three critiques Kant carried through the revolution inherent in the emergent modern conception of the human being which Descartes had commenced. The first work was followed by a critical approach to ethics which establishes that the ultimate good is that good which the human being wills. The third and final critique, The Critique of Judgement (1790), establishes a framework for the interpretation of beauty and human judgement. It is the crowning achievement of Kant's critical philosophy and is foundational to the thinking of German Idealism.

Concerning human education, Kant was essentially optimistic. The employment of discipline would help to perfect the human being. He contrasted the animal instinct with the human lack of instinct in order to indicate the necessary role of reason in human life:

> Animals are by their instinct all that they ever can be; some other reason has provided everything for them at the outset. But man needs a reason of his own. Having no instinct, he has to work out a plan of conduct for himself. Since, however, he is not able to do this all at

> once, but comes into the world undeveloped, others have to do it for him.[15]

Reason fulfills man whose lack of instinct leaves him helpless before nature without education: "Man can only become man by education. He is merely what education makes of him."[16] Man requires culture to fulfill himself; through the upbuilding of education man might improve.

German Idealism

In German Idealism one sees an effort to think man in God. Man has an essential place in the process in which the Absolute achieves full possession of itself in Absolute Knowledge. This raises the question of how man in such a framework could be free and how evil came to be. This problematic became the central preoccupation of Friedrich Schelling (1775-1854).

In German Idealism the concern for man came to the fore again in great force in the works of G. W. F. Hegel (1770-1831) and Schelling. Hegel's *Phenomenology of Mind* established a philosophical idealism which articulated a vision of an underlying rational unity in lieu of the universal dichotomy Kant's philosophy had established:

> For Hegel, the difficulty with Kant was the cul-de-sac in knowledge caused by so overloading the subject side of the subject-object relationship that there was no obvious vehicle for reaching the object.[17]

Hegel's thought moves in the other direction--seeing that the objects taken as appearances are in essence the "making known" of the Spirit. Man appears in Hegel's Absolute Idealism as a finite manifestation of Spirit, or the Spirit becoming conscious of itself in merely finite modes.

Schelling carried the doctrine of Idealism to the question concerning the essence of human freedom. He fell heir to a set of problems concerning freedom and the human capacity to choose evil as opposed to a system of mechanical necessity wherein human freedom is an epiphenomenon either of the natural order or of God (pantheism). If God is in all and all is in God, then it becomes increasingly difficult to account for the presence of evil in the world and for the human capacity to choose evil over good. Human culpability emerged as the central concern of philosophical anthropology at the same time the theodicy failed to account for the problem of evil in a world created by an omniscient and benevolent deity. The emergence of philosophy of man as a specific discipline coincided with the lapse of theodicy as a branch of natural theology. The problem of the contradiction inherent in God's omnipotence in the face of real evil and human suffering transmuted into a philosophical concern for man as man, as a free being enmeshed in evil in a primordial way. But more, what is at stake is the nature of human choice, the philosophy of freedom.

Schelling maintained that the artist as genius is the revelation concerning the ground where freedom and nature are united. Schelling writes of the power of art in contrast to philosophy to reveal man:

> Philosophy attains, indeed, to the highest, but it brings to this summit only, so to say, the fraction of a man. Art brings <u>the whole man</u>, as he is, to that point, namely to a knowledge of the highest, and this is what underlies the eternal difference and the marvel of art.[18]

Art is for Schelling the "universal organ" of philosophy, and has the potential to manifest truth. German Idealists established man as potentially divine where the divinity of man is announced in artworks of genius.

It fell to Schelling not only to account for evil in an Idealist Philosophy, but at the same time to work out a place for human freedom in the fall-out of Kant's Critical Philosophy. Hegel's philosophy laid such a strong emphasis upon the inevitable self-becoming of the Absolute that ". . . the transmutation of God into the world must again become a problem."[19] This is essentially a theological problem. Schelling attempts to account for this by the method of theosophy, a mystico-speculative doctrine. The _Treatise on the Essence of Human Freedom_ (1809) is a systematic attempt to justify personal free will for good and evil in a world created by God, and to account for the finite world as independent from absoluteness. Material things possess a metaphysical independence from God. This accounts for the human capacity to freely choose evil.

Schelling announces a system of freedom which offers a positive philosophy of the absolute. His system takes into account the negativity which was the fall-out of Kant's Copernican Revolution and, at the same time, puts forth a discourse of the absolute. Schelling retrieves the absolute, but in the aspect of its decomposition or "fallenness." He maintains that a more primordial fall grounds man's fall into sinfulness. This discourse is the only possible discourse concerning the absolute which can account for the ground of fallenness and the proneness of human beings to sin. Schelling's system of freedom takes the _via negativa_ by accentuating nihilism to account for human freedom. "The survey of total negativity offers the only positive possibility for apprehending the Absolute seen in its fallenness."[20]

As such, Schelling's system of freedom inaugurates a "philosophical religion" which accounts for human redemption metaphysically by establishing a discourse of the fall of the absolute. Such is the saving task that the philosophy of man bears. Be that as it may, it is worth noting that Schelling's work

challenges the practical result of the fall-out of the Critical Philosophy that funnels religion into the limits of reason alone. One must ask whether Schelling's "religion" is yet within the limits of reason alone. On the other hand, Schelling's treatise is somehow a working-out of the latent potential of the unthought in Kant's transcendental philosophy.

The Nineteenth Century

The philosophy of the nineteenth century announces a confidence in progress, inherited in part from the project of the Enlightenment. This progress is understood in scientific (positivism, scientism) and social terms (socialist, communist and utopian blueprints of revolution and an ideal society). The conception of man insofar as he is conceived socially and scientifically is optimistic. However, in contraposition to German Idealism, and in particular opposition to the absolute idealism of Hegel, the philosophical conception of man in the nineteenth century is largely characterized by a negative conception of man. A philosophical interpretation of man emerged which negates all that Idealism asserted about man. The attempt is made to think man without God, either making man God or denying God's Being. We find this humanistic atheism in several forms: Marx; Comte; Nietzsche; and Freud, to name a few. To a large extent, the contemporary philosophy of man finds its origin in this negative reaction to Hegel. Two principal streams of thought are worth considering: _existentialism_; and _Marxism_.

Soren Kierkegaard (1813-1855) is the first proponent of an "existential" philosophy. This thinking holds onto man's finitude and limitation in the name of Christianity against the self-divinization of German Idealism. Kierkegaard's philosophical position is a patent negation of Hegel's absolute idealism. His attempt to salvage religion in an idealist framework failed, but later regained influence at the beginning of the twentieth century.

Karl Marx (1818-1883) was significantly influenced by Hegel, but he did not accept Hegel's idealistic conclusions. Marx was influenced by the negative theology of Ludwig Feuerbach, who emphasized a conception of man as a finite, dependent creature who projects an image of God as the antithesis or perfection of all that man is not. The nineteenth-century philosophical interpretation of man is characterized by atheism (i.e., God is a creative projection of man) and by nihilism (i.e., an emphasis on all that man is not, an emphasis on man's limitation and finitude). Feuerbach's negative theology influenced not only Marx, but also Friedrich Nietzsche (1844-1900) and Sigmund Freud (1865-1939). Both Nietzsche and Freud theorized about man, employing this "negative" method. Such an a-theistic and man-centered conception of the cosmos is not entirely new, and bears traces of humanism. The applications of this thinking, however, are novel. If man is not a "creatio Dei" then he is a product of sociological or economical material forces in history. August Comte (1798-1857) sought to apply the insight that man and his beliefs are generated through the control of society in an effort to "engineer" society through entirely rational motives. Similarly, Marx argues that philosophy ought to transform the material and economic determinants of human life in order to facilitate the historical advent of dialectical materialism. In the nineteenth century, man came to be seen as a self-creator, hence inaugurating a fully anthropocentric conception of life.

The conception of man which emerges in the nineteenth century is that human being is an entity that creates itself out of a number of pre-given, materialistic conditions. This being organizes, legislates, and constitutes its own government, establishes its own hierarchy of values, and reviles the past. As man realizes his capacity to create himself as a further development in self-understanding, a technological interpretation of the world and man's place in it sequesters the human being to the periphery of a technic a-cosmos. The world is no longer seen as benevolent or well-ordered, but the capacity for change is amplified.

The Twentieth Century

In the twentieth century one tries to think man from the perspective of man himself. This can take different forms, from nihilistic pessimism (Sartre) to humanism, to an attitude that combines a philosophy of radical finitude with the attitude of religious faith.

A benevolent element in the twentieth-century philosophy of man is the influence of Edmund Husserl (1859-1938). Husserl inaugurates a pure phenomenology which provides thinking with a method for achieving a rigorous foundation. Husserl attempted to give philosophical reflection a revolutionary new beginning. Max Scheler (1874-1928) applied the phenomenological method to the philosophy of man. Scheler gives a phenomenological account of man's place in the cosmos.

Scheler's chief contribution to twentieth-century philosophical anthropology is his notion of ek-static man. Human beings possess consciousness which makes possible that man can take distance from instinctual nature. This possibility of standing apart from nature underlies the ability to consciously apprehend one's place in the cosmos. As such it underlies man's capacity to conceptualize and make objects present to consciousness. The _ekstatic_ character of the human person is man's essential distinction which defines man's place in nature. Furthermore, the ability to take distance from one's instinctive nature for self-preservation constitutes the ground of man's freedom. Scheler indicates these ideas in his treatise, _Die Stellung des Menschen im Kosmos_ (1928).[21] Human freedom makes possible that man is an ek-static being, "outward bound." The objective attitude is the ground of human transcendence. Scheler's philosophical interpretation of man culminates in the concept of the person. The person is at the center of the transcendental capacity to isolate essence from existence. From this foundational power of the human spirit all other human capacities are derived.

Scheler's anthropology, which places a premium on human freedom as man's essential nature, underlies the direction philosophical anthropology takes in the decades following his death in 1928. Certainly Heidegger (1889-1976) concurs with Scheler's conception of man as "outward bound." In France, Scheler's anthropological emphasis upon human freedom is linked with Jean-Paul Sartre (1905-1980). Sartre created his own version of a philosophical doctrine called "existentialism," a school with which many thinkers and writers were correctly or incorrectly identified. To mention a few: Maurice Merleau-Ponty (1908-1961); Albert Camus (1913-1960); Gabriel Marcel (1889-1973); and the Russian emigres, Lev Shestov (1866-1938) and Nikolai Berdiaev (1874-1948) were all affiliated to some degree with a Christian existentialism.

In the twentieth century, the concern for man appears in the works of the great anthropologists Adolf Portman, Max Scheler, and

Nicolai Hartmann (1882-1950). Michael Landmann's Fundamental Anthropology gives an account of the rise of philosophical anthropology as a university discipline in Germany--how it usurped the Lebensphilosophie of Dilthey, the phenomenology of Husserl and Scheler, as well as the existentialism of Karl Jaspers.[22] It is also paramount in the philosophies of Heidegger, Sartre and Camus, and many others, even though the latter may reject a separate philosophical anthropology as a philosophical discipline. Yet, it is clear that in the twentieth century, too, a concern for the essence of man is still central in philosophy and that human freedom is taken to be constitutive of the essence of man.

On Truth in Art and Philosophy

Several twentieth-century philosophers have made the claim that in their philosophical conceptions of man they were deeply influenced by the novels of Dostoevsky. This is true for Heidegger, Sartre, Berdiaev, and Camus. This raises the issue of how and why artists and particularly novels and poems can make an important contribution to the philosophical conception of man.

I rely upon Heidegger's idea that Dichtung (poetizing) is irreducible to Denken (thinking). Hence, philosophy cannot directly apprehend the meaning of an artwork, while art cannot directly present Denken. Even so, the thoughtful interpreter can learn something of value from the artwork. I cite Gadamer's Truth and Method for considerations that apply to interpreting artworks from the perspective of hermeneutic-phenomenology which addresses the ontological character of the artwork.

The Work of Art

Archeological evidence demonstrates that artworks are as old as mankind. Cave paintings in the Dordogne region of France reveal 25,000 year-old depictions of rhinoceros. The first philosophical reflections upon art emphasized "beauty" and this concept was often linked to the following notions: order, harmony, proportion, splendor, and simplicity.

In the fourteenth century in Italy and in the fifteenth and sixteenth centuries in France, artworks gradually began to lose their original meaning and place in the life of the community. The desacralization of art starts to occur in the Renaissance and with the birth of the modern state. A later stage occurs in the eighteenth century when art grows independent of the community, capital and power. It no longer has the same religious (or political didactic, edifying function.[23] For example, artworks both pictorial and musical, went from the church and palace into <u>musea</u>, and concert hall. Although salons and exhibitions existed earlier, the emergence of the museum concurs with Napoleon. Philosophers at this time attempted to understand the importance of artworks in terms of the "experiences" from which they flow and the experiences which they evoke in the spectators. Between Burke and Kant, this was a common conception among rationalists and empiricists. It is still found in most contemporary empiricist and neo-Kantian views. "Experience" here has the sense that Hume and Kant employed and in connection with artwork most often stands for feelings or even emotions.

In Schelling, Hölderlin, and Hegel, this view is given up on the ground that one does not know anything about these so-called feelings except through the works. They saw the true meaning of an artwork in its original contribution to the revelation of the truth of all that is.

In our contemporary world, this view of German Idealism is accepted in principle by most hermeneutic philosophers, notably by Heidegger and Gadamer. Yet instead of speaking of the Absolute or the "whole," hermeneuticists want to respect the limits set upon human reason and, thus, to defend the view that each work of art is important as a work of art to the degree that it reveals something of the truth of what is, i.e., of "Being," the world, or the totality of meaning on the one hand and of man taken as "ek-sisting" on the other.

Hermeneutic-phenomenology defines experience as follows: "Speaking in general terms we could say that experience means the giving of meaning in an encounter with things in the world."[24] Thus, for hermeneuticists Dostoevsky's works are philosophically important works of art to the degree that they make a contribution to the truth concerning world and man. And they do so in two important ways: first of all, the truth they bring concerning man is concretely understood ("experienced") immediately by anyone who understands Dostoevsky's works. Secondly, what is so understood cannot be articulated in any other way except through the work. Thus, there is no substitute for an experience with a work of art. Whatever you say about the meaning of the work of art, the explication can never replace the work.

Many important things have been said by the various sciences that concern themselves with artworks. In the case of dramas and novels one can discuss the plot, the style, the genre, the "psychology" involved, and so on. Yet, the truth which the work presents to the one who has an experience with it cannot be presented in any other way than how it is encountered in the work of art. Concerning the interdependence of the truth of the artwork and its production, Heidegger's view is as follows: "But in contrast to all other produced things, the work is distinguished by being produced in such a way that its having-been-produced becomes an integral part of the work."[25] The how of the artwork is central to its capacity to bear truth. Heidegger is concerned with the "how" of how truth comes-to-pass in the artwork. With the artwork, the "how" of its presentation is equiprimordial with the "what" of the artistic presentation.

The thing-character and work-character of the artwork are modalities of the being of an artwork, two ways of being and being seen. This accords with Heidegger's conception of phenomenology. In discussing the meaning of the concept "phenomenon" in its root meaning of "self-showing" [phainomenon] Heidegger has this to say:

> One speaks of "appearances or symptoms of illness." What is meant by this are occurrences in the body that show themselves and in this self-showing as such "indicate" something that does not show itself. When such occurrences emerge, their self-showing coincides with the objective presence of disturbances that do not show themselves. Appearance, as the appearance "of something," thus precisely does not mean that something shows itself; rather, it means that something makes itself known which does not show itself. It makes itself be known through something that does show itself. Appearing is a not showing itself [italics in original].[26]

The artwork taken as phenomenon, then, shows forth something, but this something is not shown in the appearance. Yet, this does not mean that there is a "hidden meaning" in the artwork. The artwork is like a symptom in that it announces the truth of its "art" through its medium and yet does not coincide with this medium. But neither does art lurk somewhere beyond or behind such a medium, isolated from the artwork. Just as the awareness of illness is inextricably linked with the appearance of its symptoms, so too is the truth of the art linked to its medium of expression. Accordingly, a phenomenological-hermeneutic interpretation treats Dostoevsky's artwork as a concrete way of letting the truth concerning man be seen.

The Ontological Perspective on the Artwork

The experience of artwork is a hermeneutic phenomenon because it centers upon the act of understanding. The understanding of an artwork belongs to the encounter with the work of art itself. The understanding which belongs to the encounter with an artwork can be illuminated only on the basis of the mode of being of the work itself. "All reading that is understanding is always a kind of reproduction and interpretation."[27]

In Truth and Method, Gadamer concerns himself with the ontology of the work of art: "Literature as an art-form can be understood only from the ontology of the work of art, and not from the aesthetic experiences that occur in the course of the reading."[28] According to Gadamer the ontology of the work of art is not to be equated with the aesthetic experiences derived from reading. To understand the work properly it is necessary to identify the "level of the artwork." Further, the literary artwork also bears communion with man's historical being:

> Thus it is by no means the case that world literature is an alienated form of that which constitutes the mode of being of a work according to its original purpose. It is rather the historical mode of being of literature that makes it possible for something to belong to world literature.[29]

Dostoevsky's work does not find its place in world literature by chance. On the contrary, its translation into so many languages, across so many times and places all over the globe is a testimony to its capacity to reveal truth concerning man.

Translation

A thoughtful interpreter or hermeneut engages an artwork in its poetical character. In this way, thinking is brought to bear upon the artwork's unique, inviolable integrity. Thinking does not embrace the artwork, and there always stands a veil between the artwork and its interpretation. The role of going over to the artwork and returning is the role of understanding which is described by the hermeneut. The hermeneutical function is in this sense metaphorical, a _metapherein_. The hermeneut plays the role of the go-between who carries back or translates from an original experience with artworks to a description of the understanding that underlies this opening to the artwork. Such a "crossing-over and returning" is the unique provenance of man, and is irreducible. The integrity of the artwork is not emptied-out in the act of interpretation, and neither is the integrity of thoughtfulness abandoned in the face of the splendor of the artwork. A hermeneut crosses over and brings back something to say concerning the truth that the artwork bestows upon man.

The going-over to artwork originates in the understanding that opens man to artwork. The return to thoughtfulness articulates this understanding into a meaningful re-telling. The hermeneutical translation is first translation. Consequent translations, such as translation into foreign languages or critical commentaries, are fundamentally grounded on the first original translation that understanding performs. The task of the thoughtful hermeneut is to sustain the originality of the first translation and to speak with regard to this while standing before the artwork.

Hermeneutics and Artworks

Dostoevsky's literary works reveal an interpretation concerning the nature of the human being which is novel and which has greatly influenced twentieth-century thinkers. In this dissertation I would like to examine to what degree the works of Dostoevsky contain ideas which would lead philosophers to a relatively new way of looking at the truth concerning world and man. In so doing I shall write from a hermeneutic perspective, i.e., from the perspective initiated and put forward by thinkers such as Heidegger, Merleau-Ponty,[30] Gadamer, Ricoeur[31] and many others. It is not the task of this dissertation to justify or even explain this view in detail. I assume that the reader has some familiarity with these basic ideas. Yet I will very briefly indicate some very important insights that will be essential to understand what follows in the chapters to come. In addition to the hermeneutic conception of man already mentioned, I would like to touch on the following topics: 1) The way in which hermeneutics conceives of truth and moves from a correspondence theory of truth, according to which a claim is true when it states what the state-of-affairs is, to a view in which truth is conceived of as a process, in and through which the meaning of things or events is brought over from a state of concealedness to a state of standing open in the truth (<u>a-letheia</u>); and 2) The relation between thinking and poetizing.

The Essence of Truth

Traditionally, truth has been conceived as a correct correspondence between a human judgement, a proposition, and a factual state-of-affairs in the world. Thomas Aquinas's statement "<u>veritas est adaequatio intellectus et rei</u>" points toward a possibility that a statement is in harmony with what _is_. The possibility of truth for Thomas is the guarantee that God stands behind the world which depends upon Him. Likewise, Descartes' epistemology relies upon the existence of a truthful God in order to establish the possibility of real human knowledge against the metaphysical doubt which "_le malin génie_" ushers in. To sum up, provided that man is not in a state of delusion, truth occurs when man's judgement is in accord with a state-of-affairs in the world. Traditionally, God is the guarantor of the correctness of this correspondence.

If we are to understand the meaning of this conception of truth, we must ask what are the inner conditions that allow such a correspondence between human judgement and the world to be possible. Heidegger pursues this matter in an essay entitled, "On The Essence of Truth."[32] The condition of possibility which allows us to speak meaningfully of a correspondence between human judgements and facts, is that the things referred to are indeed made manifest immediately in an act of seeing; i.e., they must first have been brought from a state of hiddenness into a state of unhiddenness or non-concealment [_a-letheia_]. As will become clear in what follows, this new conception of truth is, in turn, intimately related to a corresponding, new conception of human freedom. Heidegger elaborates a primordial insight concerning the nature of man and freedom which the correspondence theory of truth harbors.

Despite its fidelity to the state-of-affairs, we must realize that the correspondence theory presupposes another question. How did this truth become constituted? By whom and by what process was the truth about "x" brought to light? How was it brought over from being hidden to standing there in front of us "in the open"? Thus the question of what truth is presupposes the answer to another question. The answer to this question is truth as the process of aletheuein, the process through which man brings the hidden to a state of unhiddenness.

This process is not anthropocentric. In this process human beings do not occupy the privileged position because in that process they always must presuppose the totality of meaning articulated by what we call our "world," our "culture," our present "civilization." As finite beings, humans can only bring something from unhiddenness by projecting it upon that "totality of meaning" that we call our "world" which is, in the final analysis, the totality of all conceivable meaning.

Freedom is the ultimate condition of the human ability to project the hidden upon the world and upon being and to let beings be what they are (for us). For the ability to go from "nature" to "culture" is what we call our basic freedom. To be free means not to be locked up in nature but to be allowed to enter civilization and culture. Each human being enters the world of meaning in his or her own way, and one can project what was hidden in more than one way upon the open of the world. In each case one shows concretely what it means to be a human being. For Mary or John it is not determined in advance what to be human concretely will mean; they will determine this and they will be responsible for their basic choices.

Thinking and Poetizing [Dichtung]

Heidegger maintains that man possesses two equiprimordial capacities: thinking and poetizing. Thinking does not exhaust the meaning of an artwork. The form of an artwork is its own means of articulating meaning. The artwork, so to speak, has something to say. For example, Dostoevsky's <u>The Brothers Karamazov</u> "speaks" of, or makes present, a world where a conception of what it means to be a human being appears. Referring to the power of this novel to speak of human freedom is not to suggest that the revelation that the work bears concerning human freedom could be translated into a verbal message. Heidegger calls this irreducible "saying" of the artwork <u>Dichtung</u> or "poetizing." Poetizing is the capacity of an artist in his artwork to present a revelation concerning the world and the self in an original, irreducible articulation.

Poetizing is the essence of all art and has this modality:

> By naming the beings for the first time, language brings them first to word, brings them first to appearance, and lets them be what they are. The naming of language nominates the beings and calls them into their Being from the Being of the beings, i.e., from Being itself.[33]

Poetizing relates to truth in the following way: "Poetizing is the <u>saying</u> of the non-concealment of the beings" [italics mine].[34] Note the use of the word "saying" here such that saying underlies the revelation in pictorial art, in plastic art, in music, and in poetry. The poetizing bestows upon the thinker a new horizon for the interpretation of truth. A philosopher engages in thinking while aiming to articulate an original discourse concerning the truth of man, the world and their correlation. Inasmuch as the artwork through its poetizing opens up a clearing where an original revelation of the world is made present, and insofar as man is drawn into this experience in which an original revelation concerning the self ensues, a horizon unfolds whereby thinking encounters the unifying intuition of truth.

An artwork is truthful in this sense; it opens up a clearing where man might stand in a more original confrontation with himself and the world. As a result of an experience with an artwork, man is changed and his world is changed. Aristotle in his Poetics indicates that a poetic account of the life of a man possesses a more "philosophical" and hence, more truthful, account than does a historical account. He refers to poetry as more philosophical and a higher thing than history, ". . . for poetry tends to express the universal, history the particular."[35] S. H. Butcher comments upon Aristotle's work:

> The first distinguishing mark, then, of poetry is that it has a higher subject-matter than history: it expresses the universal [ta katholou] not the particular [ta kath' ekaston], the permanent possibilities of human nature [hoia an genoito]; it does not merely tell the story of the individual life, "what Alcibiades did or suffered."[36]

Aristotle, in reply to those who would say that poetry is untrue because it is fiction, writes that poetic creations are not real but refer to a higher reality, that is, "what ought to be, not what is."[37]

Hermeneutic Retrieval

In Being and Time (1928), Heidegger advocates that philosophy relate itself to its tradition in an authentic way by a process he calls Wiederholung ("retrieval"). The task of thinking is to lay hold of the unthought-of possibilities in the great philosophical texts of the Western tradition (Heraclitus, Parmenides, Plato, Aristotle, Augustine, Aquinas, Duns Scotus, Descartes, Kant, Hegel, Nietzsche).[38] "Retrieval" is the task of reading these works in such a way that the unthought-of possibility of meaning is brought to light. This is the specific provenance of a hermeneutic interpretation. Such an interpretation is a primordial translation--the translation which manifests the coming-to-meaning of the artwork is primordial or fundamental in the sense that it precedes any linguistic translation or literary interpretation.

The retrieval is twofold in its revelation. Not only does retrieval bring a work to light in its unthought-of possibility for meaning but it also reveals an unthought-of possibility for interpreting man's own essential self-understanding. An interpretation of such works in light of a hermeneutic retrieval is a revelation concerning the essential possibility for being human, an illumination of what it means to be human. This is the task which hermeneutic philosophy sets before thinking as a matter to be thought.

The approach to the artwork that Heidegger suggests makes it eminently clear that the artwork provides for the interpreter a concrete working out of the fundamental philosophical question concerning the being of man and time. Dostoevsky's literary work in particular is a privileged site for an interpretation which seeks a concrete revelation concerning the truth of being human.

Survey of Some Philosophical Issues Raised by Dostoevsky's Literary Work

The significant contribution to philosophical anthropology that Dostoevsky's works have made is testified to by the number of philosophers who have made the claim that in their philosophical conceptions of man they were influenced by the novels of Dostoevsky. In particular Heidegger, Berdiaev, Sartre and Camus testify to this influence.

In the secondary literature (English, Russian, German, and French) there are a number of topics, central to a philosophical conception of man derived from Dostoevsky's literary work which have already been discussed in the literature. Below is a catalogue of issues which are central to Dostoevsky's "philosophical anthropology." Discussion of the secondary literary sources shall be dealt with in conjunction with the chapters which treat the individual novels.

English-Language Literature

In England and in the United States commentators have shown a great deal of interest in Dostoevsky's literary work, especially in light of formal and poetic concerns.[39] At the same time, no prominent philosopher has undertaken Dostoevsky's literary work as a theme of analysis; neither were any panel discussions held on Dostoevsky at meetings of The American Philosophical Association. This is not to say that quite a number of commentators have not provided useful insights into philosophical features of Dostoevsky's literary opus. In some cases, the insights illuminate, albeit indirectly, a philosophical conception of man. In 1981, an international conference on the occasion of the centenary of Dostoevsky's death was held at Hoftra University. The proceedings of this conference were published as _Dostoevsky and the Human Condition after a Century_.[40] In what follows I shall cite several examples where Dostoevsky's thought has been mentioned within the philosophical literature.

Walter Kaufmann's popular work, _Existentialism from Dostoevsky to Sartre_, which includes excerpts from the literary work, has gone a long way toward reinforcing the image of Dostoevsky as an existentialist or at least as a forerunner of existentialism. In particular Kaufmann singles out the first part of _Notes from the Underground_ (1864) as the "greatest overture to existentialism ever written."[41]

The _Encyclopedia of Philosophy_ includes an entry for Dostoevsky written by Edward Wasiolek.[42] In a moderately brief article, Wasiolek describes the novelist as a forerunner of existentialist thought, emphasizing that freedom is at the center of his thought concerning man. The Underground Man is presented as an example of a totally free man.

Frederick Copleston's Philosophy in Russia devotes a full chapter to the philosophical relevance of Dostoevsky's literary works.[43] He discusses Dostoevsky's thought in relation to Russian thinkers before and after him. He emphasizes the centrality of anthropology in Dostoevsky's thought and suggests the possibility of working out a Dostoevskeian philosophical anthropology along the lines of the exercise of individual freedom.

An example of a prominent literary figure in English letters whose treatment of Dostoevsky suggests a relevance for philosophical anthropology is D. H. Lawrence. In his essay entitled "The Grand Inquisitor," Lawrence points out that in the Grand Inquisitor episode of The Brothers Karamazov, Dostoevsky poses a question to the reader concerning the limits of being human.[44] Lawrence phrases the question thus, "What are the limits to the nature, not of man in the abstract, but of men, mere men, everyday men?"[45] The answer to this question encapsulates the doctrine of the Grand Inquisitor concerning the limits of human freedom. The limits which man clings to and which permanently serve to sever man from embodying and living out his freedom are miracle, mystery, and authority. The terrible wisdom that the Grand Inquisitor possesses is that man, far from cherishing the freedom which Christ urges him toward, actively seeks to postpone being free by embracing these limits. Ironically, the Grand Inquisitor presents himself as a humanitarian, and as a lover of mankind.

Lawrence understands that Dostoevsky is the first thinker to realize this devastating truth that man, by nature, cannot rise up to the demands that Christ's gift of freedom demands. However, Lawrence, rather than portraying the Inquisitor diabolically, as Dostoevsky does, sides with him. He wonders why the devil and the auto-da-fe should enter into this humanitarian disclosure. What Ivan Karamazov has accomplished with his poem is to restate ". . . the old truth, that most men cannot choose between good and evil . . . and that most men cannot see the difference between life-values and money-values. . . ."[46] Hence, it is up to the few who can decide in these matters to act on behalf of the men who have delegated that task to them. Accordingly the few are awarded with the awe of the miracle, the cloak of mystery, and the power of authority. In exchange for his freedom, man wins security. Lawrence sides with the Grand Inquisitor's humanitarian doctrine, and finds nothing diabolical in this.

Russian-Language Literature

Articles which treat of Dostoevsky's philosophical thought, his pochvennichestvo (native soil movement) alliance, and his life appear in Zenkovsky's A History of Russian Philosophy (1953).[47] A detailed consideration of the pochvenniki (men of the soil) philosophy and its relation to Dostoevsky's literary journals Vremia and Epokha is found in Wayne Dowler's Dostoevsky, Grigor'ev and Native Soil Conservatism and in several of Ellen Chances' articles.[48] A valuable source of Russian philosophy texts which includes Dostoevsky is a three-volume set edited by Zeldin, Kline, et al.[49] Finally, in the newly published A History of Russian Philosophy (2 vols.) edited by Valery Kuvakin in Moscow in 1994, there is an engaging chapter treating Dostoevsky's philosophical thought.[50] This is not to mention many other important monographs and scholarly articles.[51] In what follows are three principle interpretations which bear the philosophical relevance of Dostoevsky's work: Lev Shestov, Nicholai Berdiaev, and Viacheslav Ivanov. These were the so-called "philosophers in exile," Russian-born thinkers and writers who emigrated from Russia to France and who interpreted Dostoevsky to the French.

Lev Shestov (1866-1938)

In what follows I shall refer to the three principle texts of Shestov which concern the philosophical interpretation of Dostoevsky's works. These are: Dostoevsky and Nietzsche: The Philosophy of Tragedy (1903); Sur la Balance de Job (1929); and "Kierkegaard and Dostoevsky" (a paper read at the Russian Academy of Religion and Philosophy in 1935).[52]

Shestov identifies Notes from the Underground as the monumental work in Dostoevsky's oeuvre. This work ushers in a new age: "there ends for man the thousand-year reign of reason and conscience; a new era begins--that of 'psychology.'"[53] In bringing the Underground Man to the fore as an example of irrationalism, Shestov emphasizes his thesis that human reason is the fruit which man won in disobeying God. Reason is the prize for man's Fall, it is Original Sin.

Shestov finds that human knowledge has not brought man to freedom, but has only succeeded in delivering man to anangke (fate). This is particularly true of Hegelian Rationalism. Like Kierkegaard, whose primary thrust is against Hegel, Dostoevsky prefers faith, which promises unlimited and infinite possibilities, to a reason which would ultimately strip man of his freedom and deliver him over to rational necessity. For Shestov, the beginning of philosophy is better represented by Job than by Socrates. According to Shestov, Notes from the Underground is a bona fide "critique of pure reason" which establishes that man's true freedom lies not in the kingdom of reason but in its abdication.

Nikolai Berdiaev (1874-1948)

Berdiaev, while agreeing with Shestov to the extent that totalitarian domination is a thing to be avoided and that human freedom is a good, nonetheless finds in Dostoevsky a place for reasonable freedom. Berdiaev's Dostoievsky: An Interpretation (Mirosozertzanie Dostoevskago [1923]) emphasizes two important ideas: 1) the "epochal" character of Dostoevsky's thought; and 2) the centrality of anthropology in Dostoevsky's worldview.[54]

Berdiaev writes, ". . . [Dostoevsky] marks an absolutely new stage in anthropological knowledge, one that is neither humanist nor yet Christian in the traditional sense of the fathers of the Church."[55] The historical epoch was determined by the Orthodox Church and its conception of a transcendent world farther and farther from this world:

> This process could only lead to positivism, gnosticism and materialism, that is, to the utter dispiritualiza- tion of man and his universe. The transcendent world itself was pushed back into the unknowable and all the ways of leading to it were closed, till at last its very existence was denied.[56]

It is against this temporal-historical backdrop of atheism and nihilism that Dostoevsky reveals a novel conception of man in his literary work.

It was not until the twentieth century that Dostoevsky's work could be truly understood:

> Dostoievsky [sic] arrived at the moment when modern times were coming to an end and a new epoch of history was dawning, and it is likely that his consciousness of the

> inner division of human nature and its movement towards the ultimate depths of being was closely related to this fact.[57]

For Berdiaev, Dostoevsky's thought has an "epochal" character to it. Man in Dostoevsky's work has a fundamentally different place in the cosmos than in Dante's medieval anthropology or in Shakespeare's Renaissance vision of man. Dostoevsky begins from a qualitatively new starting-point, in a new epoch of the history of mankind. All Dostoevsky's work illustrates this:

> Therein Man has a very different place from that given to him by Dante or Shakespeare: he neither forms part of an unchangeable objective order nor exists on the surface of the earth or of his own soul.[58]

Hence, for Berdiaev, Dostoevsky reveals a novel image of man, and this image is inextricably historical.

Dostoevsky's works give a conception of man that is inseparably linked with freedom. Berdiaev calls his interpretation a "pneumatology," but this comes closer to what we call philosophical anthropology. Dostoevsky's vision is primarily dynamic and anthropocentric, and Berdiaev writes that enquiries which are solely psychological or emphasize merely the formal aspect of art cannot enter into Dostoevsky's vision of the world. "Dostoevsky devoted the whole of his creative energy to one single theme, man and man's destiny."[59] According to Berdiaev, freedom is at the center of man's being, however, unlike Shestov, this freedom is a rational freedom.

Viacheslav Ivanov (1866-1949)

As with Berdiaev's conception of the epochal significance of Dostoevsky's thought about man, Ivanov states that Dostoevsky reveals the essential characteristic of present-day self awareness. Further, his work changes as we do. Dostoevsky's artwork is implicated in human life and reveals something true about human life. In addition to these insights, Ivanov's Freedom and the Tragic Life[60] is the first significant work to treat philosophically not only the "thought" in Dostoevsky's work but also the "how" of its expression.

> In "Dostoyevski and the Tragedy-Novel," Ivanov made the first significant attempt in Russian criticism to deduce the ideas and world-view of Dostoyevski by the method of beginning with an analysis of the formal structure of the novels and then proceeding to an analysis of the ideological content.[61]

In order to get his ideas across, Dostoevsky needed an art form equal to the task before him.

> His work is the most striking example we know of identity of form and content--in so far as by content we mean the original intuitive perception of life, and by form the means of transmuting this by art into the flesh and blood of a new world of living entities.[62]

Dostoevsky discovered the means of expressing his original intuitive perception of life in the novel-tragedy.

Tragedy, according to Ivanov, is an infringement either upon a cosmic order or upon the rules of society. When tragedy is enacted it reveals something essential about man, i.e., something which other types of studies of man cannot fathom:

> His own most private experience has led him, in the fathoming of the depths of the human heart, far beyond what is empirically definable or definite; and it is just this insight into the supra-empirical nature of free will that sets the stamp of tragedy upon his primitive intuition of life.[63]

In Dostoevsky the central category of tragedy is crime. Crime too is an infringement upon either social or cosmic order which reveals the nature of man as free. Ivanov remarks that crime is at the center of all Dostoevsky's work. It is the basic antinomy in the novel-tragedy.

French-Language Literature

The French secondary literature is significant in terms of Dostoevsky's philosophical anthropology for the following reasons: 1) As we have seen, some of the most insightful interpretations of Dostoevsky's works were written by the Russian emigre philosophers, the so-called "philosophers in exile," who wrote their treatises in French. In particular, Shestov and Berdiaev were among the earliest interpreters of Dostoevsky's work to associate his ideas about human freedom with existentialist themes in Kierkegaard and Nietzsche. 2) The philosophical explication of the meaning of freedom in human life has been a central preoccupation of French philosophy, and, whether correctly or incorrectly, Dostoevsky's literary work has been cited as a crucial influence upon the existentialist conception of man.[64] In the following section, I will look at four principal interpretations of Dostoevsky's works in French written by Eugene Melchior de Vogüé, André Gide, Albert Camus, and Jean-Paul Sartre.[65]

Count Eugene Marie Melchior de Vogüé (1848-1910)

Despite the fact that many of his insights now seem inaccurate, the credit for introducing the Russian novel to the French-speaking literary world is given to Count Eugene Marie Melchior de Vogüé. His work entitled Le roman russe (1886) includes a chapter which gives a general introduction to Dostoevsky's literary opus.[66] De Vogüé's interpretation is significant not only because of its primacy in French literary criticism, but also because it opened up a certain way of looking at Dostoevsky's work to the French-speaking world. The author offers a first-hand account of the first French translations of Dostoevsky's literary works. De Vogüé's central interpretive concept is "la religion de la souffrance." This phrase,

"the religion of suffering" is the formulaic expression which compresses the universe of Dostoevsky's literary creation in the French critic's overview. He highlights those passages of Dostoevsky's novels that emphasize the suffering of the characters: "On sent la plaie vive dans ses lettres, on la sent chez les héros de ses romans, en qui son âme est si visiblement incarnée; tous sont torturés par une vergogne ombrageuse."[67]
Accordingly, de Vogüé argues that the novelist's goal in writing about such hurt and humiliation was salutary: "tel est le cas de Dostoïevsky. Il a écrit pour guérir."[68] The prevailing theme in de Vogüé's book is that Dostoevsky employed his literary work in order to express his own maladies and thus to bring about healing for the reader vicariously. No matter how flawed his conception, de Vogüé's Le roman russe influenced an entire generation of literary critics, opened up Dostoevsky's work to the French speaking world and therefore remains a monument in French language interpretation of Dostoevsky's works.

André Gide (1869-1951)

Gide's interpretation of Dostoevsky's literary work is found in the volume entitled Dostoïevsky, which comprises a series of addresses delivered at M. Jacques Copeau's School of Dramatic Art in Paris in 1922, together with an early essay (1908) on Dostoevsky's correspondence.[69] Gide's interpretation moves beyond de Vogüé's effort in a number of ways. First of all, Gide advances beyond general, sociological observations concerning the "russianness" of Dostoevsky's work toward a thoughtful reflection upon Dostoevsky's philosophical conception of man. Secondly, Gide criticizes de Vogüé's "la religion de la souffrance," for providing a catch-all formula which for many French readers summed up Dostoevsky's "philosophy" in too facile a manner. Finally, Gide criticizes de Vogüé's interpretation of Dostoevsky on the score that it is limited by a French aesthetic sensibility which would reject Dostoevsky's massive and complex novels (The Brothers Karamazov, in particular) in favor of literary works that bear more of the French image: "A ne vouloir admettre de l'étranger que ce qui déjà nous ressemble, où nous puissions trouver notre ordre, notre logique, et, en quelque sorte, notre image, nous commettons une grave erreur" (Conférences du Vieux-Colombier VI).[70] Whereas de Vogüé contrasts Dostoevsky's "russianness" with the French literary and cultural tradition, Gide prefers to compare Dostoevsky's "russianness" with European and Western ways of thinking.[71] He celebrates Dostoevsky's particularity rather than seeing it as a critical fault.

It is my task to show how Gide's interpretation moves beyond de Vogüé's Le roman russe toward a philosophical interpretation of Dostoevsky's image of man. In "Allocution lue au Vieux- Colombier pour la célébration du centenaire de Dostoïevsky," Gide observes, "Il [Dostoïevsky] ne l'aborde [de question si haute] jamais d'une manière abstraite, les idées n'existent jamais chez lui qu'en fonction de l'individu; et c'est là ce qui fait leur perpétuelle relativité; c'est là ce qui fait également leur puissance."[72] I would like to underline two points here. The first point concerns Gide's claim that Dostoevsky portrays characters in such a way that they embody or incarnate ideas, without becoming mere vehicles of his intention or dogmatic viewpoint. Dostoevsky's characters are not guilty of being "hollow masks" or personae through which some didactic aim is realized. Rather, through their embodiment, they manifest and incarnate certain truths concerning man. The second point which follows from Gide's comment is that the perpétuelle relativité which is specifically related to the individualization of Dostoevsky's characters, establishes the power of those characters.

Dostoevsky's characters manifest a certain truth concerning human freedom which is inalienable from its expression in individuality. Gide's observation concerning Dostoevsky's literary technique of characterization indicates to the philosophical anthropologist that the expression of individuality reveals a perpetual relativity which is at the basis of man's essential freedom. There is something more. Gide's observation also suggests that Dostoevsky's ideas could not have been better expressed had they been "brought into line," for example, in a philosophical discourse: "S'il avait été philosophe au lieu d'être romancier, il aurait certainement essayé de mettre ses idées au pas et nous y aurions perdu le meilleur" (Conférences du Vieux-Colombier I).[73] The very means of expressing these ideas in characterization is itself the most adequate realization of those ideas. If Dostoevsky had been a philosopher he might have attempted to rationally describe how man's individuality is linked with his freedom, but then there would be a certain truth concerning man's freedom and perpétuelle relativité which by necessity he would fail to express. These two observations concerning Dostoevsky's approach to characterization are primordial and central for Gide's interpretation of Dostoevsky's work. They are valuable to us because they present a nascent conception of "polyphony" which Gide was to develop to the greatest extent in his most complex novel, Les faux-monnayeurs.[74] This is not to say that Gidean "polyphony" is akin to Dostoevsky's but his critical remarks on Dostoevsky's work certainly prefigure Bakhtin's important work on Dostoevsky's poetics.[75]

Now I would like to briefly examine several elements in Gide's interpretation which reveal an "existentialist" conception of man, and which point the direction which ensuing readings of Dostoevsky's work have tended to embrace. Despite the fact that it is difficult to clearly delimit the term "existentialist" in the sense of a philosophical school, I use the term in a limited sense whose value is to highlight the conception of freedom within a philosophical definition of man. Accordingly, in referring to the elements of Gide's interpretation which point toward an "existentialist" conception of man, I have in mind the emphasis upon the centrality of the individual as the revelation of truth, including features which are at times illogical, irrational, abnormal, but which, nevertheless reveal some essential truth concerning human nature. The following elements of Gide's interpretation fit within this framework.

After describing Balzac's penchant for creating characters who are logically consequent with themselves, the sort of character the French critic has a predilection for, Gide tells us that "inconséquence" seems to be Dostoevsky's chief interest. "Il semble que ce soit là ce qui intéresse le plus Dostoïevsky: l'inconséquence" (Conférences sur Dostoïevsky III).[76] By "inconsequence," Gide means the cohabitation of contradictory statements within the same character. "Cette cohabitation paraît souvent chez Dostoïevsky d'autant plus paradoxale que les sentiments de ses personnages sont poussés à bout, exagérés jusqu'à l'absurde."[77] Such contradictoriness, or duplicity within a character, is rendered all the more absurd because Dostoevsky brings his characters to a conscious awareness of this inconsequence. Inconsequence then, is a poetic feature, a narrative strategy. Further, it reveals a paradoxical feature of human life.

L'inconséquence in characterization reveals a polymorphous capacity within the human being. Any given action of a human being can be interpreted in a number of ways. It is possible for a person to meaningfully contradict logic. Gide points to Raskolnikov's simultaneous love and hate for Sonia, as an example of such inconsequence. With his discussion of inconsequence Gide opens up a consideration of the meaning of Dostoevsky's characters' actions. Two more elements of philosophical relevance unfold in Gide's interpretation: the gratuity of acts, and the meaning of the absurd which Dostoevsky reveals.

A locus to consider l'acte gratuit in Dostoevsky's work is in Crime and Punishment. The novel circles around Raskolnikov's criminal act whose motives are unclear. At the same time, the hero is inseparable from his act, which is gratuitous in precisely the manner Gide describes. The gratuity of acts is an idea that Gide introduced in his study of Dostoevsky and developed in his ironic récit, Les caves du vatican.[78] It is an act without purpose, to which no rational motive can be given. In Les caves the gratuitous act is a crime. Gide constructed the novel around the premise of the gratuitous act. Jean Hytier writes of Les caves' protagonist: "In Lafcadio, Gide has subtilized, refined, quintessentialized gratuitousness; he has aspired to a crime that is committed absolutely without reason."[79] Gide consciously employed the gratuitous act as a literary technique. For Dostoevsky, the difficulty in finding the motive for Raskolnikov's crime was certainly of major literary concern. And yet, it is not the entire pretext for the novel as we shall see in chapter four below. This problem in Crime is related to a set of ideological, metaphysical and historical concerns.

Hytier tells us that Gide's concern with the gratuitous act is primarily psychological: "On the whole, the concept of the free act is not metaphysical in Gide, it is psychological, by its connection with the idea of disinterestedness [. . .]."[80] However, Dostoevsky's concern with man is metaphysical, as well as psychological. This is why the gratuity of acts in Dostoevsky cannot count as the essential revelation about human freedom. For example, Gide's account of Kirilov's suicide is found wanting. Gide formulates the idea of a gratuity of action in consideration of Kirilov's suicide:

> Le suicide de Kirilov est un acte absolument gratuit, je veux dire que sa motivation n'est point extérieure. Tout ce que l'on peut faire entrer d'absurde dans ce monde, à la faveur et à l'abri d'un "acte gratuit", c'est ce que nous allons voir. (Conférences du Vieux-Colombier VI).[81]

Gide seems to be fascinated with the idea that the motive for Kirilov's suicide is entirely self-determined. It is not the consequence of depression or tragedy. But this is not all. For Gide the gratuitousness of Kirilov's suicide reveals absurdity. Hence, Gide is not only emphasizing the autonomy of the human act from external determinants, but the curious fact that when taken to its extreme as with Kirilov's suicide in _The Possessed_, it reveals absurdity. However much Gide sees of the gratuitous act in Kirilov's suicide, a question must be posed whether this is an accurate reading. Many critics would read this not as an _acte gratuit_ but as a more complicated symptom of Russian nihilism and an inversion of the idea of Godmanhood (i.e., Soloviev's _bogochelovechestvo_).

The term "_l'absurde_" has demonstrated a vibrant career in the world of French letters, having been employed in a number of ways and taken on varying shades of meaning.[82] Martin Esslin contrasts philosophers of the absurd with dramatists of the absurd:

> Yet these writers [Sartre, Camus, Anouilh and others] differ from the dramatists of the Absurd in an important

> respect: they present their sense of the irrationality of the human condition in the form of highly lucid and logically constructed reasoning, while the Theatre of the Absurd strives to express its senselessness of the human condition and the inadequacy of the human approach by the open abandonment of rational devices and discursive thought.[83]

Esslin argues that philosophers and dramatists differ in their approach to the absurd. One might argue that Esslin has wrongly allocated Camus as a philosopher of the absurd. According to Camus, philosophers of the absurd attempt to describe absurdity in terms that are still rational. He cites Sartre's existentialism is the best example of this.[84] Camus distinguished himself from Sartre on precisely this point. Even so and despite the meaning affixed to the absurd, it must be noted that the approach to describing the absurd is as significant as the content of that description. Hence, the question of genre cannot be overlooked. Gide is clearly a writer in _Les caves du vatican_ and an essayist (even philosopher) in _Dostoïevski_. With Camus and Sartre this capacity for writing in many genres is also true, and to parallel the philosophical thought of _L'Étranger_ with _L'Être et le neant_ without taking the genres into consideration leads to difficulties in interpretation.

Gide's use of the term _l'absurde_ is related to the exaggeration with which Dostoevsky portrays his characters.

For example, the absurdity of Kirilov's predicament is his apparent lucidity which leads him to the logical conclusion that he must commit suicide. This is a theme that Camus explores at length as we shall see below. Gide's treatment of the absurd in Dostoevsky is unique in that it suggests a possibility of a positive interpretation. For example, Gide points to Kirilov's momentary revelation of bliss and rapture in contrast with Myshkin's blissful state. Myshkin's description of the mystical state of union and harmony that precedes his epileptic seizures quite resembles Kirilov's disclosure that there are moments in which he experiences eternal life in the present. Both characters manifest a religious transformation which Gide associates with the Gospel teaching, "Except ye be converted and become as little children, ye shall not enter into the Kingdom of Heaven." And yet, Kirilov will be driven to suicide, being fully lucid of these moments where eternal life bursts the temporality of before/after revealing an eternal now. The similarity between Myshkin's pre-epileptic rapture and Kirilov's idea of eternal life is striking, and suggests a possibility of a positive view of the absurd or at least a possibility of interpreting Kirilov and Myshkin in light of a similar blissful state of realization.

Gide's study of Dostoevsky continues to speak to us. In a paradoxical way, the lectures manifest the very ideas that he was teaching. For example, Gide says concerning his tendency to identify his own thinking with the Russian: "C'est aussi, vous l'avez bien compris, et je vous le disais dès le début, que Dostoïevsky ne m'est souvent ici qu'un prétexte pour primer mes propres pensées" (Conférences du Vieux-Colombier VI).[85] This is in part an apology, but also a revelation. By discovering in Dostoevsky a pretext to talk about his own sensitivity, ideas and literary practice, Gide is praising Dostoevsky's "modernity." Gide's artistic works echo the ideas we find in his discussion of Dostoevsky. To elucidate this literary "kinship" is not my aim here; however, if one were to look for this affinity in Gide and Dostoevsky beyond the two works mentioned (Les caves du vatican and Les faux-monnayeurs), he or she would be strongly rewarded through the study of the early lyrical work, Les nourritures terrestres, or the ironic tandem works, La porte étroite and L'immoraliste. Gide's Journals include several essays which present religious and ethical ideas which both echo and bear affinity with some ideas that are prominent in Dostoevsky's work. For example, Numquid et tu?; Et nunc manet in te; Ainsi soit-il.

Albert Camus (1913-1960)

Camus attributed a great deal of importance to Dostoevsky's writings, particularly in their literary impact in France. In a 1957 letter in the New York Herald Tribune entitled, "The Other Russia," he asserts: ". . . without Dostoevsky, French literature of the twentieth-century would not be what it is."[86] The significance of Dostoevsky's work and thought for Camus himself, is as follows: "At first I admired Dostoevsky because of what he revealed to me about human nature. Reveal is the word. Because he tells us only what we know but refuse to see" [italics mine].[87] A close reading of this letter written at the height of the Cold War, indicates that Camus, fully aware of the effects of political totalitarianism and fascism, is able to suggest a certain politically prophetic character in Dostoevsky's work which neither of the earlier French interpreters, de Vogüé nor Gide, could have foreseen.[88] Camus discerned in Dostoevsky a prophet of the dire consequences of nihilism in European political life.

Early in the 1940s Camus began to discover the contradiction between man's reason and the irrationality of the war. In light of the stupidity of the war, he wrote succinctly of the incommensurability of human reason and the world in Lettres à un ami allemand: "Nous avons longtemps cru ensemble que ce monde n'avait pas de raison supérieure et que nous étions frustrés."[89] It is this split between man's rationality and the world's irrationality that gave Camus a basis to speak of absurdity. He also finds this revealed in Dostoevsky's Devils. Recall that Gide connected the theme of l'absurde with the gratuity of Kirilov's suicide with particular emphasis laid on the gratuity of Kirilov's act. Camus reads absurdity in Kirilov differently. Camus finds in Dostoevsky a means of demonstrating his conception of absurdity and political nihilism. This analysis of absurdity appears in the essay subtitled "essai sur l'absurde," Le mythe de Sisyphe.[90]

In the preface Camus points out that his essay is concerned with une sensibilité absurde, and he distinguishes this from the "absurd philosophy" which his time had not known. Camus was familiar with the existentialism of his time. Elsewhere, he has written that he disagrees with its conclusions:

> If the premises of existentialism are to be found, as I believe they are, in Pascal, Nietzsche, Kierkegaard or Chestov, then I agree with them. If its conclusions are those of our existentialists, then I no longer agree because they contradict the premises.[91]

He takes l'absurde as a point of departure and not a conclusion stating that his essay will provide a description of this human phenomenon: "On trouvera seulement ici la description, à l'état pur, d'un mal de l'esprit."[92] This malady consists in a consciousness of a certain split between the human being and his world: "Ce divorce entre l'homme et sa vie, l'acteur et son décor, c'est proprement le sentiment de l'absurdité."[93] Man's desire for logical clarity concerning his existence is based upon a contradiction: "Mais ce qui est absurde, c'est la confrontation de cet irrationnel [monde] et de ce désir éperdu de clarté dont l'appel résonne au plus profond de l'homme."[94] The absurd sensibility is neither in the world nor in man but is based upon man's relation to the world.

For Camus, Kirilov's "logical suicide" exemplifies l'absurde in its contradictory, logical clarity. Kirilov realizing that there is no immortality concludes that he must kill himself. However, Kirilov also feels that God is necessary and must exist. Faced with this contradiction he commits suicide. Kirilov's "logical suicide" is absurd, but Dostoevsky ultimately treats it in an existential manner. Here, Camus distinguishes the "absurd novelist" from the "existentialist novelist." Concerning Dostoevsky he writes: "Ce n'est donc pas un romancier absurde qui nous parle, mais un romancier existentiel."[95] Camus is closer to being a "romancier absurde" whereas Dostoevsky is a "romancier existentiel." According to Camus, an "existential" writer discloses the absurd as a step toward religious faith. Both thinkers ask the same question concerning the meaning of life, but the "absurd" writer leaves the question hanging and attempts no answer. Camus does not make this "leap" toward faith in a future life but remains true to the experience of the absurd sensibility. Dostoevsky, at least in his Diary of a Writer, reveals the thought which lurks behind Kirilov. Belief in immortality of the soul is the normal state for humanity, and if man commits suicide because he lacks faith in eternal life, this demonstrates the necessity not of suicide, but of eternal life for man.[96] Camus is aware of Dostoevsky's conclusion which renders Dostoevsky's treatment of suicide "existential" and not "absurd." Camus, for his part, rejects suicide as a valid option based upon absurd reasoning: "La conclusion dernière du raisonnement absurde est, en effet, le rejet du suicide et le maintien de cette confrontation désespérée entre l'interrogation humaine et le silence du monde."[97] This insight provides the possibility of overcoming nihilism.

Despite the significance of Camus' interpretation of Kirilov's suicide, it leaves something to be desired. If by stating that Dostoevsky is an existential novelist who introduces in Kirilov an absurd, nihilist contradiction which necessarily leads to suicide, Camus suggests that the experience of suicide in Dostoevsky's work is uniformly "existential," then he is wrong. Suicide is multiform in Dostoevsky's work. An absurd suicide, quite unlike Kirilov's, is found in the article, "Two Suicides," in Diary of a Writer. There, Dostoevsky contrasts two suicides, both of young girls, and makes note of the humility in one, and the absurd resignation in the other. The latter is truly absurd, and left a note stating that if her suicide did not succeed she wished her resuscitation to be celebrated with a bottle of Clicquot Champagne. Also, there is a great difference between the suicides of Kirilov, Smerdiakov, and Svidrigailov. The reason for each suicide is as unique as the character himself. Camus does not indicate how individual the meaning of suicide is in Dostoevsky's work.[98]

L'Homme révolté carries forward Camus' interrogation and description of la sensibilité absurde from the discussion concerning suicide to the discussion of whether murder can ever be justified. Camus takes the absurd sensibility as a starting-point in his reasoning. Like Descartes' methodical doubt, absurdism offers no dogmatic solution to the problems that living brings. And yet, an analytical investigation of the absurd sensibility can offer the fact of rebellion as indubitable. In a passage that mimics Descartes' Méditations Camus writes:

> Je crie que je ne crois à rien et que tout est absurde, mais je ne puis douter de mon cri et il me faut au moins croire à ma protestation. La première et la seule évidence qui me soit ainsi donnée, à l'intérieur de l'expérience absurde, est la révolte.[99]

Camus' method in L'Homme révolté is to consider the historical and metaphysical data of rebellion. It is here, in the data concerning la révolte métaphysique that Camus meets Dostoevsky.

In "Le refus du salut" Camus presents his interpretation of Dostoevsky's character, Ivan Karamazov. What interests Camus in Ivan is his theodicy and his anti-theism. Ivan does not deny that God exists, but rejects this world in which children must suffer: "Ivan Karamazov prend le parti des hommes et met l'accent sur leur innocence."[100] If theodicy is the attempt to justify God's purity and omnipotence in the face of suffering and evil present in the creation, then Ivan inverts theodicy accusing God of the suffering of innocents. Camus remarks that Ivan's rebellion is not the blasphemous rebellion of a romantic whose aim is to put oneself in the place of God (Kirilov). Ivan's rebellion advances one step further in that he does not wish to replace God, but to put God on trial to account for His creation before the tribunal of human justice. Camus highlights the fact that Ivan rejects God's creation because he maintains justice as a higher value than truth. Hence when Ivan says, "Mon indignation persisterait même si j'avais tort,"[101] Camus emphasizes the "même si" to stress that this is not a simple atheism but rather a profound theological argument concerning suffering in human history. This is why Ivan Karamazov is central to Camus' essay.

Camus labels Ivan's rebellion, ". . . une sorte de donquichottisme métaphysique."[102] He concludes that like Quixote's, Ivan's rebellion borders on madness. Like Kirilov's, Ivan's logic expresses an absurd contradiction. Ivan concludes that if God does not exist, all is permitted. This conclusion, states Camus, is at the heart of contemporary nihilism: "A ce 'tout est permis' commence vraiment l'histoire du nihilisme contemporain."[103] This is an unexpected remark when contrasted with Sartre's 1946 statement: "Dostoïevski avait écrit 'si Dieu n'existait pas, tout serait permis'. C'est le point de départ de l'existentialisme."[104] Here we are facing the same starting point ("commence" and "le point de départ") but arriving at different conclusions ("l'histoire du nihilisme contemporain" and "l'existentialisme"). Sartre's statement is treated at length below.

To realize the bitter implication of the excessive sweep of human freedom means to be in a position where one must either accept murder, and the suffering of the innocents with divine resignation, or else become mad. Camus' play Caligula depicts a tyrant whose whim becomes the decree of the state. He is a type of absurd hero: "Mais je ne suis pas fou et même je n'ai jamais été aussi raisonnable. Simplement, je me suis senti tout d'un coup un besoin d'impossible."[105] He desires what he cannot have, and demands money and then the lives of his people. At the conclusion of the play he realizes his guilt but concludes that it has no meaning. Facing himself in the mirror he shouts, "Caligula! Toi aussi, toi aussi, tu es coupable. Alors, n'est-ce-pas, un peu plus, un peu moins! Mais qui oserait me condamner dans ce monde sans juge, où personne n'est innocent!"[106] This theme echoes in La Chate's hero, Jean-Baptiste Clamence, whose conscience suggests complicity in a suicide he was too cowardly to stop. Caligula must exercise the power of his calling, and ultimately destroy himself because of his inordinate freedom. Similarly, Ivan Karamazov must go mad.

Ivan cannot and will not accept God's creation. Even though he is aware of the saving wisdom of Zosima, he knows that ultimately there is no responsibility to be assigned for the sufferings of the world. As Camus puts it: "Je sais seulement que la souffrance existe, qu'il n'y a pas de coupables, que tout s'enchaîne, que tout passe et s'équilibre."[107] This is the same knowledge which the holy man teaches, the knowledge that all men are bound together in sin and that all men are redeemed together through the love of God. This is the affirmation of a believer and mystic, and yet, Ivan refuses to accept God's creation if suffering is the necessary result of its ongoing existence.

Camus demonstrates that Ivan prefers justice to truth and that his rebellion is based upon his belief in the insuperable value of justice. Yet, Ivan becomes entangled in an absurd impasse when he complicitly commissions his father's murder. The reason for this impotence is that he cannot escape the passive anarchy which his "tout est permis" has thrown him into. Camus tells us: "Pour le moment, Ivan ne nous offre que le visage défait du révolté aux abîmes, incapable d'action, déchiré entre l'idée de son innocence et la volonté du meurtre."[108] Despite Ivan's ethical quiescence, his literary creation, the Grand Inquisitor, embodies Ivan's deification of justice over truth. Camus presents the Inquisitor as the embodiment of Ivan's inverted theodicy when acted out in the sphere of political-theology. Whereas Ivan will wallow in despondency and eventual insanity, the Grand Inquisitor will usher in a new religion, a religion of the kingdom of heaven upon earth. Camus interprets this utopic empire as the apocalyptic unification of the world which nihilism demands: "L'unité du monde qui ne s'est pas faite avec Dieu tentera désormais de se faire contre Dieu."[109] Hence, what begins as a quest for justice ends in its complete overthrow.

At the heart of Camus' discussion of absurdity is the realization that one aspect of human freedom is not determined by sets of affairs either in the world or out of the world. Therein lies its autonomy and its horrifying sense of inescapability. The possibility of affixing meaning to the world is a manifestation of human freedom. In fact, this is _the_ central revelation about freedom. The essence of freedom lies in its ability to affix meaning to any given fact in the world. Were this not so, then human action could not be free--another story would preclude it. The "world" of the literary text also consists of meaning which the interpreter affixes to it. This world, like the world it mimes, is governed by rules and structures, and yet, the analysis of such structures cannot exceed its store of meaning.

Camus' treatment of the absurd relies on a type of indifference. For example, he notes that Kirilov is driven to commit suicide by a realization which is, in essence, mystical. He experiences the same bliss which Prince Myshkin knows, and yet, he kills himself. This is absurd. Likewise, Ivan Karamazov is not simply an unbeliever. While he possesses the same beatific realization: "everything will be fine" which is afforded to mystics and saints, yet still he refuses to accept the world if the suffering of innocents is the price of its ongoing history. The Grand Inquisitor provides the political and theological solution to Ivan's dilemma in proposing a utopic, totalitarian state in which human beings will suffer no longer. Kirilov, Prince Myshkin, Ivan, Alyosha, Zosima and the Grand Inquisitor all incarnate and exemplify _l'absurde_. It is as though they were all looking at the same terrible knowledge but deriving unique and often contrary courses of action therefrom. Camus illuminates absurdity in the following way, "L'existence est mensongère _et_ elle est éternelle" [my emphasis].[110] With this insight,

Camus brings us a heuristic with which to view the workings of human freedom in Dostoevsky's work.

It is confusing that Camus is labelled an "existentialist" when he makes clear that he is not. In his eyes, Dostoevsky is an existential novelist. Through characters like Kirilov, Dostoevsky has predicted the effects of nihilism. But, he has not shown the way beyond nihilism as does Camus. In a preface to the American edition of Le mythe published in 1955, Camus states: "Written fifteen years ago, in 1940, amid the French and European disaster, this book declares that even within the limits of nihilism it is possible to find the means to proceed beyond nihilism."[111] Camus' goal is to introduce a type of thinking "la pensée du midi," which allows man to live in the face of the desert. Such a mode of thinking avoids the vanity of absolutism, and yet attempts to understand man's responsibility for evil.

Jean-Paul Sartre (1905-1976)

If Camus rejected the epithet "existentialist," Sartre, on the contrary, was the self-proclaimed founder of French atheist existentialism. The most succinct presentation of Sartre's defense of existentialism is found in his popular essay, L'existentialisme est un humanisme (1946). Though Sartre's thinking on human freedom is more artistically presented in his novels (esp. La Nausée [1938]), and plays (Huis-clos [1945] and Les mains sales [1948]); and though his philosophical conception of man is treated more systematically in his philosophical treatise, L'Être et le Néant, this little essay offers the most straightforward exposition Sartre's conception of human freedom, man's essential being, and of existentialism as a doctrine of humanism.[112]

Sartre writes, "Je voudrais ici défendre l'existentialisme contre un certain nombre de reproches qu'on lui a adressés."[113] While acknowledging Christian existentialism (Karl Jaspers and Gabriel Marcel), this work is a defense of Sartre's brand of existentialism against criticism it suffered from communist and catholic writers. The work is thus also a defense of a certain conception of freedom and a vision of man--an existentialist interpretation of human existence that centers on the reality of human freedom. Our concern is with Sartre's treatment of what he takes to be Dostoevsky's teaching concerning man and his freedom. In contrast to Camus, who chose _The Brothers Karamazov_ (_Brat'ia Karamazovy_) and in particular, Ivan Karamazov's rebellion, as the center point of his discussion on human freedom, in Sartre it is only a passing reference. Sartre writes, "Dostoïevski avait écrit 'si Dieu n'éxistait pas, tout serait permis'. C'est _le point de départ de l'existentialisme_" [my italics].[114] Sartre associates Ivan's denial of God with existentialism. He takes Dostoevsky's statement as the beginning of a reflection that he will take farther. This "echo" is significant because of the precise manner in which Ivan's denial is linked with the assertion of human freedom. In fact, Sartre does not equate atheism with existentialism:

> L'existentialisme n'est pas tellement un athéisme au sens où il s'épuiserait à démontrer que Dieu n'existe pas. Il déclare plutôt: même si Dieu existait, ça ne changerait rien; voilà notre point de vue.[115]

In this point of view Sartre reveals a subtle dimension of human freedom. Freedom eludes the controversy between theism and atheism, if indeed nothing is changed by God's existence (or non-existence).

Sartre develops a conception of atheism which is positive, optimistic and humanistic. Sartre concludes his essay with these words:

> En ce sens, l'existentialisme est un optimisime, une doctrine d'action, et c'est seulement par mauvaise foi que, confondant leur propre désespoir avec le nôtre, les chretiens peuvent nous appeler désespérés.[116]

Atheistic existentialism appears to be despairing for Christians, but this attitude is based upon a mistaken bad faith. Even so, Sartre is not seeing the world through rose-colored glasses. Freedom is a burden for man who is anguished by his choice. Without God, man is condemned to be free. Sartre vividly represents the full weight of man's choice in his theatrical works Huis clos and Les mains sales.

To contrast Sartre's atheistic existentialism with Ivan Karamazov's ideas about human freedom illustrates first of all that Sartre's thought is not identical to Ivan's. Hence, it is not possible to read L'existentialisme as a continuation and amplification of Ivan Karamazov's rejection of God. However, there are very certain echoes of Dostoevsky's ideas in Sartre's essay. Sartre's conception of freedom has the advantage that it incorporates a great deal of Zosima's theistic interpretation of freedom along with Ivan Karamazov's rebellion. That is why Sartre is able to attach words like "optimism" and "humanism" to an atheistic way of thinking that in Ivan Karamazov's terms must surely lead to despair.

Sartre has written of The Brothers Karamazov that each classical novel has a crystallizing moment or "knot" around which the action centers. "Dans le roman classique l'action comporte un noeud: c'est l'assassinat du père Karamazov. . . ."[117] It is revealing that he chose Fyodor Karamazov's murder as the central knot in this work. This perspective is discordant with Dostoevsky's, who speaks of the "culminating points" of the novel as books five and six of part two.[118] The culminating points are Ivan's poem, "The Grand Inquisitor," and the teachings of Zosima. It is possible that Sartre's emphasis on Ivan's "existentialist" declaration of freedom renders him blind to

Zosima's and Alyosha's pronouncements to the same. Hence he discounts the central significance of Zosima's theistic teaching on freedom while emphasizing how human freedom is linked with atheism and sees Fyodor Karamazov's murder as the central act in the novel. Even though Sartre incorporates "positive' dimensions of freedom into his interpretation of man in L'existentialisme, in the final analysis, his teaching does not grasp all that he asserts--that man is free, that free choice brings anguish, that man is inescapably responsible for his actions--is true within a theistic as well as an atheistic framework. This assertion will be made clear in chapter five with a consideration of how Dostoevsky's final literary work enacts a conception of human freedom that transcends the antinomy between theism and atheism.

German-Language Literature

In the German secondary literature, a significant philosophical interpretation of Dostoevsky is presented by Friedrich Nietzsche. Even though we know that his familiarity with Dostoevsky was limited, and he makes only a few passing references to him, nonetheless, it is reasonable to assume that the author of Human All too Human was smitten with the Underground Man.[119] Furthermore, even if Nietzsche's "overman" [Übermensch] is not the same as Kirilov's "man-god," it bears a striking resemblance to the essence of this idea, as well as to Raskolnikov's obsessional "Napoleonic Idea" and to Shatov's idea of the one-tenth who shall rule the majority. Each of Dostoevsky's "supermen" characters (man-gods) bears a certain prophetic gait of Man-on-the-way, or, as the Underground Man says: "budushchii chelovek" (future man) set against the backdrop of an apocalypse where man is nihil (i.e., nihilism).[120] Perhaps it is a case of kindred souls or ideas "in the air," but even so, the reception of Nietzsche's thought concerning human freedom certainly influenced the manner in which Dostoevsky's work was appropriated at least in philosophical circles, for example, by Camus and Heidegger.

Another German thinker, Reinhard Lauth, in his Die Philosophie Dostojewskis claims on the basis of existing secondary literature, that there is a positive and a negative philosophy in Dostoevsky.[121] The negative philosophy deals with the meaninglessness of life, the absence of God, the idea that God is dead, that there is no immortality, no moral law, that everything is permitted, the notion of power, the will to freedom, suicide, nihilism, etc. The positive philosophy is really identical with the Christian view on life as Dostoevsky understood it. For example, in The Brothers Karamazov, Lauth finds a systematic presentation of Dostoevsky's positive philosophy of religion; this is found particularly in the doctrine of Starets Zosima.

Lauth tells us that in Notes from the Underground Dostoevsky deals with the problem of free will, intellectualism, the question concerning the meaning of voluntarism, and man's inner schism.

In "Meditation devant le corps de Marie Dmitrievna" (16 April 1864) a brief essay which Dostoevsky wrote on the occasion of his wife's death (16 April 1864), he speaks about man's development toward the Christian ideal and about immortality.

In Crime and Punishment (1866) Dostoevsky explains what Nietzsche will later call the "will to power," which implies that there are two kinds of human beings: sheep and rulers; all of this centers on Raskolnikov's "idea."

In The Idiot the problem of freedom and the question concerning the last Ground of the universe are treated.

In The Devils Lauth finds reflections on immortality, the meaning of religion and mortality, the moral consequences of atheism and nihilism.

Various articles in The Diary of a Writer address philosophical matters like the impact of the environment upon the criminal, the problem of responsibility for one's actions, freedom of will. In "Suicide and Immortality" Dostoevsky examines the question concerning the meaning of life; he also asks the question of whether a human being could live without the notion of an immortal life of the soul. In "The Dream of a Ridiculous Man" Dostoevsky speaks about the will to live, suicide, the Fall of man, and about moral indifference.

Conclusion: The Work at Hand

In this first chapter of my dissertation, I have touched on a few topics whose familiarity is presupposed in the research I shall be concerned with in the chapters to follow. The first of these topics has to do with the origin and development of what is called "philosophical anthropology." The second issue deals with the relationship between "thinking and poetizing," i.e., with the view that both the philosopher and the poet or novelist can make an important contribution to the truth in the sense that both, each in its own way, can present insights about issues of meaning and truth.

The preceding reflections on philosophical anthropology were meant mainly to show that the question concerning the essence of man cannot be formulated and answered once and for all, but that the question recurs and must in each era be asked again and again. In each era it is a pressing question that demands careful attention. This is so because there is not one necessary eternal, invariant conception of the essence of man, of what it means to be a human being. In the West, human beings have tried to define the essence of man in several ways, certainly since the time of Plato and Aristotle. As the history of philosophy clearly shows, the essence of man has been defined as a "rational animal," a rational creature created by God, a thinking substance, a mode of the divine substance, a transcendental subject, consciousness, and so on. In other words, the question of what it means to be a human being is not a question of metaphysics or logic; it is above all, an "historical" question. The real question is time and again: what is each human being to make him or herself be, and on the basis of what overall conception of the nature of man is this question to be answered? In the past different conceptions were proposed. Some of these have been mentioned in the preceding pages by way of example. Contrary to what at first sight seems to be the case, these conceptions do not conflict with each other; rather historically, they follow one another in some orderly sequence. Yet this sequence appears undetermined. It is neither necessary nor arbitrary. What we can say is that the sequence can be understood once it has come about.

A second issue presupposed in this first chapter of the dissertation is the insight that speculations about what it means to be a human being are not just the business or the privilege of professional philosophers; the question is a vital one for every human being who wishes to understand himself or herself fully. It is not even the case that only professional philosophers are allowed to have opinions about this question and to unfold possible answers. For poets and novelists too, have come to remarkable insights about the nature of man, and have articulated their insights. Yet where the philosopher unfolds his ideas systematically and critically, the poet and novelist does it "poetically."

In developing these ideas in relation to the novels, it is not my intention to show what philosophical influences Dostoevsky himself underwent in his life and career. Undoubtedly it would have been significant to focus on the influence of Immanuel Kant, or of Michel de Montaigne on Dostoevsky, and so on. In this thesis I have decided not to do so. However, where such influences are obvious, I have made the suggestion clear. Establishing such influence is not my major concern here. On the other hand, it is not my intention to detail the concrete influence of certain statements about man made by Dostoevsky on the ideas developed by Nietzsche, Scheler, Heidegger, Sartre, Merleau-Ponty, and Camus. Such a task would lie far beyond what one person can achieve in one book. What I try to do is the following: I want to show that in the novels of Dostoevsky, ideas about man's nature and freedom are proposed or suggested which anticipate basic conceptions about the mode of being of human beings explicitly defended by the philosophers mentioned.

Contrary to what is the case for plants and animals, the mode of being of human beings is not determined in advance. This agrees with Nietzsche's idea that man is the being whose mode of being is not determined yet. When a human being is born, he or she is no more than a promise, a center of possibilities. Those that become actual are largely determined by each human being. In determining what options to materialize each human being is deeply influenced by events and factors over which he or she has no full control. Yet man is, and remains inescapably free.

Furthermore, freedom is not just a characteristic of actions that proceed from choices; it is also a characteristic of <u>who you are</u> as a human being. Man is responsible not only for what he has done, but also what he is. Dostoevsky pondered the implications of this realization within the framework of his Christian belief. The same is true for people such as Gabriel Marcel, Karl Jaspers, Heidegger, Merleau-Ponty, Gadamer, to mention a few. Yet, there are many others who cannot ponder these issues within a framework that rests on grace and faith. Like many atheist existentialists, but long before them, Dostoevsky must have seen the possibility that for these people there is simply no hope because there is no exit.

Notes

1. Michael Landmann, Fundamental Anthropology (Washington, D.C.: Center for Advanced Research in Phenomenology and University Press of America, 1982), 19. This work is the best overview on the subject of philosophical anthropology, its origin and meaning.

2. Jesse Mann and Gerald Kreyche, Reflections on Man (New York: Harcourt, Brace and World, 1966), 6.

3. Wilhelm Windelband, A History of Philosophy (New York: Macmillan, 1919), 276. ". . . Augustine far transcended his time and likewise the immediate following centuries, and became one of the founders of modern thought" (ibid.).

4. Jos DeCorte, Lecture Notes (Leuven, 1986). "To know (oida) is to see (idein), to contemplate essential truths or forms (eidos)," 1.33.

5. Ibid., 1.35.

6. Windelband, History of Philosophy, 276.

7. Pico quoted in Landmann, 127.

8. Giovanni Pico della Mirandola, On the Dignity of Man (Indianapolis: Bobbs-Merrill, 1965), 4.

9. Jan Van der Veken, Lecture Notes (Leuven, 1986), 11.

10. Albert Hakim, Historical Introduction to Philosophy (New York: Macmillan, 1987), 291.

11. Robert Wernick, "Declaring an Open Season on the Wisdom of the Ages," Smithsonian (May 1997), 72-83.

12. Robert Darnton, The Great Cat Massacre and Other Episodes in French Cultural History (New York: Basic Books, Inc. 1984), 200.

13. Hakim, Historical, 411.

14. Ibid., 413.

15. Immanuel Kant, Education, trans. Annette Churton (Ann Arbor: University of Michigan Press, 1991), 6.

16. Ibid.

17. Hakim, Historical, 477.

18. Friedrich Wilhelm Joseph von Schelling, System of Transcendental Idealism, trans. Peter Heath (Charlottesville, Va.: University Press of Virginia, 1978), 233.

19. Windelband, History of Philosophy, 616.

20. Pierre Kerzsberg, Lecture Notes (Pennsylvania State University, November 1994).

21. Max Scheler, Man's Place in Nature (Boston: Meyerhoff, 1961). On the occasion of Scheler's death in 1928, Heidegger pronounced him the greatest thinker in contemporary philosophy.

22. Landmann, Fundamental Anthropology, 19-33.

23. Hans-Georg Gadamer, Truth and Method (New York: Crossroad, 1982), 78.

24. Joseph Kockelmans, "Unity and Multiplicity in the Sciences According to Hermeneutic Phenomenology," in Being Human in the Ultimate: Studies in the Thought of John M. Anderson, ed. Georgopoulos and Heim (Atlanta, Ga.: Rodopi, 1995), 281.

25. Joseph Kockelmans, Heidegger On Art and Artworks (The Hague: Martinus Nijhoff, 1985), 178.

26. Martin Heidegger, Basic Writings (New York: Harper and Row, 1977), 76.

27. Gadamer, 142.

28. Gadamer, 143.

29. Gadamer, 144

30. For Merleau-Ponty's views on literature see especially "Metaphysics of The Novel," Chapter Two in Sense and Non-sense, trans. Hubert and Priscilla Dreyfus (Evanston, Ill.: Northwestern University Press, 1964).

31. For Ricoeur's conception of interpretation see Essay Four, "Explanation and Understanding" in Interpretation Theory: Discourse and the Surplus of Meaning (Fort Worth, Texas: The Texas Christian University Press, 1976) and the essay "The Task of Hermeneutics," in Philosophy Today (Celine, Ohio: Messenger Press), 112-28.

32. I present a summary of Heidegger's "On the Essence of Truth," in Basic Writings, trans. John Sallis; ed. David Krell (New York: Harper and Row, 1993).

33. Kockelmans, Heidegger on Art, 188.

34. Ibid., 189.

35. Aristotle, The Poetics in On Poetry and Style (Indianapolis: The Library of Liberal Arts, 1958), 3-62.

36. S. H. Butcher, Aristotle's Theory of Poetry and Fine Art (New York: Dover Publications Inc., 1951), 164.

37. Concerning the discussion about truth in art and in particular validity in literary art I consulted the following essays and articles: St. Thomas Aquinas, in Introduction to St. Thomas

Aquinas, ed. Anton Pegis (New York: The Modern Library, 1948); Monroe C. Beardsley, Aesthetics; Problems in the Philosophy of Criticism (New York and Burlingame: Harcourt, Brace and World Inc., 1958); Arthur C. Danto, The Philosophical Disenfranchisement of Art (New York: Columbia University Press, 1986); M. Dhavamony, "Truth in Art According To Aquinas," Proceedings of The Fifth International Congress of Aesthetics (The Hague: Mouton, 1968), 287-91; John Hospers, "Implied Truths in Literature," in Philosophy Looks at the Arts, ed. J. Margolis (New York: Charles Scribner's and Sons, 1962), 199-214; Vera Maslow, "Heidegger and Ortega On Truth In Poetry and Art," in Proceedings of The Fifth International Congress of Aesthetics (The Hague: Mouton, 1968), 298-302; Iris Murdoch, The Fire and The Sun: Why Plato Banished the Artists (Oxford: Clarendon Press, 1977); Jose Ortega y Gassett, Meditations on Quixote (New York: W. W. Norton and Co., 1961); Laurent Stern, "Truth in Literature," Proceedings of The Fifth International Congress of Aesthetics (The Hague: Mouton, 1968), pp. 337-40; Meir Sternberg, "Polylingualism as Reality and Translation as Mimesis," Poetics Today, 2 no. 4 (1981): 221-39.

38. Joseph Kockelmans, Heidegger's "Being and Time": The Analytic of Dasein as Fundamental Ontology (Washington, D.C.: Center for Advanced Research in Phenomenology and University Press of America, 1989), 6.

39. Helen Muchnic's Dostoevsky's English Reputation, 1881-1936 (New York: Octagon Books, 1969) provides a detailed account of Dostoevsky's earliest reception in England and in the United States. She cites Edward Hallett Carr's biography, Dostoevsky (1821-1881): A New Biography (Boston and New York: Houghton and Mifflin and Co., 1931) as a definitive account of the writer's life. D. S. Mirsky's A History of Russian Literature (New York: Alfred A. Knopf, 1969) delivered a critical view of Dostoevsky from the viewpoint of a Russian Count. Works that helped to establish Dostoevsky's reputation in the early part of this century were Middleton Murry's Fyodor Dostoevsky: A Critical Study (New York: Russell and Russell, 1924; and Janko Lavrin's An Introduction to the Russian Novel (London: Methuen and Co. Ltd., 1942).

40. A. Ugrinsky et al., eds., Dostoevsky and the Human Condition after a Century (New York: Greenwood Press, 1986) records the proceedings of a fascinating conference.

41. Walter Kaufmann, Existentialism from Dostoevsky to Sartre (New York: Meridian, 1975), 14.

42. Paul Edwards, ed., The Encyclopedia of Philosophy (New York: Macmillan, 1967).

43. Frederick Copleston, S. J., Philosophy in Russia: From Herzen to Lenin and Berdyaev (Notre Dame: Search Press, 1986), 142-67.

44. D. H. Lawrence, "The Grand Inquisitor" in D. H. Lawrence, Selected Literary Criticism, ed. Anthony Beal (New York: Viking, 1961), 233-41.

45. D. H. Lawrence, quoted in F. M. Dostoevsky's The Brothers Karamazov, The Norton Critical Edition, ed. Ralph Matlaw (New York: W. W. Norton and Co., 1976), 830.

46. Ibid., 836.

47. V. V. Zenkovsky, A History of Russian Philosophy (2 vols.) trans. George Kline (New York: Columbia University Press, 1953). A short and succinct presentation of Zenkovsky's view of Dostoevsky's ideas appears in his article, "Dostoevsky's Religious and Philosophical Views," in Dostoevsky: A Collection of Critical Essays, ed. Rene Wellek (Englewood Cliffs, N.J.: Prentice-Hall Inc., 1962), 130-45.

48. Cf. Chapter 7 in Wayne Dowler, Dostoevsky, Grigor'ev and Native Soil Conservatism (Toronto: University of Toronto Press, 1982), 116-29. Two informative articles treating of native soil ideology in Dostoevsky's periodicals: Ellen Chances, "Pochvennichestvo: Ideology in Dostoevsky's Periodicals," MOSIAC 7, no. 2 (Winter 1974): 77-88; and "Pochvennichestvo--Evolution of an Ideology," Modern Fiction Studies (Spring 1974-Winter 1975): 543-51.

49. James Edie et al., Russian Philosophy (Chicago: Quadrangle Books, 1965).

50. Valerii Kuvakin, ed., A History of Russian Philosophy from the Tenth through the Twentieth Centuries, (3 vols.) (Buffalo N.Y.: Prometheus Books, 1994).

51. A fine presentation of the early Russian language criticism is to be found in Vladimir Seduro, Dostoevsky in Russian Literary Criticism, 1846-1956 (New York: Columbia University Press, 1957).

52. Lev Shestov, Dostoevskii i Nitshe--filosofiya tragedii published in English as Part II of Dostoevsky, Tolstoy and Nietzsche, trans. Bernard Martin (Athens, Ohio: Ohio University Press, 1969); Sur La Balance de Job: Peregrinations à travers les âmes (Paris: Flammarion, 1971); "Kierkegaard and Dostoevsky," in Edie et al., Russian Philosophy, Volume Three (Chicago: Quadrangle Books), 227-47. For a detailed Shestov bibliography, see Andrius Valevicius, Lev Shestov and His Times (New York: Peter Lang, 1993), 146-52.

53. Shestov, Dostoevsky, Tolstoy and Nietzsche, 174.

54. Nicholas Berdiaev, Dostoievsky: An Interpretation trans. Donald Attwater (New York: Sheed and Ward Inc., 1934). Berdiaev is also considered to be an existentialist, although cut from quite another variety than Shestov.

55. Ibid., 61.

56. Ibid., 36.

57. Ibid., 60.

58. Ibid., 49-50.

59. Ibid., 39.

60. Viacheslav Ivanov, Freedom and the Tragic Life: A Study in Dostoevsky, trans. Norman Cameron (New York: Noonday Press, 1960).

61. Seduro, 58.

62. Ivanov, 7.

63. Ivanov, 15.

64. The term "existentialist" has been used in so many ways. French thinker Emmanuel Mounier indicates that in 1947, existentialism was associated with a style made famous by Sartre and flouted in cafés and mixed up with all sorts of thinking. However, Mounier realized that existentialism was really nothing new and that it is perennial to philosophical inquiry about man. Speaking of this current in modern thought, he writes: "En termes trés généraux, on pourrait caractériser cette pensée comme une réaction de la philosophie de l'homme contre l'excès de la philosophie des idées et de la philosophie des choses." (Emmanuel Mounier, Introduction aux existentialismes (Paris: Editions de Noël, 1947), 8. Existentialism is a philosophy which takes the existence of man as its starting-point. This is a very broad definition, but it is adequate. According to Mounier, existentialism has many predecessors, including Socrates, the Stoics, Saints Augustine and Bernard, and Kierkegaard, to name a few. It is worth noting that Dostoevsky is not named in Mounier's "l'arbre existentialiste."

65. A succinct review of the early French criticism of Dostoevsky's work is found in the introduction of Part Three in Henri de Lubac's Le Drâme de l'humanisme athée (Paris: Spes, 1944). Henri Peyre reviews Dostoevsky's literary influence in France in a chronological order in "French Literary Imagination and Dostoevsky," in his work, French Literary Imagination and Dostoevsky (Tuscaloosa, Ala.: University of Alabama Press, 1975), 1-56. An abbreviated article deals with this same theme: "The French Face of Dostoevsky," in Dostoevsky and the Human Condition after a Century, ed. Ugrinsky et al. (New York: Greenwood Press, 1986).

66. Count Eugene Marie Melchior de Vogüé, Le roman russe (Paris: Plon, 1886).

67. Ibid., 207.

68. Ibid.

69. André Gide, Dostoïevski: Articles et causeries (Paris: Gallimard, 1964).

70. André Gide, Oeuvres Complètes d'André Gide (Paris: Nouvelle Revue Française, 1932-1939), Vol. XI, 305. Gide's Dostoïevsky is published in its entirety in Volume XI of his collected works. I cite references to this text with the title of essays from which they are derived.

71. Gide writes: "Pour ne choquer personne, disons, si vous le préférez, que la comédie humaine de Balzac est née de contact de l'Évangélie et de l'esprit latin; le comédie russe de Dostoïevsky du

contact de l'Évangile et du bouddhisme, de l'esprit asiatique" (Oeuvres Complètes, Vol. XI, 209).

72. Ibid., 150-51.

73. Ibid., 161.

74. André Gide, Les faux-monnayeurs in Romans: Récits et soties, oeuvres lyriques (Paris: Bibliothèque de la Pléiade, 1958), 931-1248.

75. Gide identifies a feature in Dostoevsky's poetics that is not only poetically, but philosophically significant. Ideas are a function of individual characters and their perpetual relativity. This insight parallels and antedates Bakhtin's description of Dostoevsky's deployment of ideas in "The Idea in Dostoevsky." "In Dostoevsky, two thoughts are already two people, for there are no thoughts belonging to no one and every thought represents an entire person" (Bakhtin, Problems of Dostoevsky's Poetics, 93). To say that Gide in some way prefigures ideas that were central to Bakhtin's monumental 1929 work should not surprise. Bakhtin himself indicates as much in the following sentence, "In the voluminous literature on Dostoevsky, the chief distinctive features of his poetics could not, of course have gone unnoticed . . ." (Bakhtin, 3). Gide, like the other commentators Bakhtin cites, sees the distinctive feature of Dostoevsky's poetics, i.e., his "polyphony," but fails to establish this insight in a rigorous and systematic fashion as does Bakhtin.

76. Gide, Oeuvres, Vol. XI, 224.

77. Ibid.

78. Gide, Romans, Les caves du vatican, 677-873.

79. Jean Hytier, André Gide, trans. Richard Howard (Garden City, N.Y.: Anchor Books, 1962), 102. Contains eight public lectures given at the Faculté des Lettres of the University of Algiers, from February to May 1938.

80. Ibid., 97.

81. Gide, Oeuvres, Vol. XI, 295.

82. For a clear exposition on the notion of the "absurd" in contemporary French literature, see Martin Esslin's The Theatre of the Absurd (Garden City, N.Y.: Anchor Books, 1969).

83. Ibid., 6.

84. Albert Camus, "Albert Camus . . . A Final Interview," Venture 3(4):25-39 (1960).

85. Gide, Oeuvres, 282-83.

86. Albert Camus, "The Other Russia," in The New York Herald Tribune, December 19, 1957. See Miriam Sajkovic, F. M. Dostoevsky: His Image of Man (Philadelphia: University of Pennsylvania Press, 1962).

87. Ibid.

88. Concerning Dostoevsky's role as a prophet of the political consequences of nihilism Camus wrote, "For me Dostoevsky is first of all a writer who, long before Nietzsche, knew how to discern modern nihilism, to define it and predict its disastrous consequences and to try to indicate the road to salvation" (ibid.).

89. Albert Camus, Lettres à un ami allemand (Paris: Gallimard, 1948), 75.

90. Albert Camus, Le mythe de Sisyphe: Essai sur l'absurde (Paris: Gallimard, 1942).

91. Albert Camus, "Albert Camus . . . A Final Interview," Venture, III, 4 (1960), 36.

92. Camus, Le mythe, préface.

93. Ibid., 18.

94. Ibid., 37.

95. Ibid., 150.

96. See "Two Suicides," and "The Verdict," vol. 1, 468-73 and "The Dream of a Strange Man: A Fantastic Story," vol. 2, 672-90, in Dostoevsky's Diary of a Writer, trans. and ed. Boris Brasol (New York: Charles Scribner's and Sons, 1949). For the most straightforward and succinct statement of Dostoevsky's conviction concerning the immortality of the human soul see "Will I Ever See Masha Again?" (Dostoevsky, PSS 20:172). Here, Dostoevsky contrasts the belief of the materialists with the "true" philosophy. The true philosophy consists in the realization that inertia will be abolished. This thought sees that matter and the apparent form of the universe will ultimately be abolished. God is the center of the universe and consubstantial with eternal life and the abolition of inertia and matter.

97. Albert Camus, L'homme révolté (Paris: Gallimard, 1951), 16.

98. For a source which treats solely of suicide in Dostoevsky's works see N. N. Shneidman's Dostoevsky and Suicide (Oakville, Ontario: Mosaic Press, 1984).

99. Camus, L'homme, 21.

100. Ibid., 75.

101. Ibid., 76

102. Ibid., 77.

103. Ibid., 78

104. Jean-Paul Sartre, L'existentialisme est un humanisme (Paris: Les Editions Nagels, 1946), 36.

105. Albert Camus, Le malentendu suivi de Caligula (Paris: Gallimard, 1958), 111.

106. Ibid., 225.

107. Camus, L'homme, 78.

108. Ibid., 82.

109. Ibid.

110. Camus, Le mythe, 152.

111. Albert Camus, The Myth of Sisyphus (New York: Vintage Books, 1959), v.

112. Sartre, La Nausée (Paris: Gallimard, 1938); Huis clos (Paris: Gallimard, 1945); Les mains sales (Paris: Gallimard, 1948); L'Être et le Néant (Paris: Gallimard, 1932).

113. Sartre, L'existentialisme, 9.

114. Ibid., 36.

115. Ibid., 95.

116. Sartre, L'existentialisme, 78.

117. Jean-Paul Sartre, Situations I (Paris: Gallimard, 1947), 71.

118. See Chapter 5 below.

119. Friedrich Nietzsche, Human All Too Human: A Book for Free Spirits, trans. Marion Faber, with Stephen Lechman (Lincoln: University of Nebraska Press, 1984).

120. "Buduschii chelovek" is the Underground Man's expression. For more on "the future man" see my Chapter 3 below.

121. Reinhard Lauth, Die Philosophie Dostojewskis (München: Piper, 1950).

CHAPTER 2

NOTES FROM THE HOUSE OF THE DEAD (1860)

Despite the overwhelming success of its first publication, the significance of Notes from the House of the Dead [Zapiski iz mertvogo doma] (hereafter referred to as Dead House) both in terms of its literary merit as well as its "thought," had been for a long time overlooked in the secondary literature.[1] The neglect of this work in France has been noted: "Les Récits de la Maison des Morts demeurent un chef d'oeuvre injustement négligé dans la création de Dostoevskij et Pierre Pascal a raison de le déplorer, lui qui fit tant pour les faire apprécier du public français."[2] The reasons for this work escaping critical notice are manifold.

One reason for the literary dormition of Dead House is its alien character. This is a strange work. Joseph Frank writes:

> From a purely artistic point of view, House of the Dead is probably the most unusual book that Dostoevsky ever produced--unusual not so much in Russian literature, despite the novelty of its depiction of prison life, but rather in the context of his own production.[3]

It is an "unusual" work, not only in purely artistic terms, but also in terms of "thought." The work possesses a documentary quality, and the tone of the narration is detached, with a description of prison life "from the outside." This differs greatly from Dostoevsky's later novels (esp. Notes from the Underground and Crime and Punishment, where internal monologue emerges as Dostoevsky's chief means of narration).

Dead House is unusual in that it can be read as fiction or autobiography. This unique character determines the narrative strategies and the approaches to be used in exploring its treatment of the meaning of man. The work ". . . contains an unprecedented analysis of the irrational lengths to which the human personality will go in quest of a sense of freedom."[4] Dead House demonstrates not only technical, poetic mastery but also a profound meditation upon the meaning of human freedom. Edward Wasiolek suggests that in this work, Dostoevsky ". . . is brought to the terrifying perception of the moral abyss of human nature."[5]

A number of themes relevant to philosophical anthropology emerge from this work: life and its limits; death and its limit; human suffering and joy; comradeship; wonder; prayer; faith in God; drunkenness; hope; and criminality. But above all, the question of the meaning of being human is raised, along with a consideration of the meaning of human freedom. Two primary senses for freedom become clear in the text: 1) there is svoboda, a word which connotes an absence of obstacles in the exercise of one's own personal will, and 2) volia, a word which connotes the will as a psychic capacity. A deeper look at the meaning of these terms follows below. Before addressing the denotative interpretation, there are a number of preliminary considerations to make concerning issues of narration, genre, and temporality.

Because the narrative unfolds with a "view from the outside," considerations which are based on the analysis of dialogue, and polyphony (cf. Bakhtin) are of little use. The meaning of being human is best interpreted in terms of the meaning of freedom.

It is convenient to approach freedom from several angles highlighting narrative strategies which I have split under five general headings which the works suggests. The first section presents an analysis of several narrative strategies which reveal the meaning of human freedom. The second section takes a closer look at the dead house as the primary metaphor in this work and presents an interpretation of the meaning of freedom within its world. The third section considers the prisoners who dwell in the dead house. Section four addresses the symbolic depiction of freedom in the dead house. Finally, section five presents a philosophy of crime according to Gorianchikov's memoir and concludes with a reflection upon the philosophical meaning of freedom.

Narrative Strategies in "Dead House"

The reader approaches this text as an alien world. He/she must pry open the meaning of this work, not only in terms of its linguistic and descriptive difficulties but in terms of the "first translation." Hans-Georg Gadamer's hermeneutic approach to literary works entails what he calls a dialectic of question and answer. Each text presents a central question to the reader. "Thus interpretation always involves a relation to the question that is asked of the interpreter." Further Gadamer writes: "The reconstruction of the question to which the text is presumed to be the answer takes place itself within the questioning through which we seek the answer to the question that the text asks us."[6]
The central question that the narrator of the Dead House asks is, how can a man go on living in an unlivable environment? The answer that the work gives is in fact Gorianchikov's memoir. Dead House is itself the answer to the question it poses. The interpreter, however, must reconstruct the work at this, and not another, level of meaning.

The interpreter meets various forms of alienation when facing this text, some literary, others linguistic, still others philosophical or cultural. And yet, the task of understanding is accomplished when the alien horizon that the text presents is "brought home." Gorianchikov's memoir makes present how he goes on living in a dead house because he possesses a capacity to adapt. This in fact is Gorianchikov's definition of man. Man is an "adapting" being [privykaiushchii].

While freedom and adaptation are not synonymous, adaptation reveals man's essential freedom. Pico della Mirandola identifies man's "unfinished" character as that which distinguishes him from other animals. Other animals have to be what they are, but man must finish himself. This implies that in talking of human adaptation we are not simply talking about survival. In order to survive in the dead house, the prisoner must discover a way to go on existing which requires some meaning which transcends mere physical survival.

And yet, freedom is portrayed within the narrative as having its meaning only within a certain limit or boundary. Beyond this, freedom ceases to have its meaning. The idea of "total freedom" is related to impossible dreams and unattainable illusions. This can still be understood in terms of a "negative freedom" i.e., a freedom from some obstacle or hindrance. It follows that in attaining release from such walls, the prisoner succeeds in becoming "free," at least in the negative sense. However, this has only opened up the horizon for our question: What is the positive meaning of freedom? If we take freedom as essential to his being human, we realize that man is free in a way that even prison walls do not eradicate.

A contrary idea states that the convict's life situation is so exceptional that it cannot teach us much about man's essential freedom.[7] For example, Soviet scholar Valerii Kirpotin has argued that Dostoevsky has too easily generalized from the convict population to the people outside the prison gates concerning human freedom. To be sure, the convict inhabits a unique world and ought to be considered exceptional. This world is a "special" world, set apart. The narrator relates:

> Here was our own world, unlike anything else; here were our own laws, our own dress, our own manners and customs, here was the house of the living dead, a life like no other upon earth, and people who were special, set apart. It is this special corner that I am setting out to describe. (E: 27; PSS 4:9)[8]

The primary descriptive feature of the dead house is the "special" character of its world. It might be objected that the uniqueness of this world makes its description of man irrelevant to all inhabitants of the world outside the dead house. I want to argue that it is, on the contrary, the uniqueness of the dead house, and its special laws and customs which reveal the essential features of human freedom. In the extreme wilderness, in the remote regions of Siberia lies the dead house. It is a boundary situation which reveals human nature and reveals man in his essential freedom. We learn from it the essential meaning of freedom in human life, as though by negative example. Dostoevsky describes the prison life in such a way that the question of the meaning of human freedom is set in relief in all that he describes. The "negative space" of the Omsk Stockade opens up a horizon in which the narrator's question is written large in every face and on every door.

The Fictional Narrator

We now want to indicate features of how the narration of Dead House reveals the meaning of human freedom. In a manner reminiscent of his literary hero, Alexander Pushkin, Dostoevsky distances himself as far as he can from the narrative by using a frame device. Much in the same way that Pushkin introduced the narrator Ivan Petrovich in Tales of Belkin [Povesti pokoinogo Ivana Petrovicha Belkina],[9] Dostoevsky introduces his reader to a fictional narrator, Alexander Gorianchikov, in a preface in order to present (as well as to disguise) his prison memoir. The choice of the fictional narrator brings to the interpreter certain problems. For example, there is the problem of narrative reliability, the question of authority within the narrative--"I" and the problem of the horizon of interpretation. While the use of a fictional narrator hides the facts of Dostoevsky's prison experience, it also grants the reader a liberty to stand at a remove from the historical events which underlie this narrative. The peculiarity of Dostoevsky's autobiographical "I" opens up to a more universal sense of humanity, thanks to the fictional narrator. Hence, what might be read as a memoir, bound to its author in temporality, can be read as fiction with a much broader horizon of interpretation.

The narration of this work employs two framed narrators. The first narrator is "the publisher of these notes by the late Alexander Petrovich Gorianchikov," and the latter is the primary narrator, the fictional narrator of Dostoevsky's work, Alexander Petrovich Gorianchikov ("gore"; grief, misfortune). In addition to resemblance to Pushkin's collection of tales (povest'), the narrative frame of Dead House is in the "zapiski" tradition.[10] Framing one's work as "notes" gives an author organizational control over a fictional manuscript to which only he has access. By publishing such notes, the author is making known to the public what would otherwise remain unknown. The notes open up a window to a human life that would otherwise remain entirely opaque. A closer look at the narration in this work reveals the "exotic" world of the inhabitants of the "dead house."[11]

Except for narrative insertions, for example at the beginning of Chapter VII, Part Two, in which "the publisher of these notes by the late Alexander Petrovich Gorianchikov" inserts almost a page, Gorianchikov's memoir serves as our eyes and ears in the alien world of the dead house. He informs the reader of the ultimate limitations of his observation: "I found at the beginning of my time in the prison that I was unable to penetrate the inner fabric of this life . . ." [proniknut' vo vnutrennuiu glubinu etoi zhizni] (E: 305; PSS 4:197). This narrative assertion reveals not only a statement of fact concerning Gorianchikov's incapacity to fully understand life in the prison, but also points to a capacity to recognize that there is such an impenetrable depth in human life. Just as words reveal and conceal in such a way that the reader finds the narrator's silence on a given matter to be meaningful, so too with matters of "narrative perception." Robert L. Jackson indicates the manner in which "seeing" in Dostoevsky's work is revelatory of a deeper comprehension of things: "To 'see,' in Dostoevsky's aesthetics, as in the etymological sense of the Slavic word 'videt',' 'to see,' is always 'to understand'; and to understand is to penetrate to the depths of a phenomenon."[12]

It is precisely when he realizes his former blindness that Gorianchikov recognizes his fellow prisoners as comrades, and hears kindness in their words that he never noticed before. He finds himself opening up to nature--his eyes behold "God's world" [bozhii svet] and the pure, uninhibited freedom of nature. Viacheslav Ivanov discusses Dostoevsky's realism precisely in such terms of spiritual penetration:

> Clearly this mode of thought is not based upon theoretical cognition, with its constant antithesis of subject and object, but upon an act of will and faith approximately corresponding to the Augustinian "transcende te ipsum." Dostoevsky has coined for this a word of his own: proniknovenie, which properly means "intuitive seeing through" or "spiritual penetration."[13]

Ivanov parallels Augustine's expression "transcende te ipsum" with Dostoevsky's "proniknovenie." Augustine's original statement appeared in De Vera Religione. Here it is: "Do not go abroad. Return within yourself. In the inward man dwells truth. If you find that you are by nature mutable, transcend yourself." [Noli foras ire, in teipsum redi. In interiore homine habitat veritas. Et si tuam naturam mutabilem inveneris, transcende et te ipsum.][14] That truth dwells within man, that it is not to be found in exteriors alone, is a conviction common to both Augustine and Dostoevsky. When Gorianchikov reports that he was unable to penetrate the inner fabric of the prison life, he at least substantiates that interior life by referring to it negatively.

The narrative form of Dead House manifests this spiritual "inward seeing." A type of spiritual penetration is at work when we recognize the fictional character of our narrator, and we do not interpret his narrative as a factual description of Dostoevsky's experience. Thanks to the frame, the reader is able to read his statements in another light. Dostoevsky as author has chosen to show us the truth of his prison experience through the limitations of this frame vehicle. Even so, that which reveals, also conceals. And vice-versa.

Another limitation in the observation is the fact that the world described is colored to a certain extent by the narrator's affect. The perspective made possible by Gorianchikov's narration is colored by his feelings and reveals gaps:

> The anguish, the depression I experienced during that first year were unbearable, and they made me bitter and irritable. Because of them I failed to notice much of what was going on around me in the first year. I closed my eyes to it all and did not want to look. (E: 278; PSS 4:178)

That which the narrator fails to notice is most likely unavailable to the reader's perception. Limitations in what appear as narrator's perception equal limitations in the knowability of prison life. Yet, the reverse is also true, the world that the narrator makes present is available to the reader and is knowable insofar as it is presented. The narrator's notes "open" and "close" the world of the dead house. A consideration of what is said as well as of what is unsaid reveals a fuller picture of the world the work makes present.

Genre

Narration possesses a double capacity, or freedom for interpretation. The question of genre poses an even larger obstacle for interpretation. Jacques Catteau enumerates a number of generic designations which *Notes from the House of the Dead* has earned: "a novel, a documentary novel, literary memoir, a work in the "*zapiski*" (notes) tradition, even a religious autobiography."[15] If, as E. D. Hirsch argues, "All understanding of verbal meaning is necessarily genre-bound,"[16] then *Dead House* presents a certain problem for understanding, since its genre is not so easily ascertained. Presumably, we cannot arrive at a meaning for the work until we discern its genre. One solution suggests that this work is a "boundary work" which can be read by at least two different sets of generic codes.[17] Another point of view is that genre is inherently unstable. Thomas Beebee writes, ". . . [T]he truly vital meanings of a text are often contained not in any specific generic category into which the text may be placed, but rather in the play of differences between its genres."[18] Whether we take genre to be the regulative principles guiding interpretation, or whether we see genre itself as problematic, the consideration of genre figures centrally in any interpretation of Dead House, for it is precisely in the interplay of Dostoevsky's fictional narrator and the facticity of Dostoevsky's narrative world that the features of his thinking about man are revealed.

The work traditionally falls into either an autobiographical genre and is seen as revelatory of Dostoevsky's own prison experience, with the convenient addition of a fictive narrator as a device to throw off the censors; or it is seen as a fictional work which ought not to be read as a memoir of Dostoevsky's prison experience, save in a very refractory way. Frank finds both features in the work, and refers to its "double perspective":

> This double perspective is very carefully maintained, and must constantly be kept in mind if we are to avoid the error of taking the work either as an unadorned memoir or as a purely fictional construct; in fact, it is a unique combination of both.[19]

Gary Morson's concept of a boundary work seems to fit here: "In what I shall refer to as boundary works, it is uncertain which of two mutually exclusive sets of conventions governs a work."[20] The work is open to a reading as autobiography or as fiction. At any rate, whether it is taken as a novel, as fictional writing, or as an autobiography, the question of the genre of this work underscores an essential interchange between Dostoevsky's prison experience and the writing of Dead House.

Metaphysics of the Novel

Another level of narrative interpretation which has a direct bearing on how the meaning of freedom is deployed within the work is the metaphysics of the novel. Three French philosophers that have been associated with existentialism have emphasized the philosophical implications of novel writing. J. P. Sartre in an essay on William Faulkner has written: ". . . [U]ne technique romanesque renvoie toujours 'à la métaphysique du romancier."[21] Maurice Merleau-Ponty in Sense and Nonsense discusses the metaphysics of a novel by Simone de Beauvoir.[22] And for Albert Camus, the act of writing fiction is de facto already a rebellion against the world "as it is." The work of art is man's sole chance of keeping his consciousness and of fixing its adventures. The absurd place of the work of art is in its universal inexhaustibility.

Catteau's La creation littéraire chez Dostoievski (1978) attempts to analyze the function of literary creation, or the "how" of the literary work: ". . . la fonction créatrice elle-même, au sens mathématique du terme, plus exactement l'opération, l'acte, qui associe à tout élément de l'ensemble constitué par l'homme un élément de l'ensemble défini par l'oeuvre créée."[23] By reading Dostoevsky's works synoptically and comparing the notebooks of their literary genesis, Catteau arrived at an integral understanding of the literary creation and the life and mind of its creator. Catteau analyzes the fundamental structures in the literary work: space and time. Space is the "architecture" of a novel, while time is the "symphony." "Si le temps est la structure de l'expérience tragique du héros, l'espace constitue la structure de la signification, du déploiement de la conscience."[24] Time constitutes the horizon in which the heroes either accomplish their freedom or fail to do so.

Catteau's analysis is apt and particularly fitting with regard to Dead House. Chief amongst the temporal structures that Catteau considers is the repetition of cyclical time. In considering the temporality of Solzhenitsyn's One Day in the Life of Ivan Denisovich,[25] Catteau remarks that Dostoevsky's work is also a type of prolonged day in which the events of Gorianchikov's four years add up to one cyclical year. The narrative proceeds from a lengthy description of Gorianchikov's first day in prison, ranging several chapters, after this chapters present successively greater portions of Gorianchikov's prison time until he is set free. There is hence an acceleration of narrative time relative to the reader's experience. As a result of this narrative technique, the first impressions are particularly strong and unique. Catteau points out how the specific temporal structure tends toward a cyclical representation. He writes: "Plus même, pour mieux imprimer cette structure cyclique où l'esprit s'englue, l'écrivain a peu à peu associé des châinons qui sont de nature hétérogène, transformant ainsi le temps en concrétude."[26] Hence, the novelty of the first day, the first bath, the first month, or the first Christmas do not need to be replicated in the narrative. The diachrony moves toward a synchrony of "everyman's year."

Temporality of Narration

Another level of the narration in the work which figures in the interpretation of freedom is time. The double-framed temporality of Gorianchikov's narration is past-tense. This stands in contrast with the description of the convicts' psychological temporality which is primarily future-tense, based upon a temporal suspension. "No convict feels at home in prison, but rather as if he were on a visit ['v gostiakh'] there" (E: 128; PSS 4:79). The criminal's perception of the dead house is something to be gotten over. Their consciousness is future-oriented, toward life beyond the dead house. This feature of the narrative temporality--looking forward to release--is characteristic of life within the dead house. The framed narrator who gives us Gorianchikov's past-tense memoir implies a vantage point of having gone through the dead house and living to talk about it, i.e., of writing from beyond the grave and release.[27]

The Meaning of "Volia" and "Svoboda"

A number of statements appear in the narrative which reflect nuances in the meaning of freedom, chief amongst which are svoboda and volia. These two terms are not entirely synonymous, and their denotation and connotation demand distinguishing. Volia is simply the popular word for freedom. Vladimir Dal's Explanatory Dictionary of Living Russian [Tolkovyi slovar' zhivogo velikirusskogo iazyka] (1882) gives among others the following definitions for svoboda:

> . . . svoia volia, prostor', vozmozhnost' deistvovat po-svoemu.
>
> [One's will, space, possibility to acting of one's own accord. . . .][28]

Volia is defined:

> . . . dannyi cheloveku proizvol deistviia; svoboda, prostor' v postupkakh. . . .
>
> [. . . man's gift (capacity) for arbitrary actions, freedom, latitude in conduct. . . .][29]

The Soviet Academy of Sciences Dictionary (1984) gives as a primary meaning for svoboda: "The means for man to act in accordance with his own interests and goals, resting upon a perception of objective necessity."[30] A secondary meaning describes the absence of political and economic oppression. In the same dictionary, volia finds as its primary meaning: "One of the qualities of the human mind, expressed in the method to attain to the realization furnished in front of the goal itself, the realization of striving."[31] A second meaning refers to desire, want, demand. A review of the adjectival meanings of "svoboda" [svobodnyi] indicates that svoboda has a broader range of meaning and can refer to non-human phenomena, while "volia" refers primarily to a quality which the human being possesses (except for metaphorical usage). Nonetheless, it is evident that svoboda and volia possess a ground of common meaning and that insofar as svoboda refers to a capacity of action within man, it relies upon volia. Volia we might say is the capacity within man to exercise svoboda.

Deprivation of volia is constitutive of the being of the prisoner:

> Ves' smysl slova "arestant" oznachaet cheloveka bez voli; a, tratia den'gi, on postupaet uzhe po svoei vole. (PSS 4:66)
>
> [The whole meaning of the word "convict" implies a man without a will of his own; when he spends money, however, he is acting from his own will.] (E: 109)

Volia, further, is associated with wanting (khotenia), wish (okhota), desire (zhelanie) and the untrammeled assertion of one's own will power no matter what the cost. It is evident in the manner in which Gorianchikov describes the prisoners' sprees, the drunken free-for-all. In Dead House Gorianchikov observed that for the illusion of freedom, a convict will: ". . . go on the binge, brawl, annihilate someone with crushing insults and prove to him that he can do this, that all this is 'in our hands'. . ." (E: 109).

The convict will go to any length, take any risk to assert his freedom, even if it is entirely contrary to reason. The ultimate goal of such lashing out is svoboda:

> Nakonets, vo vsem etom kutezhe est' svoi risk, --znachit, vse eto imeet khot' kakoi-nibud' prizrak zhizni, khot' otdalennyi prizrak svobody. (PSS 4:66)
>
> [But in the end all this excess carries with it its own risk--and this means that it is all imbued with an illusion of life, an illusion, however remote, of freedom.] (E: 109)

The power of the spree or drinking binge lies in its relation to freedom. It should be noted that money is essential to the spree. Money is intimately linked with the exercise of one's own will. The spree is more valuable than money for the reason that it is tied up with the illusion of freedom. "What will a man not give up for freedom?" Gorianchikov asks. The dream of the spree is one of the few avenues that a convict has to grasp for his freedom. Even though it is an illusion, and even though he loses all, he is exercising the power of his will, and this is the most significant point. Dreaming of the spree has at its heart the quest for freedom which is as essential to human life as air or water. The freedom of a convict is certainly curtailed and yet the exercise of one's own will is intensified. This seems to suggest a freedom which is more primordial than the apparent freedom which is hindered by prison walls.

The Dead House as Structure and Metaphor

Its Inhabitants

Having considered the narrative strategies which enact freedom within the text, we now turn to the meaning of the dead house and its world. The "dead house" is a primary metaphor for the world of the prison which is self-contained in which men are cut off from vital relations with their families, and their homelands, living as though buried alive. The chief descriptive feature of the prison is its epithet "the house of the dead" or "dead house" [mertvyi dom].[32] As in English usage whose "house" can be seen both as building: "house" or habitation: "home," the word "dom" can translate either a house (building) or a home. In both cases "a dead house" is a paradox for "dom" which suggests living rather than death. As a metaphor, a dead house suggests a world beyond life, or even a tomb; it embodies the meaning of the boundary of life, and establishes a paradoxical "life" in a "dead" house.

The "dead house" is a very rich metaphor. Still, what the reader is directly confronted with is the fictional frame which grants the reader access to the strange and distant world of the dead house. This means that the world that Gorianchikov describes is the primary referent. For example, even though the dead house stands metaphorically for death,[33] the underground,[34] hell,[35] alienation,[36] and a number of other things; it must not be forgotten that the dead house refers primarily to the Siberian prison. It is necessary to stabilize the referential meaning of the primary metaphor of the dead house within the world in which it stands before applying secondary metaphors which may in fact undercut the primary reference.[37] The method of securing such a reading is to treat Dead House as a literary artwork which reveals a world which can teach us something essential about human freedom:

> . . . anyone entering a prison can feel that this entire body of men has been assembled here against its will [". . . ne svoieiu okhotoiu . . ."] and that, whatever measures are taken, it is impossible to convert a living man into a corpse: he retains his feelings, his thirst for vengeance and life, his passions and his desire to satisfy them. (E: 78; PSS 4:44)

The expression which translates: "ne svoieiu okhotoiu" above as "against its will" is echoed in the expression "bez voli" cited above. The noun okhota standardly means will or desire but can also mean in another context "hunt" or "chase." There is an element of cat and mouse in that the convict is caught and held prey. Even so, the convict remains a hunter who still possesses a thirst for life, and a will of his own.

The People

In order to get a better idea of the people that inhabit the particular world of the dead house, let us look at Gorianchikov's observations concerning people in the narrative. Even though he is a prisoner, the tone of his narrative description of prison life in its details is that of a tour guide, as though an outsider keeping an outside look at all he describes: "As you enter the enclosure, you see several buildings in it . . ." (E: 27; PSS 4:9). Likewise, the description of the culture and life of the prisoners within the dead house is so sober, restrained and distant that his narrative resembles a scientific documentary describing the categories of prisoners in their specific ethnic and cultural habits. We might call his observations a "prison anthropology."[38]

The prison wall is not merely a physical boundary, but moral as well. Freedom in an aberrant sense is implicated in the meaning of prison. The prison fortress is as Gorianchikov describes--". . . [A] high stockade in the form of an irregular hexagon . . . " (E: 27; PSS 4:9). It is also a moral structure held in place by the tension between the act that placed the criminal in prison and the will he retains to live beyond the prison wall.

This world that is set apart is peopled with a strange community. Membership in its society is afforded only by criminals or presumed criminals. It should be noted that this world is not only extreme in the sense of being geographically remote in a severe climate, but that it is also morally an extreme type of community. One of the essential features of this community is its negativity. First of all, the presence of other human beings in forced communal existence is for the narrator yet another torment of prison life. Add to this torment the forced penal labor, and the atrocious food, prisoners with bad habits, and bad attitudes, and you have a picture of a rather depressing society.

Despite the negative picture of the communality in the narrative, Gorianchikov also cites some positive, redeeming features. For example, one positive aspect of this community is the Christmas holiday with its theatrical production. Gorianchikov also relates favorably to the Church and the ritual services at Christmas and Easter. Finally, Gorianchikov takes a great deal of solace from the company of animals, especially Sharik, the dog. As though in a portrait freedom is depicted in this tension between the dark, negative space of the dead house, and the rays of light that pierce its dark day.

Another positive influence on the community in the dead house is that of the girls of the village who sell "kalatches" and breads to the prisoners to lighten their burden. The Russian folk call criminals "unfortunates" [neschastnye] (PSS 4:46). Gorianchikov pays special attention to this epithet asking what is its significance:

> It is not for nothing that the common people throughout Russia call crime a misfortune, and criminals "unfortunates." This distinction is of profound significance. It is even more important because it is formulated unconsciously, instinctively. (E: 80; PSS 4:46)

The significance of this way of referring to criminals is precisely that it emerges straight from the speech of the real Russian "folk" and reveals a nonjudgmental view of the convict (cf. PSS 21:13-23).

Gorianchikov's description of the first impressions of the other convicts falls into a neat classification. Later, when he discovers that he is attempting to categorize the prisoners into too rigid a configuration, he states that life is not such that it allows such strict definitions:

> Reality is infinitely various when compared to the deductions of abstract thought, even those that are most cunning, and it will not tolerate rigid, hard-and-fast distinctions. Reality strives for diversification [Deistvitel'nost' stremitsia k razdrobleniiu.] (E: 305 [italics mine]; PSS 4:197)

I cite this quotation because it indicates a metaphysical point of view. This tendency to refrain from strict rational classification of the prisoners and their life makes our narrator more of a descriptive than an analytical anthropologist. Perhaps it is more accurate to say that Dostoevsky's narrator is a talented philosophical anthropologist.

Gorianchikov begins his narrative by telling us that there were 250 men of great national variety, and that each crime was represented:

> I think that each province, each zone of Russia had its representative here. There were non-Russians as well, there were even some convicts from among the mountain tribesmen of the Caucasus. They were all divided according to the degree of their crime and consequently according to the number of years their sentence carried. I suppose there was no crime that did not have its representative here. (E: 29; PSS 4:10)

The concatenation of such men from all parts of the Russian Empire betrays not a pan-Russian phenomenon, but one that is not ethnically Russian. Gorianchikov comments not on the commonalities but on the distinctions in a prisoner's nationality and religion, for example, the Old Believer from Starodub, or Isai Fomich, the Jew, or, for example, Ali, the Mohammedan. Perhaps the primary descriptive fact in his narrative description of the other prisoners is the distinction between nobles and peasants. His own status as a noble did not allow him equal peerage with the peasant prisoners. I shall comment on this important distinction below.

Gorianchikov observes that all of the prisoners are dreamers. Paradoxically, the prisoners who harbor the most unrealizable dreams hold onto them all the more strongly.

> The more unrealizable were the hopes of these men, and the stronger their own sense of their unrealizability, the more stubbornly and chastely they would keep to themselves, unable, however, to renounce them. It was quite possible that they were privately ashamed of these hopes. (E: 304; PSS 4:196)

Non-convicts play their roles in the dead house as well. There are doctors, the villagers who are described in the narrator's introduction, bread bakers, prostitutes, a priest, the girls who sell kalatches, and so on. Then there are prison authorities: Governor, Major, sentries and so forth.

An Important Distinction

"The Complaint" (Part II, Chapter 7) is one of the rare places in the text where Dostoevsky's fictive narrator, "the publisher of these notes," inserts his voice. It is in this chapter where one might find Dostoevsky asserting his voice as well. Dostoevsky's two fictive narrators act like filters between himself and the narrative which conveys his memoir. The fact that he chose to remove himself as far as possible from the narration is meaningful. Of course, it has its practical aim in deterring censorship. More importantly for our consideration is the lesson to be learned in the revealing/concealing movement from the "truth" of Dostoevsky's imprisonment to the "poetry" or fiction of this framed narrative. Here are several assertions which seem to resonate beyond the fictiveness of the narration.

A special note should be made concerning the special distinction that Gorianchikov draws between nobles and muzhiks. He makes a clear effort to clarify this issue. Despite well meaning efforts of humanitarians to equate muzhiks and nobles, Gorianchikov resolutely declares that this is not possible. That this is an issue that is significant to our narrator he makes clear in the chapter called "The Complaint." The complaint is twofold: there is the prisoners' plan to complain to the Major concerning the miserable quality of the prison food, and then there is Gorianchikov's complaint which stems from the fact that he cannot participate in the formal complaint.

When Gorianchikov attempts to participate in an official complaint to the Major concerning the wretched quality of the food he is made painfully aware that this is none of his business, that he is not an equal to the peasant and never will be. He went out into the line like the peasant prisoners, who found it strange that he showed up. He is mocked by the peasants and urged to return inside. When Gorianchikov asks Petrov, a peasant convict whom he trusts, whether the peasants are angry at the nobles, Petrov doesn't understand. Gorianchikov states, "We ought to have gone along with you--as your companions." Petrov answers, "But what kind of companion could you ever be to us?" Gorianchikov was made to realize that the muzhik is a special kind of human being and that to equate him with the nobleman is simply naive:

> My conviction comes not from books (<u>ne knizhno</u>), or from speculation, but from lived experience, and I have had a great sufficiency of time in which to put my conviction to the test. Possibly one day everyone will realize the extent to which it is justified. . . . (E: 308; <u>PSS</u> 4:199)

The narrator defends his conviction, masking Dostoevsky's true sentiment at the time of the writing. The three dots (. . .) only serve to emphasize his challenge. The conviction which comes from books or speculation is the humanitarian theory which Gorianchikov is familiar with:

> I am familiar with this proposition, have heard it bandied about of late, have read about it. The foundation of this idea is a sound and humane one. It is that all are people, all are human. But as an idea it is far too abstract. (E: 306; PSS 4:197)

The text gives the interpreter a riddle to consider: namely that the conviction of the narrator "does not come from books" [ne knizhno] when in fact the publication of Gorianchikov's conviction is nothing if not "bookish" [knizhno]. It is for this reason we perceive a chink in the fictive armor and suggest to hear the author speaking.

The strength of Gorianchikov's position is based upon his struggle to be an equal of the peasant. It is not as if he made no effort to make a rapprochement. But it simply did not work. Perhaps Gorianchikov, like Dostoevsky, once sided with the humanitarians but reality and lived experience taught him how theoretical the idea of equality between noble and muzhik is.

When Gorianchikov realizes that the inequality is clear, it makes him resentful and even envious. The nobleman suffers to a greater extent in prison than does the peasant. He is not at home [u sebia doma] like the peasant. It is not in a physical sense that he suffers more, being more refined or educated, but that he is never welcome amongst his peasant prisoners as a brother and an equal. "There is nothing so terrible as to live in a social environment that is alien to one" (E: 307; PSS 4:198). As if to make the gulf between himself and the peasant felt more clearly, Gorianchikov transcribes a dialogue between the muzhiks in their peasant dialect, as if to make it clear that even the speech excludes the nobleman and is scarcely intelligible to him (cf. PSS 4:23-25). In the chapter that follows the complaint, Gorianchikov describes his "companions" who are the fellow Polish and Russian nobles in prison.

Prison Anthropology

Is there any way to draw parallels between the world of the dead house that the narrative reveals and the truth about human freedom? As mentioned, one clue is already given in the meaning of "prison." A prison is not merely a physical, material construct, but it implies the tension of human freedom and the moral dilemma of crime. In what follows, the philosophical significance of the dead house is considered in light of philosophical anthropology. I assert that the extreme nature of this world both in terms of its geography and its community reveals something essential concerning the nature of human being and human freedom. The dead house can be read as the "limit" which raises questions concerning the meaning of being human. The narrative asserts two fundamental "theses" concerning man.

Thesis One: Man is Adaptable

The question arises in Gorianchikov's prison memoir as to how man goes on living in an unlivable circumstance and environment:

> I always found it hard to come back into our barracks from outside. It was a long, low unventilated room, dimly lit by tallow candles, with a heavy suffocating smell. I do not understand how I managed to live in it for ten years. (E: 29; PSS 4:10)

His answer follows ". . . man has great endurance. Man is a creature who can get used [privykaiushchii] to anything, and I think that is the best definition of him" (ibid.).

During the first month Gorianchikov found himself musing upon the idea that some day he might regret having to leave the prison:

> The thought that I might in time be sorry to leave this corner filled me with horror: even then I had some inkling of the monstrous extent to which human beings are capable of getting used to anything.
> [. . . do kakoi chudovishchnoi stepeni prizhivchiv chelovek . . .] (E: 95; PSS 4:56)

The narrator has an inkling of the monstrous (the stem "chud-" also connotes "miracle, wonder") extent man adapts to anything. As time went by, after the first month, Gorianchikov gradually grew accustomed to prison life:

> Already I walked about the prison as though I were at home, I knew my place on the plank bed and even seemed to have managed to get used to things I never would have believed I could have grown used to in all my life. (E: 126; PSS 4:78)

The first answer to the question how can man live in a dead house is provided by Gorianchikov when he states that man can adapt to anything. The narrative shows how this life is possible, not only for Gorianchikov but the other prisoners as well.

Purposive Work

Man adapts to prison life because he is capable of adaptation. This insight accords with Max Scheler's conception of man as "outward bound."[39] Man has a "flexible nature" which is freed-up from the dictates of his environmental and natural instincts in such a way that free consciousness is possible. That man is capable of taking distance from his instincts and affixing meaning to his conscious activity is the essential possibility of meaningful human freedom. This is freedom in its most primordial, anthropological sense. Man's outstanding capacity for adaptation stands forth as an essential revelation concerning man's nature. However, this freedom to adapt and to go on living implies a still more primordial and philosophical sense of freedom. Before we discuss this, let us see how this "anthropological" freedom takes sense in the text.

What are the characteristic features which constitute Gorianchikov's adaptation to penal life? The chief fact of human adaptation is that man needs to work in order to maintain a sense of purposiveness. Paradoxically, work is perhaps the chief feature of life in the dead house. Prisoners were expected to and are compelled to do penal labor. Labor made up a big part of Gorianchikov's life in prison and accordingly he provides a detailed account of the work conditions and a thoughtful analysis of the meaningfulness of such labor.

The character of penal labor and what gives it its penal feature is that it is imposed upon a man without his will:

> The work itself, for example, did not seem at all like the hard, *penal* labor it was supposed to be, and I realized only much later on that its hardness and *penal nature* consisted not so much in its being difficult or unalleviated as in its being *forced*, compulsory, done under the threat of the stick [italics in original]. (E: 43; *PSS* 4:20)

What makes penal labor so difficult, then, is not its physical aspect, but its moral aspect. Gorianchikov comments that if one wanted to truly crush and break man, one need only assign to them useless and meaningless toil, for example pounding sand or moving dirt from one pile to another. Therein lies the upshot of Ecclesiastes' lament and Sisyphus' tragedy.[40] It is worth noting that even though he sees the penal labor as morally difficult Gorianchikov resolves to find meaning in his labor: "I had a feeling that work could be my salvation . . . " (E: 129; *PSS* 4:80). It appears that purposive work is essential to the ongoing life of a human being.

It should be noted that in addition to penal labor convicts did their own work, whose significance Gorianchikov rates highly:

> Without work and without lawful, normal possessions a man cannot live, he grows depraved, turns into an animal. And for this reason every man in the prison had, as a consequence of a natural demand and an instinct for self-preservation, his own craft and occupation. (E: 38; PSS 4:16)

Thus, there are some natural constraints to man's adaptability. Man can adapt to anything provided that he can find his own meaningful endeavor. Prisoners find meaning in their work, and through this they are able to sustain hope by projecting their thoughts toward freedom beyond the meaninglessness of penal labor.[41]

Hope

The prisoners maintain an attitude which consists of statements like, "I will really live then." This attitude provides perhaps the only real possibility for the convict to go on living. It is not only a coping mechanism but reveals a philosophical necessity. While Gorianchikov resolves to live and to find meaning in his labor, Isai Fomich, we are told, will take a wrinkle formula so that he will find a wife "after my prison sentence--then." Hence, Gorianchikov reveals that the condition of possibility of meaningfulness in prison life is living in hope toward an indefinite future. George Dolnikowski said, "You will be free at last (for the time being)."[42] Every stage in life can be likened to a prison, and every person moves on and graduates from one prison to yet another and ever and anon.

The prisoner while he may adapt to life in the dead house, never feels at home there, and lives always toward the indefinite future in which he will be free:

> No man can live without some goal to aspire towards. If he loses his goal, his hope, the resultant anguish will frequently turn him into a monster. . . . The goal of all

> the convicts was freedom and release from prison. (E: 305; PSS 4:197)

It is precisely this goal, the dream of release from prison which drives the prisoners on.

Hope, like work, is absolutely essential to human life. That without which a human being cannot go on being human is necessary, i.e., essential, to being human. In the latter part of his narrative, Gorianchikov points out a category of convicts without hope. He identifies an elder from the Starodubye settlements as belonging to this category. And there was another:

> The convict who went mad, the one who used to read the Bible and who went for the Major with a brick, was probably another of those who had given up every last hope; but since life without hope is impossible, he had found a way out for himself with a voluntary, almost artificial martyrdom. (E: 305; PSS 4:197)

This convict had abandoned all hope [kogo pokinula posledniaia nadezhda] and yet martyrdom represented for him a means of escape, hence he possessed this final hope.

Now, having taken careful note that man can live in the dead house and that work and hope are essential features of Gorianchikov's presentation of life in the dead house, I would like to return to the question of human adaptability. The question of man's adaptability reveals the question of man's nature. "How can man live in the dead house?" can be read as: "What are the limits to human nature?"

Thesis Two: Human Nature is Unbounded

The flip side of the question concerning man's ability to adapt is the question concerning the limits or range of human nature. If I assert that man is capable of adapting to anything ("omniadaptable") then I am asserting that his nature is indeterminate, and unbounded. If this is so, then how are we to identify the human being? If we know the conditions which make a man human, then we can also know what a man is. Obversely, if we know the point at which a man is not a man, then in knowing what a man is not, we know something about what a man is. Precisely at what point does a man cease to be man, and to become, for example, a "terrible monster"? For our narrator, a convict who ceases to be human is called a monster. We have noted above that on two occasions Gorianchikov has stated at what point a man ceases to be man; the man without his own work and possessions becomes an animal, and the man without a goal to aspire toward becomes a monster. Now let us look more closely to Gorianchikov's depiction of some men who are perhaps more monster than man.

"It is hard to imagine the degree to which human nature may become distorted" (E: 246; PSS 4:157). This remark concerns the executioner who flogs the convicts. Gorianchikov provides an extensive reflection upon those men who make flogging an art and a craft. He cites Zherebiatnikov's "pure love of the art of flogging," who took great pleasure in punishing convicts. Gorianchikov reflects that there are people like tigers thirsty for blood, men who become drunken with blood and power. One is shocked at the depravity which certain men exhibit in their love for blood and torture. One wonders whether there is a lower limit at which the tyranny in a man forces him to surrender his manhood.

Tyranny is a habit that can grow into a disease. And tyranny threatens to swallow up the human being in its drunken quest for power and blood. Gorianchikov observes that this habit can grow in even the best of men to the point where the human person is lost: "The human being and the citizen perish forever in the tyrant, and a return for human dignity, to repentance, to regeneration becomes practically impossible for him" (E: 242; PSS 4:154). Gorianchikov is presumably commenting upon the tyrannical sway of the executioner, because he desperately wanted to communicate the moral evil of the practice of flogging which is perhaps a greater wrong than the crime to which it is applied to punish. The tone of the narrator swells like that of a preacher who preaches to rout a humanitarian wrong. This is not a particular problem entirely remote from the non-convict society. He writes, "The qualities of the executioner are found in embryonic form in almost every modern person" (E: 243; PSS 4:155).

Tyranny is a feature even of respectable society and is difficult to identify. To a certain extent, the intensity of Gorianchikov's invective ought to be seen in light of the prison reforms being established at that time through Czar Alexander II. A footnote, presumably the author's, added as a footnote to the title of Part II, Chapter 3, informs the reader that the practices of torture and punishment in prison have changed since he was there.[43] It might be noted that Dostoevsky's work made an impact upon Russian society and led to reforms:

> The publication of The House of the Dead immediately unleashed a huge debate in the press about Russian justice and the system of imprisonment; all sorts of reforms were suggested or advocated as a result of the information it provided.[44]

Once again this insertion into the narrative in the form of a footnote is significant because it throws a different light upon the fictional narrative. It shows forth the "double" character of the narrative as fiction and autobiography.

Terrible Monsters

In consideration of the distortions of human nature that occur as noted in the example of the mind of the executioner, we next turn to the beings which Gorianchikov calls "terrible monsters."

Gorianchikov describes a Tatar convict named Gazin as the most violent and terrible person that he had ever met. He was exceptionally strong, ugly, and fond of murdering little children. He was in the special category of strong punishment. Gorianchikov tells us that Gazin kept silent and was contemptuous toward other convicts and that several times a year he became drunk. It was then that his barbarous traits came to the fore and he posed a real threat to other prisoners. When he attempted to take a man down with a knife, it required several men to beat him unconscious, but even then, they could not kill him. Gazin is described as though he were some sort of indomitable beast.

A man whom Gorianchikov calls a moral Quasimodo presents a special phenomenon of nature. His name is A--v. "He was an example of what the physical side of man on its own can produce if unrestrained by any inner norm or set of laws" (E: 105; PSS 4:63). This man is depicted as a moral vacuum, and yet he is described as clever, handsome, and even educated. Gorianchikov is so alarmed by the depravity of this man that he feels that society would prefer fire, plague or famine than such a man as A--v.

Another human monster that Gorianchikov describes was a bandit named Korenyev, whom he observed in Tobolsk. What shocked our narrator the most was this man's spiritual indifference:

> The flesh had gained such ascendancy over all his mental qualities that one glance at his face was enough to tell you that all that was left in him was a savage desire for physical pleasure, for sexual passion and carnal satisfaction. (E: 82; PSS 4:47)

This description highlights the centrality of the human spirit [dushevnoe svoistvo] which when overcome, leaves a being whose humanity is doubtful.

Gorianchikov introduces the recollection of Korenyev in contrast to Orlov, a convict of the special category in the dead house whom Gorianchikov met while convalescing in the hospital. Orlov is characterized as man with complete self-mastery. He is the antithesis of Korenyev. He was afraid of nothing: "It was truly a case of total victory over the flesh. . . . All that could be seen in him was an infinite energy, a thirst for activity, for revenge, and for the achievement of a predetermined goal" (E: 82-83; PSS 4:47).

Gorianchikov describes Orlov in glowing terms as though he were some type of "negative saint." Orlov was such that no authority on earth could lord over him. He looked upon everything with imperturbable tranquility as though nothing could surprise him. When Orlov leaves the hospital he shakes hands with our narrator. In attempting to account for Orlov's motive, Gorianchikov gives the following explanation in a self-critical tone: "What it boiled down to was that he could not help despising me and seeing me as a weak, pathetic, submissive creature, in every way his inferior" (E: 84; PSS 4:48). Orlov possesses a certain type of natural and moral superiority that intimidates Gorianchikov. The sheer life force of a man like Orlov also raises the question is this a man or perhaps a "superman"?[45]

The contrast between Korenyev and Orlov is illustrative of two types of Übermensch. Both are examples of unlimited power. Korenyev has attained his power in the conquest of his spirit by his flesh while Orlov has attained his power by overcoming his flesh by his spirit. The existence of such men as these present a challenge to a notion of human nature that is too narrow. These are boundary cases, men who have overcome their own nature and are brute examples of the sheer thirst for energy.

The Symbolic Depiction of Freedom in the Dead House

Having seen how freedom is depicted in terms of the dead house as structure and metaphor, let us now look to the "freedom symbolism." One of the chief ways that freedom is depicted within the narrative is symbolic. The narrative examples which I will consider are: 1) The constellation of dreaming, holidays, and theatre; and 2) Nature (in particular animals). These narrative moments are *topoi* of transcendence which show the meaning of human freedom.

Dreaming

The power of dreaming in the dead house was so great that Gorianchikov tells us that it is the characteristic feature of life in the dead house, where every prisoner is a dreamer:

> One somehow felt at once, almost at first glance, that there was nothing like this outside the prison. Here everyone was a dreamer, and this was immediately obvious. The place had a morbid feel to it, stemming from the fact that this daydreaming made most of the convicts look sullen and morose, and somehow unhealthy. (E: 303-4; *PSS* 4:196)

Despite the fact that Gorianchikov's description of the day-dreaming prisoners takes on a negative aspect, the effect of the dream is to provide an outlet to this otherwise living hell. The persistent activity of daydreaming reinforces the house of the dead metaphor as a type of perpetual nightworld beyond whose sleeping lies the dayworld, with its light and its freedom. It is against the backdrop of this darkened dreaming that Gorianchikov's narrative manifests an aspiration for freedom at whatever cost. Dreaming, like hoping, is a projection of one's will toward an indefinite future goal, toward the indefinite space of the world beyond the prison walls. The time is "then" and the place is "beyond." Even though it is indefinite and future tense, such projecting is absolutely necessary to provide meaning to the convicts' lives.

On the final day of Gorianchikov's prison sentence, he observes that the convicts tend to exaggerate freedom:

> I will observe here in passing that all our daydreaming about it and our lack of contact with it made freedom seem to us in some way freer than freedom itself, the freedom that is to be found in the real world, that is. (E: 355; PSS 4:230)

The freedom that seemed "freer than freedom itself" [kak-to svobodnee nastoiashchei svobody] is a curious concept. The vision of freedom which was necessary to propel the prisoners' hopes perhaps shone more brightly, or appeared larger than life. When one crosses the threshold toward freedom, a new horizon appears and "true" freedom once again recedes into the "then" and into the "beyond," and ever and anon. Then the "freer freedom" appears on another distant horizon. Can any insights be gleaned from the convicts' dreams concerning the nature of man in general? Certainly, if we consider that no human existence is devoid of walls, nor of projections toward eventual release. Taking into account Dolnikowski's formula: "You will be free at last (for the time being)," we see that freedom is always relative to a greater freedom.[46] Thus, in leaving one prison gate, we arrive into another prison cell and so on. While it may be true that convicts experience a life deprived of their own will to an extreme extent, this experience is not alien to non-convicts, since all human beings are hemmed-in in some manner, and no one exercises the full extent of his own will.

Dostoevsky's use of the image of the dreamer (mechtatel' [PSS 4:196]) in the present text contrasts with its use in his youthful, pre-exilic writings. A consideration of this contrast provides insight into the degree to which Dostoevsky had moved from the humanistic and utopian viewpoints of his youth. The "dreamer" motif is prominent in the early works and refers to the social-utopian ideas of French writers such as George Sand, Pierre Leroux, Cabet, and Fourier. The young Dostoevsky came into contact with these thinkers through the influence of his hero and mentor, Vissarion Belinsky. V. L. Komarovich argues that with imprisonment, Dostoevsky came into contact with pure, human evil, and realized that the premises of utopic humanism were wrong.[47] The idea that man is essentially good and has no original sin is violently contradicted in prison life. The humanistic religion which substituted for Christianity in the writings of the French socialist-utopians is powerless to account for the very real and palpable human evil that Dostoevsky met in his fellow prisoners. The reference of the word mechtatel' shifts from an optimistic mode in the early Dostoevsky to become associated with morbidity, sullenness. Both utopians and prisoners dream, however unlike the utopian who dreams of the possibility of a better society, the dream of a prisoner is not a luxury, a possibility, but is a fundamental necessity.

The Christmas Feast

One of the places where Gorianchikov's narrative rises above utter darkness is his description of the Christmas holiday. There was a sense in the dead house that something out of the ordinary was approaching. The holiday aroused great feelings and childhood memories. The holiday seemed to draw the community of convicts together in a common feeling:

> This mood of the convicts was remarkable, and could even be quite moving. In addition to his inborn sense of reverence for the great day, each convict had an unconscious feeling that by observing this feast he was in some way in contact with the whole world, that consequently he was not an outcast, a lost man, a severed limb, and that as it was in the world of men, so it was in prison. (E: 166; PSS 4:105)

Note that the feast at Christmas not only had a binding power for the prison community, but also drew the prison community into the world beyond the prison walls toward a universal human community.

The Christmas holiday brought the prisoners not only better soup, a suckling pig, bread and tea, but also gifts for the "unfortunates." A priest brought holy water to all the barracks. And the convicts put together a play. Julie de Sherbinin draws a parallel between the religious service and the convicts' theatrical.[48] She argues that the theatrical is a more authentic sacrament than religious ritual, and that within this work, "the Russian folk theatre becomes the locus of transcendental experience."[49] This is in accord with "Dostoevskij's [sic] plan to concentrate the transformative power of art at the novels' core."[50] To be sure, the play reconciled the convicts through a truly artistic experience. In a metaphorical way the theatrical is a self-reflexive miniature of the artwork as a whole. Even more, however, than the transcendence of the play's ritual action which makes communion amongst the convicts possible, the locus of transcendence in the theatrical is found in the prisoners' projected vision onto a horizon of unfettered freedom. The theatrical allowed the prisoners' imagination to go beyond the vision of their daily routines and to be released "someplace so high above the wall."[51]

> Every face wore an expression of artless expectation. The men's faces were red and wet with sweat from the heat and stuffiness. What a strange reflection of childlike joy, of pure, good-natured contentment shone on these furrowed, branded cheeks and foreheads, on these gazes which had hitherto expressed only gloom and sullenness, on these eyes which sometimes sparkled with a terrible light! (E: 192; PSS 4:122-23)

The theatre is presented as a positive, luminescent value for the prison community; it has the capacity to draw men together, to draw their imaginations toward a common spectacle, and finally, to light up their faces and to project their gazes beyond the sullen and morose gloom that was their daily bread. Likewise, the theatrical is a light shining in the darkness of the dead house narrative. Dead House is itself an artwork which mirrors the redemptive character of the theatrical, hence giving the reader, like the convicts themselves, a moment of transcendence.

Nature

Perhaps the clearest symbolic expression of freedom in Gorianchikov's narrative description of the dead house is nature. Nature in his narrative consists of the description of the seasons, which embodies the cyclical time of the year, and the open space, for example, the steppe beyond the Irtysh river where the nomads live, and the prison animals. In a chapter entitled "Summer," Gorianchikov gives us a lyrical description of life beyond the prison. He begins this chapter in April, and relates that a man yearns for freedom more in the Spring than in the Winter or Fall. The prisoner's yearning for freedom is related to season and climate. The human being is prone to seasonal shifts and variations. Summer is the time for "runners" and escaped convicts:

> As well as this being the time when in the warmth of the bright sun you feel with all your soul, with all your being the boundless strength of nature as once more it rises from the dead all round you, the time when the closed-in prison, the guards and the will of others become even more difficult to bear; this is also the time when, with the first skylark, vagrancy begins all over Russia and Siberia: God's people escape from prison and take to the forests. (E: 271; PSS 4:174)

As though responding to a natural call, the convicts yearn to escape into vagabondage. Note the lyricism and the light imagery in this passage; the warmth of the bright sun [v teple, iarkogo solntsa], nature . . . rises from the dead [voskresaiushyi], and the first skylark [s pervym zhavoronkom] appears. Vagabondage is itself a suggestion of freedom and flight, but one rarely achieved. What is startling is that although ninety-nine out of a hundred prisoners dream of escape, only one will decide to do it. Like so many other unrealizable convict dreams, the dream of flight is a "necessary illusion" as much as the dream of unlimited freedom.

Perhaps the dream of escaping is like one of the impossible dreams that is characteristic of the Russian prisoner and is deemed unrealizable. Even those who do escape realize that this is not an escape into pure freedom:

> No man who runs away really plans to escape into total freedom--he knows that this is well-nigh impossible-- but either to end up in another institution, to get into a settlement, or to be retried for a fresh crime which he will commit during his vagrancy. (E: 273; PSS 4:175)

The idea of vagabondage in wild nature looks like a pure symbol of freedom, but Gorianchikov notes that even this "freedom" is relative to the new set of circumstances the escapee will find. Freedom has its meaning within a certain range or horizon; beyond this range, freedom ceases to have meaning. The convict continuously projects his freedom toward an unattainable horizon. To do so is essentially human, and yet it is contradictory. The essential interplay of human freedom is seen in the convicts' "impossible dreams," precisely in their unattainability. And yet, this unattainable horizon from which all such dreaming recoils defines a realm where human freedom is meaningful. This dynamic is, philosophically speaking, the locus of transcendence.

The banks of the Irtysh are the central place where Gorianchikov labored pounding alabaster and breaking up a boat hull. In some ways the river bank is the physical limit of the dead house, and what goes on beyond the river is described in symbols of freedom: "But on the river bank one could forget oneself: one would look at that immense, vacant landscape in the way a prisoner looks out at freedom from the window of his cell" (E: 277; PSS 4:178). Gorianchikov's description of the world beyond the river Irtysh is lyrical. He sees God's world in the free and uninhabited steppes. There dwell Kirghiz nomads in their yurts; he notices the clear blue sky and the birds.

A wonderful transposition occurs when a figure from the world beyond the river enters into the world of the dead house. One day the prisoners find an eagle with a broken wing. It was a small eagle, a Karakus variety from the steppes. The prisoners fed and kept it in prison for two months. Finally the men decided it ought to be released:

> Some said it ought to be taken out of the prison. "Let it die if it's got to, but not in prison," they said. "Its a wild bird, you know, it needs its freedom, you'll never teach it to live in prison," others agreed. "It's not like us, then," somebody added. "Don't be stupid: it's a bird, and we're human beings aren't we?" (E: 301; PSS 4:194)

Because the men grew sympathetic to the eagle they realized that it did not belong in prison like them. Finally, they release the bird to fly free. As he flies away, the prisoners watch to see which way he will go. The eagle soars toward the Autumn sky above the steppe, toward his freedom. The freedom of the eagle is the freedom to live in nature according to its instincts. Human freedom refers to something quite different from instinct. In fact, freedom means the capacity to live outside of one's instincts, or even more precisely, that man has no instinct, only freedom.

Prison Animals

Gorianchikov devotes a chapter of his narrative to the description of prison animals. Perhaps the most loving description we find in the narrative is of the prison dog named Sharik. Gorianchikov looked upon Sharik as a friend sent to him by fate. In the darkest moments of his early days in prison Gorianchikov's world was lighted up by his love for this mongrel prison dog:

> And I remember that I would derive great satisfaction from the thought--as though taking pride in my own agony of spirit--that there was in the whole world left to me only one creature that loved me, that was devoted to me, my friend, my only friend--my faithful dog Sharik. (E: 126; PSS 4:77)

In this prison animal Gorianchikov was able to find solace and comfort.

Gorianchikov is very fond of animals, and he views them in a positive light. He reports that the other prisoners would have cared for animals if they were allowed to. Another prison animal that he describes is a bay horse named "Gnedko." Gorianchikov tells us that when the convicts fed him with salt or bread, he would ". . . eat it and toss his head again, as if to say: 'I know you, indeed I do! I'm a nice horse and you're a good man'" (E: 294; PSS 4:189).

This is a telling observation on the narrator's part. Gorianchikov projects a non-judgmental gaze onto this horse. His description of the geese, Vaska the goat, and the dog named Kultyapka all reveal an implicit judgement about man. The direct juxtaposition of descriptions about animals tells us a great deal about man. The position of the horse in the narrative is beyond the prison; even though he is physically within the prison wall, he is not the same as the prisoner. It is this difference which highlights the role of human freedom.

To summarize, freedom is depicted within the world of the dead house in the prisoners' dreaming and in their fantasy. The Christmas Feast allowed the prisoners to experience childlike joy and to find communion beyond the walls of the prison. The theatre was another window which allowed the prisoners to go beyond the sullen gravity of day-to-day prison life. Another window where freedom is depicted in Gorianchikov's memoir is nature, and in particular the prison animals. Freedom is depicted concretely within the world of the dead house by means of these symbols, and the light imagery they bring to the darkness. Now let us consider the philosophical meaning of this freedom in light of the prisoner.

The Philosophical Meaning of Freedom in the Life of a Convict

Having surveyed the narrative world of the "dead house," its temporality and spatiality, its surrounding nature, and the convicts who people it with an eye toward the meaning of freedom that is embodied there, it is now necessary to turn from the "prison anthropology" to the meaning of crime itself. Since crime is the constitutive act which establishes the criminal, and criminality is the decisive fact which founds the penal institution, it is Gorianchikov's meditation upon crime which provides the central philosophical conception of freedom within the work.

As indicated above, the meaning of freedom as transcendence depicted in the narrative world of the dead house possesses a significance that goes beyond the inhabitants of the dead house. Freedom appears in the convicts' world as an impossible, unattainable dream. And yet, paradoxically, the convict must project himself toward such an unrealizable freedom in order to find the meaning to go on living as man. The realm of meaningful human freedom is delineated by the tension between the world of light, "_bozhii svet_," and the dark walls of the dead house. The freedom that is delineated here is not only meaningful in the life of a convict, but reveals an essential structure of any human freedom whatsoever.

When we considered the constitutive features of the inhabitants of the dead house, we found the reason why they reveal a privileged site for the interpretation of the working of human freedom. The interpretation of the meaning of freedom in the lives of the inhabitants of the dead house revealed _in extremo_ what is true of every man. The criminal aspires toward an unlimited range of expression, and acts (transgresses) in accordance with this projection. It is a world in which the expression of his will is unbounded. It is a freedom that is greater than freedom, but is it possible, or merely a fantasy? The convict thirsts for a greater and greater freedom like a drunkard thirsts for yet another bottle of vodka. Just like the prisoner dreams of a spree and projects an imagined realm of unlimited freedom, the criminal projects an unreal, fantasy world in which his crime is enacted. And just as the prison wall makes the convict recoil from his fantasy, the criminal, insofar as he is human, must recoil from his wild expression of freedom and must thirst for a moral limit. But where is he to find his limiting moral wall? Freedom does not mean the absolute lack of restraint nor even the absence of restraining bonds. A man's freedom follows him wherever he goes. It is no less essential to life within the prison walls than without. Freedom to do whatever one wishes is a purely negative concept which must land upon some morally limiting concept in order to be truly human.

This picture depicts the meaning of freedom and its deployment in human life. Man is a unique being in that his being is not thinglike. The inner essence of man is not a dictate or structure, but is an act of will. In order to be man one must be free. To be free, man must be capable of free action, and be autonomous, i.e., free from the constraints of natural laws, or of any other predetermining or heautonomous will. This is the necessary condition of human freedom; however, it is not a sufficient condition. Something else is needed. Human freedom is the freedom to be human. In order to be human, a man must choose his humanity. What is the essence of this humanity that must be chosen in order for man to be human? Let us take a closer look at our narrator's thinking about crime in order to find out concretely what the convict can teach us concerning human freedom.

A Philosophy of Crime

In many ways, this work is Dostoevsky's most patently philosophical work. It is worthwhile noting that the narrator does not save his philosophical reflection for a conclusion at the end of his work, but begins to philosophize during the first chapter and continues until the end. When it comes to an understanding of crime, Gorianchikov admits to an inability to penetrate to the deepest core of the prisoners' lives within the dead house. And he further remarks that a philosophical understanding of crime is more difficult to achieve than has been commonly imagined: ". . . It seems that crime cannot be comprehended from points of view that are already given, and that its philosophy is rather more difficult than is commonly supposed" (E: 36; PSS 4:15). This comment is oriented toward the question of the moral reform of the criminal by means of labor and imprisonment which was being widely debated in Russia at the time Dostoevsky wrote Dead House. Frank suggests that several passages in this work cannot fail to reflect ideological polemics:

> A few passages, however, can hardly be read except as manifest thrusts against some of the notions, strenuously propagated by Chernyshevsky, which had now attained the status of irrefutable truth among the younger generation.[52]

The "points of view that are already given" cited above presumably refers to Chernyshevsky's theory, which emphasizes the deleterious effects of some deprived environments upon a man which causes him to commit crimes.

Despite his reservations, our narrator has some insightful observations to make concerning reform, a philosophy of crime, and the relation between freedom and criminality. Paradoxically, the ideal subject for the study of human freedom is in many ways the man deprived of his freedom, i.e., the prisoner. The relation between criminality and freedom is seen in the contrast between a prisoner's overwhelming thirst for freedom and the curtailment of that freedom which comes about in prison. One characteristic of the convict is his concentrated "lust for life." With a superman like Orlov, Gorianchikov is able to demonstrate the indestructibility of certain men's spirits. Perhaps it is this brute drive for life, regardless of moral constraints, which enables these convicts to adapt to the most strenuous demands of prison life and punishment (to flogging, in particular).

Another manifestation of freedom is the "convulsion of the will" which leads a convict to lash out regardless of the consequences simply because he needs to demonstrate the use of his will. Even men who have acted quietly for years can all of a sudden lash out:

> But all the while the cause of this sudden outburst in the man of whom one least expected it is nothing more than an anguished, convulsive manifestation of the man's personality [. . . sudorozhnoe proiavlenie lichnosti . . .], his instinctive anguish and anguished longing for himself, his desire to declare himself and his humiliated personality, a desire which appears suddenly and which sometimes ends in anger, in frenzied rage, in insanity, fits, convulsions. (E: 110; PSS 4:67)

It is difficult to identify the cause of such outbursts, which seem to be in principle irrational. This is a central thesis which appears again in a central role in Underground.[53]

The primal lust for life is related to human freedom, but is not synonymous with it. Lust for life is a purely undefined and unconscious drive; it is animal or brute strength:

> . . . anyone entering a prison can feel that this entire body of men has been assembled here against its will and that, whatever measures are taken, it is impossible to convert living man into a corpse: he retains his feelings, his thirst for vengeance and life, his passions and his desire to satisfy them. (E: 78; PSS 4:44-45)

A man is still a man and not a corpse as long as he possesses this "thirst for life." Thirst for life [zhazhda zhizni'] is not the same as freedom [svoboda]; however, the way Gorianchikov uses it here, it means the most basic instinct for life that man possesses. In this context, it means freedom in the most natural, or instinctual sense. As such, the thirst for life may be primordial and undisclosed to rationality.[54] Thus, like so many other insoluble mysteries in prison such as the inequality between peasants and nobles, the lack of remorse for crimes committed, the existence of human monsters, and the impossibility of a complete eradication of the evil will, Gorianchikov cannot rationally explain this phenomenon. The prisoner is still a man and it is not possible make him stop being a man without turning him into a corpse.

Freedom, on the other hand, has a specific moral "container." A thirst for freedom seems to be unbounded in the criminal and recognizes no limit. Yet, this same thirst for freedom leads the criminal to a wall, to the limit which is discovered when it is overstepped:

> To the prison came men who had gone too far, had overstepped the limit when they had been free . . . [Prikhodili v ostrog takie, kotorye uzh slishkom zarvalis', slishkom vyskochili iz merki na vole . . .], so that in the end it was as if their crimes had not been committed by them personally, as if they had committed them without knowing why, as if in a fever or a daze; often out of vanity, raised in them to an extraordinary degree. (E: 32; PSS 4:13)

I have quoted the expression in Russian because it throws a particular light upon the state of the convict with regard to freedom. This statement is very emphatic, literally: "The ones who came to the prison were those who had gone too far too much, had leapt out too much from the common measure in freedom. . . ." The men who came there had already gone too far ["uzh slishkom zarvalis: zarvat'sia:" (to go too far; to overstep the mark)] overstepping the limit when they were free. This expression further emphasizes the distance that these men had leapt (like a wild horse) too strongly beyond a common measure in free society ["vyskochili iz merki na vole . . ."]. At the heart of this action is the limit, measure, mark [merka] which is transgressed.

The criminal does not recognize this limit but society does and the criminal realizes it when he is imprisoned. "But in our prison they were soon brought to heel, in spite of the fact that some of them, before they came here, had been the terror of whole towns and villages" (E: 33; PSS 4:15). Thus, it is in the dead house where the criminal finally recognizes a limit, unrecognized in his thirst for boundless freedom but stepped over in his crime.

Of special interest to Gorianchikov's narrative is the description of the criminal who has no remorse. This is a startling phenomenon:

> I have already said that for a period of several years I saw among these people not the slightest trace of repentance, not one sign that their crime weighed heavily on their conscience, and that the majority of them consider themselves to be completely in the right. This is a fact. (E: 35; PSS 4:15)

Gorianchikov is quite alarmed at this strange fact. The educated man with a strict conscience suffers far more harshly within his own heart than any punishment could render, while another considers himself to be in the right, and yet another prefers the prison life. He realizes the great inequality in prison that while some convicts are dying away others might even enjoy the society in the dead house(!):

> Here is a man wasting away in prison, melting down like a candle; and here is another who before he came here had no idea that there was in the world to be found such a merry existence, such an agreeable club of lion-hearted companions. Yes, men like these come to prison, too. (E: 76; PSS 4:43)

All of these comments appear in the context of Gorianchikov's discussion concerning the possibility of moral reform of the criminal, but also reveal a more disturbing question concerning the true meaning of crime and punishment.

Gorianchikov was alarmed by the fact that the convicts felt no remorse for their crimes. This requires two observations: 1) Moral regeneration cannot be expected to proceed naturally by virtue of the power of guilty conscience in a convict who, for all practical purposes, admits of no binding moral law; 2) Physical punishment will not bring about moral regeneration within a convict since the essence of crime is a moral fact. If crime results from fundamental aberration in the will, or rather, in a fundamental misconception of the unbounded powers of freedom, then the only restoration that prison can serve a criminal is the reality of a limit within society where men who are never shocked by anything live. This is a strange type of limit, but nonetheless it is a limit that all of the convicts recognize.

The nature of the limit which the prison society imposes upon a convict in the dead house is, of course, material punishment in the extremity of the place, forced communality of the dead house and forced labor. Yet, the prisoner does not discover his limit solely in these features but in a moral fact of this society:

> You could discern at first glance one single glaring characteristic that was common to all this strange family: even the strongest, most original personalities who dominated the others without trying, even they attempted to fit in with the general tone of the prison. (E: 32; PSS 4:12)

It is in this "general tone" [obshchii ton (PSS 4:12)] of the prison, at this final outpost on the Siberian frontier that the men who have gone to the farthest limits of human action, who are men "at the frontiers" of being human, discover a moral limit to their freedom.

Is the limit which the convict finds in the "general tone" of the dead house enough to count as an objective moral absolute? Certainly it is not a concrete moral absolute in the sense of a moral law that says: "Thou shall not murder" (Exodus 20:13). Nonetheless, it is objective since all of the men recognize it. It plays the same function vis-a-vis the convict who will admit no remorse before any moral law on account of his transgression. The limit which was so eagerly overstepped in freedom [na vole] is re-discovered in the "general tone" of the prison which breeds a certain conformity, even in the most monstrous of criminals. A distinctive feature of this "general tone" of prison life is that a convict realizes that he cannot surprise anyone here:

> Looking around him, the new convict soon realized that he had come to the wrong place: that there was no one here whom he could surprise, and imperceptibly he grew resigned and fitted in with the general tone. (E: 33; PSS 4:13)

To my way of thinking, this phenomenon of no longer being able to surprise constitutes perhaps the only common moral wall which these convicts recognize. This phenomenon is not an objective moral absolute, but for some of these men was the only societal and moral fact which curtailed the unbounded use of their freedom. Granted it is minimal, but it is at the heart of this community.

Concluding Reflection

I have attempted to make explicit that Dead House gives the thoughtful reader a great deal to consider concerning man's essential being and being free. As such this effort is not so original. The work has been interpreted along these lines from the very beginning. Even so, the effort to discern the question of freedom's meaning in this work and to "think it through" remained a task. I have indicated the significant places in the text which lend themselves to interpretation along these lines. Manifold approaches to the text reveal how freedom is at work in the artwork and how the work opens significant questions concerning the being of man. Freedom is apparent not only as a patent thematic which is unfolded in this most philosophical work, but also as a symbol and a metaphor which the narrative world of the dead house makes present.

The artwork embodies and incarnates essential thought concerning human freedom in the how of its presentation. The meaning that freedom takes on can also be investigated in terms of the language of the text, where the meaning of significant terms like freedom [svoboda], will [volia], and crime [prestuplenie] are at question. It is fitting that a work which takes as its task the discovery and explication of the meaning of human freedom in Dostoevsky's literary work begin with Dead House. It grounds and establishes Dostoevsky's thought concerning freedom which is at play in the consequent works considered below. Its philosophy of crime is clearly at work in Crime and Punishment, a work whose epilogue mirrors Gorianchikov's narrative musing upon the timeless steppe beyond the river Irtysh.

Freedom can be taken in a number of senses. In its mechanical conception, man is understood to be "free" insofar as he or she is undetermined by an external causality. Such a freedom is referred to as negative, since it is a "freedom from" causation. Because Dead House focuses upon the life of convicts within a prison, it portrays freedom for the most part in this sense. Following Heidegger, contemporary philosophy of freedom emphasizes a more primordial and essential sense of freedom.[55] In short, to be free means to determine what it will mean to be a human being. The free human being is not only undetermined but also undefined. The nature of man is a task that must be performed. The thinking which takes as its task the delineation and description of the positive meaning of freedom is central to this dissertation.

Dead House provides us with a clue as to the positive meaning of human freedom and does so in the following manner. Dostoevsky depicts men deprived of their citizen rights who possess very little freedom of action, to wit: one of the introductory rituals in the dead house is the forging of shackles. The dead house is composed of limits, walls, chains, gates and fences; it is in short a place where unfreedom is made manifest. Nevertheless, the narrative points beyond the immediate hindrances of prison life in order to ask after the meaning of human life within such a dead house. It becomes clear that the narrative is searching for freedom in a more primordial and philosophical sense than "freedom of action." While providing no clear and concise answer to the question, the text explicitly offers it up as a matter to be thought. And this leads to the next work.

Notes

1. Joseph Frank, Dostoevsky: The Stir of Liberation, 1860-1865 (Princeton: Princeton University Press, 1986), 214-15.

2. Jacques Catteau, "De la structure de La maison des morts de F. M. Dostoevskij," Revue des etudes slaves 54 (1982): 63-72.

3. Frank, Stir, 224.

4. Ibid., 7.

5. Edward Wasiolek, Dostoevsky: The Major Fiction (Cambridge, Mass.: M.I.T. Press, 1964), 25.

6. Hans-Georg Gadamer, Truth and Method (New York: Crossroad, 1975), 337.

7. Valerii Kirpotin, Dostoevskii v shestidesiatye gody (Moskva: Izdatel'stvo Khudozhestvennaia Literatura, 1966), 332. Kirpotin writes: "Dostoevskii ne delal popravki na ekstsentrichnost' sredy, v kotoruiu popal, na iskusstvennost' ee podbora, na osoboe prelomlenie morali i psikhologii v katorzhnom 'narode'." I translate this as follows: "Dostoevsky did not make corrections for the eccentricity of the surroundings into which he fell, for the irregularity of its assortment, for the special refraction of morals and psychology in prison 'folk.'"

8. Fyodor Dostoevsky, The House of the Dead, trans. David McDuff (London: Penguin Classics, 1985). This English translation will be referred to throughout the chapter and is identified as "E" followed by the page number. The Russian text is drawn from Dostoevsky's collected works, Polnoe sobranie sochinenii, 30 vols. (Leningrad: Nauka, 1972-90), and is identified as PSS, followed by the volume and page number.

9. Alexander Pushkin, Povesti pokoinogo Ivana Petrovicha Belkina in Polnoe sobranie sochinenii v desiati tomakh (Leningrad: Izdatel'stvo Nauka, 1978), 54-57 ('Ot izdatelia').

10. Bagby addresses the meaning of the tradition of literary works entitled, "notes" (zapiski). Ivan Sergeyevich Turgenev's Zapiski okhotnika (1854) [Notes of a Huntsman (Chicago: Russian Language Specialties, 1965)] as well as Dostoevsky's own Selo Stepanchikogo, iz zapisok neizvestnogo cheloveka (1860) [The Village of Stepanchikovo, From the Notes of an Unknown Man, trans. Ignat Avsey (Ithaca, N.Y.: Cornell University Press, 1987)] and of course, his famous Zapiski iz podpol'ia (1864) [Notes from the Underground]. It is a mystery to me why a translator like McDuff omits the word "notes" in his translation of "Zapiski" iz mertvogo doma when its designation is so central to the generic tradition in which Dostoevsky placed his work. He calls it simply The House of the Dead.

11. Andrei Bitov compares Gorianchikov to Robinson Crusoe in his article "Novyi Robinzon: K 125-letiiu vykhoda v svet 'Zapisok iz mertvogo doma'" (Moskow: Znamia, Dec. 12, 1987), 221-27 emphasizing

that the prison, like America is an exotic destination which the notes provide access to. Likewise, in his article on prison literature Hugh McLean notes the exoticism of prison: "The prison is exotic territory, outside the range of ordinary experience. A prison memoir is thus a travel book, a journey to an unknown land . . ." (258). See Hugh McLean "Walls and Wire: Notes on the Prison Theme in Russian Literature," International Journal of Slavic Linguistics and Poetics (1982): 253-65.

12. Robert Louis Jackson, The Art of Dostoevsky: Deliriums and Nocturnes (Princeton: Princeton University Press, 1981), 354, n. 28.

13. Viacheslav Ivanov, Freedom and the Tragic Life: A Study in Dostoevsky, trans. Norman Cameron (New York: Farrar, Straus and Cudahy, 1960), 26. According to Ivanov, penetration refers to a realm of understanding that is beyond or rather within ordinary perception in which the subject and object are fused: "It is a transcension of the subject. In this state of mind we recognize the other Ego not as our object, but as another subject" (Ivanov, 26). Ivanov sees this process as central to all of Dostoevsky's major creation. He has located and identified a poetic structure within Dostoevsky's work which is correlative to the revelation of a conception of man's essential freedom.

14. Aurelii Augustini, De Vera Religione, Liber Unus, ed. K.-D. Daur, in Sancti Aurelii Augustini De Doctrina Christiana et De Vera Religione (Turnholti: Typographi Brepols Editores Pontifici, 1962), ch. 39, no. 72. This work, part of Corpus Christianorum, Series Latina, is published in this series as volume 32: Aurelii Augustini Opera, Pars IV, 1. The page quoted can be found on page 234, 12-16. English: Augustine: Earlier Writings, trans. John H. S. Burleigh in The Library of Christian Classics, vol. 6 (Philadelphia: The Westminster Press, 1953), p. 262.

15. Catteau, "De la structure," 64.

16. E. D. Hirsch, Validity in Interpretation (New Haven: Yale University Press, 1965), 76.

17. Gary Saul Morson, The Boundaries of Genre: Dostoevsky's "Diary of a Writer" and the Traditions of Literary Utopia (Evanston, Ill.: Northwestern University Press, 1981).

18. Thomas Beebee, The Ideology of Genre: A Comparative Study of Generic Instability (University Park, Pa.: The Pennsylvania State University Press, 1994), 249-50.

19. Frank, Stir, 214.

20. Morson, Boundaries, 48.

21. Jean-Paul Sartre, Situations I (Paris: Gallimard, 1947), 71.

22. Maurice Merleau-Ponty, Sense and Non-sense (Evanston, Ill.: Northwestern University Press, 1964). See Chapter Two, "Metaphysics of the Novel."

23. Jacques Catteau, La creation littéraire chez Dostoievski (Paris: Institut D'Etudes Slaves, 1978).

24. Ibid., 565.

25. Alexander Solzhenitsyn, One Day in the Life of Ivan Denisovich, trans. Ralph Parker (New York: Dutton, 1963).

26. Catteau, "De la structure," 67.

27. Jackson identifies the meaning of the dead house in its potential for resurrection. Cf. "Freedom in the Shadow of the Dead House," in Jackson's The Art of Dostoevsky: Deliriums and Nocturnes (Princeton: Princeton University Press, 1981), 144-70.

28. Vladimir Dal', Tolkovyi slovar'zhivogo velikirusskogo iazyka tt. 1-4 (Sankt Peterburg: Bodwina de Kurtene, 1882), t. IV str. 151 "svoboda" (Moskva: Russkii Iazyk, 1978-1982).

29. Ibid., 238.

30. Akademiia Nauk SSSR Institut Russkogo Iazyka, Slovar' russkogo iazyka v chetyrekh tomakh, (Moskva: Izdatel'stvo 'Russkii Iazyk', 1981), t. IV str. 52 "svoboda".

31. Ibid., Vol. I, 209.

32. Cf. T. S. Karlova's "O strukturnom znachenii obraza 'Mertvogo doma' in Dostoevskii: Materialy i issledovanii I. Redaktor G. Fridlender (Leningrad: Nauka, 1974), 135-46.

33. Harriet Murav, "Dostoevskii in Siberia: Remembering the Past," Slavic Review 50, no. 4 (Winter 1991): 858-66.

34. Robert Louis Jackson, Dostoevsky's Underground Man in Russian Literature ('S-Gravenhage: Mouton and Co., 1958).

35. Alexander Herzen, quoted in Jackson, Dostoevsky's Underground Man, 6.

36. Gary Rosenshield, "The Realization of the Collective Self: The Rebirth of Religious Autobiography in Dostoevskii's Zapiski iz mertvogo doma," Slavic Review 50, no. 2 (Summer 1991): 317-27.

37. A succinct statement of the "collectivist" interpretation of the House of the Dead which tends to undercut the primary meaning of the dead house as the prison is found in Rosenshield. It is a widely received interpretation appearing in Shklovsky [Za i protiv, Moskva, 1957], Murav, de Sherbinin's article [see below], and most succinctly stated in Rosenshield's 1991 article. Rosenshield reads the work as "a modern religious autobiography of the Russian people" and finds The House of the Dead to be a story which identifies the Russian people as the collective "hero." This reading is unsatisfactory, because this rapproachment with the people never comes about. What is worse, Rosenshield reaches an even more inadequate view of the prison as a metaphor: "From the point of view of religious autobiography, the prison camp is less an alien, external environment from which the author seeks escape than a

metaphor for the private hell of his own benightedness and alienation from the people" (ibid., 324). On the contrary, the power of the dead house as a metaphor lies precisely in its negativity, its alienating moral community and distance.

38. Cf., Murav, "Dostoevskii in Siberia."

39. Max Scheler, Man's Place In Nature, trans. Meyerhoff (Boston: Beacon Press, 1961).

40. This observation parallels Albert Camus' remarks in Le Mythe de Sisyphe concerning human toil and absurdity. It is unfortunate that Camus did not comment there on Gorianchikov.

41. Viktor Frankl, Man's Search for Meaning (New York: Simon and Shuster, 1963).

42. Professor George Dolnikowski, personal interview, February 5, 1995.

43. See "Note by F. M. Dostoevsky" in Fyodor Dostoevsky, The House of the Dead, trans. David McDuff (London: Penguin Books, 1985), 238.

44. Frank, Stir, 215.

45. It is not difficult to imagine that Dostoevsky's Notes from the Dead House influenced Nietzsche's conception of "the overman." Jackson notes that "Nietzsche had outlined the problem of seeing for the artist-psychologist in Twilight of the Idols (written after his reading of Notes from the Underground and House of the Dead)" (Jackson 1981, 44).

46. The title of George Dolnikowski's autobiography is This I Remember: From War to Peace (Elgin, Ill.: Brethren Press, 1994). In his work he recounts his life from boyhood in Voronezh, to active service in the Red Army, incarceration in German military camps, and to his life as a Professor of German and Russian at Juniata College.

47. Cf., V. L. Komarovich, "Iunost' Dostoevskogo," in O Dostoevskom: Stat'i, introd. Donald Fanger (Providence, R.I.: Brown University Press, 1966), 73-115. "Chto stalos' s iunosheskim mechtatel'stvom za gody katorgi, chto iz nego utselelo v etom ispytanii ognem, v etoi poverke zhizn'iu, polnoi grekha, otchaianiia i zloby--vyiasnit' vse eto seichas ne iavliaetsia nasshei zadachei. No soglasimsia zaranee: dal'neishaia religioznaia zhizn' Dostoevskogo vo mnogom byla predopredelena etimi dvumia, sil'no perezhitymi i stol' raznorodnymi momentami ego mysli: 'mechtatel'naia' religiia gumanizma, otritsavshaia organicheskuiu grekhovnost' 'bozhestvennogo' cheloveka, i Mertvyi Dom, gde nado bylo byt' sledym, chtoby ne videt' dukhovnuiu iznachal'nost' grekha, gde vse v 'bozhestvennom' cheloveke smerdelo grekhom" (pp. 110-11).

48. Julie de Sherbinin, "Transcendence through Art: The Convicts' Theatricality in Dostoevskij's Zapiski iz mertvogo doma," Slavic and East European Journal 35, no. 3 (Fall 1991): 339-51.

49. Ibid., 344.

50. Ibid., 343.

51. Bob Dylan, "I Shall Be Released," Bob Bylan's Greatest Hits Volume II (Columbia CS 31120, 1971), Side 4, band 5.

52. Frank, Stir, 230-31.

53. F. M. Dostoevsky, Notes from the Underground, trans. S. Shishkoff (New York: Thomas Y. Crowell, Inc., 1969).

54. The idea of an irrational life force that drives human life is central to the philosophers associated with Lebensphilosophie. Dostoevsky was certainly swimming in the current of this return to vitalism, although it is not clear that he was directly influenced in that direction. Rather, it is possible to identify in his works certain philosophical conceptions about man that later became central to Lebensphilosophie. That is not to say that he necessarily influenced those later thinkers either, but the "thought was in the air."

55. See Chapter 1 above on Heidegger's view of freedom.

CHAPTER 3

NOTES FROM THE UNDERGROUND (1864)

The narrator of Notes from the Underground [Zapiski iz podpol'ia],[1] the Underground Man, makes an attack upon reason in the name of freedom. This freedom is based upon a conception of volia or will. As we have seen in Dead House, the deprivation of the prisoner's will is integrally related to his freedom or lack of freedom. Associated with the deprivation of "volia" is the reactive assertion of will power "no matter what the cost." All of this is evident in Gorianchikov's analysis of the prisoner's drinking sprees, and in his description of their impulsive free-for-alls. Gorianchikov concludes that this assertion of will is not an act of authentic freedom, but aims at the illusion of freedom. Whereas Dead House juxtaposes the prisoners' instinctual lashing-out against the suppression of the individual, personal will; in Underground we face the juxtaposition of a conception of wanting that is in conflict with reason. A study of this conflict centers on the concept of the human being.

It is instructive to compare the definitions of man in Dead House and Underground. Whereas Gorianchikov defines man as a creature who can adapt to anything, the Underground Man simply calls man an ungrateful biped [sushchestvo na dvukh nogakh i neblagodarnoe] (PSS 5:116). We have seen how Dostoevsky depicts the prison milieu in order to demonstrate the essential role that adaptation plays in human life. If man can adapt to life in a Siberian prison, then he can adapt to anything. It is more difficult to surmise what the epithet "ungrateful" means. The following chapter explores the meaning of human freedom which the Underground Man depicts as well as the way the terminology of wanting and willing which appear in Dead House recur in Underground with different shades of meaning.

I will demonstrate how literary and poetic factors, the very "stuff" of art, do not impede the attempt to interpret the depiction of man and freedom. In section one, Narrative Complexity in Underground, the strategy will be to investigate a number of specific literary obstacles which threaten to undermine the stability of this interpretation. For example, the problem of narrative reliability will be addressed. As narrator, the Underground Man is extremely unreliable. Even if we could take his "philosophy" at face value, we would still encounter the profound ambiguity, ambivalence, contradictoriness and paradoxicality that this text embodies. Further, the hermetic and allusive quality of Underground harbors a complex web of ideological and polemical motives. Section two, Complexity in Ideology and Polemic, addresses these matters. Jackson argues that a close reading of the text reveals neither a total irrationality nor a total victory of freedom over reason. Rather, as a character or hero the Underground Man is profoundly unfree. He admits this and says he does not know why. His confession in Part II serves only to demonstrate and amplify his incapacity for free action. Section three indicates that there are reasons to believe that this text was meant as a confession of Christian faith. Censorship excised the most patent references to the need for faith in Jesus Christ. Hence, the whole work is misleading. Even so, a close reading indicates that Underground can still be read as a crypto-confession of Christian faith, both in what is said and what is unsaid. The consideration of the meaning of what is left unsaid reveals a method of apophatic interpretation which addresses the artwork as a whole in order to describe its "saying" about freedom. Section four follows-up with a description of the image of man which the work makes present. Finally, the existentialist interpretation of _Underground_ is critically considered.

Narrative Complexity in "Underground"

The meaning of freedom in the text arises first of all in the Underground Man's description of his caprices, his lying, and the absurdity of his decisions to act. Opposing statements which address the laws of nature, and the facts that he cannot change, which are contradictory and reveal his impotence, depict unfreedom. Statements which indirectly reveal freedom as an integral component of man such as statements of blame, absurdity, chance, and so on take on specific nuances of meaning within the text. Meaning is deferred, "sideshadowed," and is made clear in conjunction with the overall literary design.[2]

Reliability of the Narrator

Serious questions have been asked concerning the reliability of the narrator. If the Underground Man is capricious, nasty and untrustworthy according to his own self-report, what kind of value are we to affix to his utterances? We must carefully consider whether the narrative structure is such that the reliability of the Underground Man's ideas is permanently held at bay.

An interpretation of _Underground_ which distinguishes the use of _volia_ and _svoboda_ can teach us a great deal about human freedom, a theme which is certainly central to the work, either _pro_ or _contra_. A close reading of the text reveals that both terms which translate "freedom" are used in a quite distinct manner, and that this usage is significant to any hermeneutic effort to describe the meaning of human freedom in the work. Such an interpretation is required because "the principal difficulty lies in the circumstance that words and other forms of expression carry many meanings."[3] Ambiguity in the meaning and use of volia and svoboda must be taken into account, as well as the manner in which narrative play and literariness determines the possible significance of the Underground Man's utterance.

Bakhtin and "Deferment of Meaning"

A consideration of the poetic structure of the work indicates the ramifications of "deferred meaning." In his study of the poetics of Underground, Bakhtin identifies the central feature of the novel in the anticipated response of the other:

> . . . The entire style of the "Notes" is subject to the most powerful and all-determining influence of other people's words, which either act on speech covertly from within as in the beginning of the work, or which, as the anticipated response of another person, take root in the very fabric of speech. . . .[4]

The significance of the influence of other's people words upon the Underground Man's discourse is his full dependence upon them and his attempt to elude any "final word" which could establish a determinate meaning for his confession:

> Say, gentleman, I hope that you won't get the idea that now I feel repentant about something, that I am asking your forgiveness for something. I am sure that you think so. . . . But I assure you that it's all the same to me even if you do. (E: 5)

Thus, according to Bakhtin, the interlocutor's (the "gentlemen's") response is anticipated in such a way that it is undermined. Further, this feature of the Underground Man's discourse is emblematic of his need to maintain his freedom. Bakhtin writes:

> The destruction of one's own image in another's eyes, the sullying of that image in another's eyes as an ultimate, desperate effort to free oneself from the power of the other's consciousness and to break through to one's self for the self alone--this, in fact, is the orientation of the Underground Man's entire confession.[5]

Entirely determined by his dependent orientation toward the other's consciousness, his effort is aimed at freeing himself from the determining "gaze" of another. Bakhtin's analysis of the Underground Man's anticipated response uncovers a structure that illustrates freedom within the narrative. The structure enacts an escape from the Gentlemen's response and leaves the Underground Man free to develop himself.

We might ask what the content of such a freedom entails and consider that it is an extremely minimal conception. Perhaps he escapes all of the others' critical gazes; he spends his entire being on maintaining this posture. He has not made himself authentically free, he has not made himself free _for_ anything. Pico della Mirandola observed that God left man unfinished and that man must complete himself. The Underground Man exercises no effort toward the goal of self-completion. His activity spent on avoidance, he avoids no one more than himself. We might ask whether the structure Bakhtin identifies reveals Dostoevsky's idea of freedom. Granted the text at least "gives" this concept of freedom. However, there is nothing in Bakhtin's analysis which could secure a "final word" on this. His analysis being dependent upon the Underground Man's literary play is also determined by it, it is also caught up in the same _perpetuum mobile_.

The Underground Man is incapable of making a simple statement about himself, and the entire narrative is discourse aimed at someone else. For Bakhtin the _perpetuum mobile_ of dialogue composed of the opposition between his own and the other's anticipated consciousness is nowhere more clearly articulated than in Underground. "But nowhere in subsequent works does this opposition appear in such naked, abstractly precise, one could even say directly mathematical, form."[6] Amazingly, it is precisely that which is abstract, even mathematical and structural within the text, that enacts human freedom. The effect upon the reader of the Underground Man's discourse is that ". . . first and foremost one reacts to it, responds to it, is drawn into its game; it is capable of agitating and irritating, almost like the personal address of a living person."[7] The structure of this narrative not only illustrates but enacts human freedom. To look more closely at the text to find out how freedom is revealed, it is necessary to consider the "underground lexicon" to reveal the semantic deployment of freedom.

The Distinction Between the Use of Volia and Svoboda in Underground

The use of volia and svoboda in Underground is not univocal. In addition to these words, a number of concepts appear in the narrative which reflect and lead up to the idea of freedom. Meaning is deferred. For example, the reader immediately meets the Underground Man's description of himself as nasty [zloi]:

> I am a sick man . . . I am a nasty man . . . . (E: 3)
>
> [Ia chelovek bol'noi . . . Ia zloi chelovek . . . .] (PSS 5:99)

A "nasty man" is not necessarily an incongruent epithet, however, the precise meaning that the Underground Man gives to it is unclear.[8] It is not necessarily redundant, and in this case may be congruent. Even though the Underground Man professes a low view of man, it is himself that he hates most of all. Man is not necessarily "nasty," on the other hand, the meaning of "zloi" reveals something significant about man, namely that man has a capacity for turning away from what is good. Dal's Explanatory Dictionary indicates that there is a meaning for "zloi" which is specifically linked to man:

> Zloi . . . o cheloveke: u kogo dusha obratilas' ko zlu, protovnik vsiakago blaga, dobra. . . .[9]
>
> [Zloi . . . concerning man: who turns his soul toward evil, against all blessings and good things. . . .]

This "turning against" is analogous of the attempt to escape the others' discourse. This does not mean, however, that man must turn away from the good toward evil. It is an indication of freedom as the potential to turn away from what is good.

The implicit linkage of "zloi" and "bol'noi" ("sick") has an ambiguous significance in the first sentence which only becomes clear as the narrative unfolds. Zloi has been translated into English in a number of ways, as wicked, evil, malicious, spiteful.[10] One translator prefers "nasty." Even so, the meaning of this "nastiness" has a unique meaning in the Underground Man's lexicon. The Underground Man as a figure embodies the meaning of "nastiness" and whatever clarity he attains is limited by the ambiguous presentation in the narrative. Its meaning is not so much that the Underground Man is evil, and that his confession is one of repentance; rather, his very manner of treating the confession as a spoof is a sign of his "nastiness." As the confession unfolds, one gets a precise sense of what the Underground Man means in his opening, self-deprecatory sentence.

In the first paragraph, the Underground Man indicates that it is from nastiness [zlost'] that he will not see a doctor. Further, he is unsure who will suffer from this, himself or the doctor. Thus, even in the first page of the narrative we find that _zlost'_ has a very idiosyncratic meaning for the Underground Man.

As an official, the Underground Man describes himself as "nasty" as well: "I was a nasty official" [Ia byl zloi chinovnik] (_PSS_ 5:99). He made trouble with a certain official and took pleasure in upsetting the "petitioners." He cannot justify this action, but in doing so he was amusing himself as though he were scaring sparrows. He amused himself without any purpose, and in vain.

At the end of Chapter V, the Underground Man attempts to account for the cause of his "nastiness." Since there is no cause for it, it can serve as a primary cause. That is, there is no other _explanandum_ which can account for its being; it is self-sufficient. On the other hand, for the very same reason, the phenomenon of nastiness can be explained away:

> Here again, because of these damned laws of consciousness, my nastiness is subject to a chemical breakdown. And so, right before your eyes the object vanishes, the reasons evaporate, the culprit is not to be found. . . . (E: 17)

The Underground Man is mixing metaphors when he speaks of "a chemical breakdown" because of "those damned laws of consciousness." This is an example of an _argumentum ad absurdum_, which serves to emphasize the parody of contemporary scientific jargon. The Underground Man's words, too, are a groundless "babbling" [_boltovnia_]. His discourse is empty, like a soap bubble [_myl'nyi puzyr'_] and amounts to nothing. Moreover, as a consequence of this type of scientific thinking, not only is the Underground Man a babbler, but it is the fate of all intelligent men to become mere babblers: "But what can you do, if the direct and sole purpose of every intelligent man is babbling--that is, intentionally shooting the breeze" (E: 18). When consciousness is strictly reduced to laws of chemical nature, then man himself is a vanity and all his deeds and words amount to nothing. Like nastiness, man appears as a dissolving phenomenon within the "chemical breakdown."

The Underground Man wriggles out of his "nastiness" in an example of what Bakhtin calls "the word with a loophole" by saying that he did not succeed in being nasty. "I lied about myself earlier when I said that I was a nasty official" (E: 5). According to Bakhtin, the word with a loophole is: "the retention for oneself of the possibility for uttering the ultimate, final meaning of one's own words."[11] Everywhere in this work Bakhtin finds an indeterminacy of meaning; nowhere does he find a fixed, monologic and final word. Accordingly, a close reading of the first chapter of Underground indicates that the meaning of the Underground Man's nastiness is not upheld by the semantics of the first sentence, paragraph, or chapter. The reader who wants to know what the Underground Man means by the first sentence must follow the Underground Man into his narrative "confession." If a meaning for the Underground Man's "nastiness" is to be derived from the narrative, the reader must engage in all of the crooked, underground logic in order to grasp it.

The notion of "nastiness" is fundamental to Dostoevsky. It is central to our consideration of the meaning of human freedom in Underground. Although it appears first of all as a quirk, and as an idiosyncrasy of the Underground Man, it appears later as the central argument against the total subsumption of human freedom within a rational-utilitarian "hedonistic calculus."[12] "Nastiness" is the first meaning that freedom takes in the Underground. Although the full content of its meaning is deferred, it is an attempt to preserve the human being against a disintegration into his best advantages. This means that there is a certain sense to the Underground Man's irrational caprice which is not entirely arbitrary and whimsical. In fact, it is ultimately related to the conception of man based on freedom. Granted that man is an ungrateful biped, still he is ungrateful for a reason. He is ungrateful precisely because either nature or society (the Gentlemen) attempt to provide him with a rational solution for living. Concerning man's ingratitude, the Underground Man has this to say:

> Go ahead, shower him with all the blessings of the earth, plunge him in over his head with happiness . . . give him such economic affluence that there would be nothing for him to do but sleep, eat gingerbread, and attend the noncessation of world history; even then, even in that case, man would, out of sheer ingratitude [neblagodarnost'], out of sheer perversity, do something loathsome. (E: 29; PSS 5:116)

Man reacts negatively to all of the blessings that would be showered upon him for a good reason--he is preserving his human freedom which is what makes him truly human.

Berdiaev argues that the defence of freedom is at the heart of Dostoevsky's literary work. Freedom propels and sustains man. It is his very core. Speaking of freedom Berdiaev writes, "Man begins to rebel in its name, ready for any misery or madness provided he can feel free. And at the same time he pursues his quest for the uttermost and final freedom."[13] Ultimately, in parading caprice, the Underground Man is underlining the role of human freedom at any cost. In emphasizing caprice in this way, Dostoevsky is defending man because man without freedom is no longer man.

Caprice

Before the Underground Man articulates anything directly about the distinction between freedom as svoboda and volia, he introduces enigmatic reflections upon a constellation of words and concepts that revolve around the idea of "caprice"--the entire confession is a "caprice"--the Underground Man's "nastiness" entails capriciousness.

Connected with caprice is whim, actions that are done in vain, without ground [_naprasno_], or done in absurdity [_nelepo_]. For example, it is a symptom of the Underground Man's caprice that he boasts of his illness. The Underground Man's use of words is even capricious. For example, a multitude of words appear in the text which amplify the meaning of human desire/wanting/willing: as in _Dead House_ the terminology of wanting [_khotenie_ and in the conversational form _khoten'e_] and wishing [_zhelanie_] re-appear many times in the text. The Underground Man goes further than Gorianchikov, obsessively burrowing into the concept of willfulness [_svoevolie_]. Caprice [_kapriz_, _proizvol_] is associated with one's very own will to do whatever one wishes: "Svoe sobstvennoe, vol'noe i svobodnoe khoten'e, svoi sobstvennyi, khotia by samyi dikii kapriz, svoia fantaziia . . ." (_PSS_ 5:113). Like a litany where the central expression of devotion is repeated, adumbrated and reinforced, the Underground Man's narrative like a spider's web circles around the concept of caprice connecting it with fantasy, willfulness, desire, choice, advantage, free will and ultimately human freedom.

Man's being, for the Underground Man, consists in the capacity to do what is wrong knowingly. If it could be demonstrated beyond any doubt that there is a manner in which man ought to behave for his own good, then man _ought_ to conform to this order. Hence, willfulness can only manifest itself as a will to agreement with the laws and systems of his best advantage. And yet, if man is truly free, then freedom consists primarily of willfulness. Freedom consists in the will to go against the totality of what is man's best interest. The proof of man's freedom is his capacity for acting in a manner that is contrary to his best advantage, and he does so knowing full well that he is acting contrary to his best advantage. The meaning of freedom is contrary to the reason that is parodied in Underground.

Complexity in Ideology and Polemic

Frank considers Underground to be a hermetic and allusive work, a work demanding the full literary and ideological acumen of his readers: "Dostoevsky, though, never again attempted anything as hermetic and allusive as Notes from the Underground."[14] A consideration of the underground as a metaphor, as a house of mirrors, highlights the self-referential aspect of this literary work which is an alien world unto itself whose features and figures determine the meaningfulness of its discourse. While Frank indicates the Underground Man's defence of freedom, Jackson describes his profound un-freedom.

Parody

Frank argues that Dostoevsky parodies Nihilistic ideology by embodying the doctrines of, for example, Chernyshevsky's rational egoism in the life of the Underground Man:

> Rather, since parody is ridicule by imitation, Dostoevsky assimilates the major doctrines of Russian Nihilism into the life of his underground man; and by revealing the hopeless dilemmas in which he lands as a result, Dostoevsky intends to undermine these doctrines from within.[15]

The arguments that the Underground Man voices in order to overturn have as their impetus and target Chernyshevsky's Anthropological Principle in Philosophy.[16] Chernyshevsky's philosophy advocates that man's wanting should fall in line with what is most of all in man's best advantage. And yet, the Underground Man states that man does not necessarily want what is "best" for him: "Man needs only and exclusively an independent wanting, whatever this independence may cost or wherever it may lead" (E: 25; PSS 5:118).

Dostoevsky emphasizes the word "samostoiatel'nogo" ("independent") which refers to a wanting "whatever it may cost" or "wherever it may lead." In consideration of man as a predominatively creative animal, the Underground Man comments that man must ". . . hew a road to wherever it may lead" (E: 31). Just as man must hew a road wherever it may lead, man must also follow his independent wanting. This parallels Gorianchikov's observation that in meaningful work he found his salvation. Just as a prisoner must find his own work and rightful possession, man must exercise his own will. It is in this quest for exercising one's own wanting that man finds his best advantage.

Frank writes: "The one 'most advantageous advantage' for man is the preservation of his free will."[17] This accords with his thesis that, taken as a parody, Underground exaggerates the irrational will in order to highlight it as the advantage which preserves human freedom from being coopted into the nihilism of Chernyshevsky.

Tragic Unfreedom

On the other hand, Jackson, in his "Aristotelian Movement and Design in Part Two of Notes from the Underground," makes a case for the Underground Man's unfreedom.

> The movement toward catastrophe is singularly linear and Aristotelian: effect follows cause swiftly and relentlessly. Every attempt by the Underground Man to introduce the irrational into his life only locks him more firmly into an irreversible course that must end in catastrophe.[18]

Paradoxically, no matter how wild, capricious, and "free" his action, the Underground Man unwittingly reinforces his unfreedom: "contrary to all his intentions, [he] brings about these model Aristotelian conditions in the drama of his life."[19] It is curious that Jackson chooses to analyze this most un-Aristotelian work in terms of the rational plot which Aristotle discusses in his Poetics.[20] Part One of Underground, having almost no plot, does not establish Jackson's argument as well as Part Two. Further, Aristotle's formal sense of irrationality has very little to do with the Underground Man's diegetic irrationality.

The action of Part Two, set sixteen years prior to the exposition of the irrational will philosophy in Part One, only makes evident the bankruptcy of what was established in Part One:

> The self-defeating, destructive nature of irrational will philosophy, of underground "spite," is already evident in part one of Notes from the Underground, though the Underground Man's polemics with rationalist-utilitarians, his tragic stance of revolt, tends to obscure the main figure in Dostoevsky's overall design.[21]

Thus, for Jackson, despite the rhetorical arguments for freedom in Part One of the narrative, the fact of the matter is that the Underground Man is profoundly and inextricably unfree. As the narrative draws to its end in chapter nine of Part Two, the Underground Man makes a confession to Liza which echoes the self-destructive narrative voice of the opening paragraph:

> And I'll also never forgive *you* for the things that I am confessing to you now! Yes--you, you alone will have to answer for all of this, because you are handy, because I am a scoundrel, because I am the most repulsive, the most ridiculous, the most petty, the most stupid, the most envious of all of the worms on earth. . . . (E: 117; PSS 5:174)

Jackson suggests that the continuity between Part One and Part Two establishes that the Underground Man is profoundly unfree.

Whereas Frank, taking into account the sociological and cultural-historical background of the Russian intelligentsia, sees the Underground Man in Part One as a parody of the men of the 1860s, and finds Part Two as a parody of the attitudes of the 1840s; Jackson interprets it as a Christian tragedy:

> The Underground Man is the embodiment of irrational behavior. Yet the singularity of his underground is that in it absolute chance is indistinguishable from absolute necessity.[22]

The only freedom the Underground Man might hope to possess, the love and self-sacrifice that Liza offers him, he refuses. According to Jackson, he could not do otherwise: ". . . he [Underground Man] has been caught in a master plot that is historical, linear and Aristotelian, a plot that he seeks, always vainly, to foil."[23] As an image of man, the Underground Man is pathetically unfree. However, Jackson himself had written in his earlier book, Dostoevsky's Underground Man in Russian Literature (1958): "If there is any work which leaves man boundless freedom of choice, and imposes a tremendous responsibility for that choice, it is Notes from the Underground."[24] One way of resolving this apparent contradiction is to consider the manner in which Dostoevsky's aesthetic philosophy sheds light on the artwork's capacity to reveal truth.

Jackson indicates the centrality of the conflict between man's ideal and reality in Dostoevsky's art. Underground depicts a failed artist and poet, and reveals a fundamental rift between art and life. The confession of the Underground Man is itself a manifestation of this unhappy consciousness. The narrative is complex, composed of two central parts. The first part of the narrative is rhetorical, and conveys a philosophical saying about human freedom which answers to the "new" image of man portrayed in the rational-utopian works of Chernyshevsky. The second part dramatizes Part One. Although not a conte philosophique, which is never a first-person narrative, Underground echoes Candide's dumbfounded discovery of the real world while his beloved conceptions of the "best of all possible worlds" fall to pieces.[25]

At the heart of this problematic is Dostoevsky's artistic conception of man. Man does not discover a world that is in accord with his ideals, but rather to the contrary, the world is impervious to man's ideals. But neither is man simply a child of the earth, devoid of ideals. It is the role of the artist to reveal man because man is revealed within this artistic representation of the conflict man discovers between his ideals and the real world. According to Jackson, Dostoevsky conceives of the artist as a creator, not an imitator, of reality:

> The role of the artist, then, is ultimately that of a seer; in him, imaginative (poetic) consciousness and religious, prophetic consciousness are one; phenomena to him are not divided into real and unreal, actual and fictitious; he reveals man to himself in the completeness of his destiny, his timeless being.[26]

This vision entails a unique role of the artist in the discovery of man, in a dynamic conception. The artwork makes possible a manifestation of a certain truth about man that is not achieved through any other means.

This accounts for the fact that despite the profound unfreedom which the Underground Man embodies, this narrative points to an image of a free man. When we look beyond the figure of the Underground Man toward the ideal which is in conflict, the work reveals an image of a free man.

Apophatic Interpretation and Human Freedom in "Underground"

In what follows I shall introduce an indirect method for the discovery of the image of man in *Underground*. The apophatic interpretation is an example of a deferment of meaning within the text on another level. Interpretation is done not on the semantic level, but on the level of the "thought" which is conditioned by the anticipatory semantics which Bakhtin describes. Just as the spiritual nature of truth cannot be directly stated, the conception of man, or the conception of freedom cannot be stated directly. This is owing to the very meaning of the concept of freedom. A true freedom which stands outside all of the laws of nature and language can be limited to a description neither within the articulation of natural science nor the system of language and logic. The philosophical meaning of freedom predetermines its presentation in language. Freedom, like the conception of a truly transcendent being, only allows a negative approach; that is, we are able to describe what freedom is not, but not what freedom is. A strictly deterministic science attempts to account for freedom as an epiphenomenon, reducible to scientifically describable events. Within this discourse freedom can only appear with its own essential meaning, as deRaison (Foucault) or something that is left unsaid.

Foucault, in his Histoire de la Folie, argues that the standard history of psychiatry could not speak of the truth of irrationality (deRaison), but could only construct a monologue of reason about madness. The voice of the insane is confined to a silence. The truth of madness cannot appear in a direct statement in a rational discourse, hence the history of madness is merely reason's monologue about madness. The French historian's goal is as follows: "We must try to return, in history, to that zero point in the course of madness at which madness is an undifferentiated experience, a not yet divided experience of division itself."[27] I cite Foucault's treatment of deRaison as a parallel. The "zero point" of freedom, the meaning of being human, the truth about religious faith, like <u>deRaison</u> cannot appear in direct statement in a literary text. Just as the truth concerning irrationality (<u>deRaison</u>) cannot appear in a rational monologue about mental illness, so too the nature of spiritual truth concerning man, his religious faith, and his freedom cannot appear in a direct statement within <u>Underground</u>.

In order to find the "saying" about freedom within <u>Underground</u>, we must recognize that the artwork "speaks" in its structural integrity, in a manner that the parts of the work cannot. In order to find the essential teaching about human freedom in the work, we must identify <u>the level of the work</u>. That is, to secure the phenomenon of the artwork, not as a system of parts consisting of confessional genre, monologue discourse, parody, and linguistic conventions, but rather the level on which the artwork moves and speaks as a unified, and integral saying. Accordingly, like a holograph, the work must be shown to speak of the truth of freedom as a whole and in all of its parts in order to arrive at the optimal interpretation. <u>Underground</u>, perhaps more than any other work of Dostoevsky, exhibits this unity of form and concept.

The Dissolution of Man

An argument appears in the beginning of Chapter VII which does not represent the viewpoint of the narrator. It claims to distinguish human advantages from human interests:

> But that if he were enlightened, if his eyes were opened to his real, normal interests, man would immediately stop making mischief, and would immediately become nice and noble, because, being enlightened and understanding his true advantages, he would see that his own advantage lies precisely in the good, and it is known that not a single man can knowingly act against his own advantage, and consequently he would, so to speak, of necessity begin to do good. (E: 18; <u>PSS</u> 5:109)

This argument asserts that when man's best interest is recognized to be compatible with his best advantage, then man will become enlightened and no longer do wrong deeds. The Underground man sarcastically rejects this argument as infantile. It is, as Frank suggests, a parody of Chernyshevsky's Anthropological Principle in Philosophy. Incidentally, if this is the case, then man must by necessity do good. The Underground Man's presentation of this idea is a strict version or interpretation of Socrates' dictum, "No man does wrong willingly."[28] This teaching is the fountainhead of enlightened views concerning the perfectibility of man.

The Underground Man argues against a number of rationalistic and enlightened views of man which would attribute to man a potential perfectibility, provided that man would realize that it is in his best interest to organize his will in accordance with a rational blueprint. However, the Underground Man exaggerates the meaning of reason in such a way that it threatens to swallow up human freedom entirely. He refers metaphorically to statistical ciphers, statistics, economic laws, mathematical tables, and engineering formulas in order to convey the idea that he is refuting. Man's own wanting [khoten'e], is the spear with which he ruptures the rational-utilitarian conception of human perfectibility.

As we have seen, Frank argues that the Underground Man's discourse is a parody of the rational-egoistic argument of a Nihilist such as Chernyshevsky. The Underground Man establishes the absurdity of the premise that if man knows what is in his best interest he will act accordingly since it leads to an absurd consequence. Paradoxically, it might not be in man's best interest to act according to his best interest. This accounts for one form of indeterminacy and incompleteness in the Underground Man's discourse.

It looks like he is building up the "Gentlemen's" argument and supporting it. However, this is only a strategy that he employs in order to ultimately overcome it. There is a way of reading the _Underground_ as an argument of the _reductio ad absurdum_ variety which defends human freedom from subsumption within a totalizing Reason.

The Underground Man finds it necessary to inquire, what after all is in man's best advantage:

> Advantage! What is this thing called advantage? And would you really be willing to take it upon yourselves to define with absolute precision exactly what constitutes man's advantage? (E: 20; _PSS_ 5:110)

The Underground Man asks an astute question concerning the possibility of defining and knowing what is man's advantage. It suggests the possibility that the Gentlemen might not know what advantage is and have assumed to know what it is.

The central term in the counterargument is "advantage" [_vygoda_]. "Advantage" is the term which serves the rational-utilitarian argument in order to indicate that man ought to choose to act in accordance with his best interest. "Advantage" is the lever with which the Underground Man overturns the argument of rational-egoism. Man possesses a "most advantageous advantage" [_samaia vygodnaia vygoda_], that is, his self-will to do whatever he wishes, albeit irrational, nasty, capricious, and even against his own best interests. This is not identical to freedom, but is a manifestation of irrational will which defends man's freedom against rational-egoism. This argument harbors a view of human freedom and human nature that is not made explicit, but which it presupposes.

The strategy of using a _reductio ad absurdum_ argument succeeds in destroying the rational-utilitarian conception of man without having to provide another image of a man in its place. The role of the Underground Man's argument is purely negative. However, it is possible to describe what freedom and self-will mean in this text, and it follows that these are essential characteristics of a philosophical conception of man even though this image of man is never stated or put forth univocally in the work. The philosophical conception of man is not articulated as such within the work; however, the work can be interpreted as an apophatic presentation of man's freedom.

As Bakhtin makes clear, the discourse of the Underground Man is unfinalizable, always waiting for a response, and indeterminate. At the end of the first part of his notes, the Underground Man declares: "But I swear to you, gentlemen, that I do not believe a word, not even one little word of all that I have just dashed off!" (E: 36; PSS 5:121). With this declaration he suspends all of what he has confessed into a fog of ambiguous meaning. Bakhtin invites us to see this dialogic unfinalizability as a unique virtue of the Dostoevskian work. On the other hand, an interpretation which indicates the significance of what is left unsaid in a text may teach us something important. Rather than establishing that the indeterminacy of words whose meanings are endlessly deferred in a perpetuum mobile is the final word about Underground, we find that the deferred meaning of the text points toward something that is not directly sayable in a determinate manner. For example, as Flath argues, the spiritual nature of truth is not directly sayable: "But a direct statement of the spiritual nature of the truth is impossible: it would be using words for something that Dostoevskij is saying cannot be expressed in words."[29]

Flath makes the case for Underground as an indirect statement which leads the reader to recognize the need for faith. Underground makes a parody of confession and the Underground hero withholds what is most precious to himself. Even if he wanted to make a "true" confession, ". . . the nature of the confession genre (or any literary form) will not allow a direct, true expression of religious faith in words."[30] The literary text cannot directly state the Underground Man's religious faith. It underscores its absence and in so doing points toward its meaning apophatically.

Meerson, citing Dostoevsky's famous letter to his brother, Mikhail, has argued that Notes from the Underground is an apophatic presentation of God: ". . . Notes from the Underground was apophatically religious, i.e., that the absence of God in the book, or rather in the Underground Man's life, was conspicuous, marked and significant."[31] The letter to Mikhail bemoans the fact that swinish censors excluded the penultimate chapter which referred explicitly "to the need for belief and for Christ." Still, when given the opportunity to restore the censored chapter within the text, Dostoevsky did not. Underground stands without the direct statement for faith and Christ. Even so, as an artwork it is stylistically and formally whole.

The Underground Man's narrative can be read as either a statement of Christian faith or atheism. The atheistic interpretation has been emphasized above all in the existentialist interpretations. Before turning to the existentialist interpretations I will indicate how it is possible to read Underground as a statement of Christian faith. Chapter X begins with the statement, "You believe in the crystal edifice indestructible for all eternity . . ." (E: 34; PSS 5:120). The Underground Man believes in something else. A close reading of Chapter X reveals two or three observations which confirm the Underground Man's thirsting for something higher:

> Well, what is to be done if I have taken it into my head that people are not living just for that [Crystal Palace], and that if one is to live at all, then one should live in a mansion? That is my want, that is my desire. You will gouge it out of me only when you change my desires. (E: 34; PSS 5:120)

He rejects the Crystal Palace in its specific connotation as ". . . a housing project with apartments for poor tenants, with a lease for a thousand years" [Ia ne priamu za venets zhelanii moikh--kapital'nyi dom, s kvartirami dlia bednykh zhiltsov po kontraktu na tysiachu let . . .] (E: 34; PSS 5:120). The "housing project" [kapital'nyi dom] is an earthly ideal and does not differ essentially from the connotation of "mansion" given above. It is simply another type of material ideal. Moreover, the Underground Man boasts that he has his underground. He does not need an apartment in the housing project. He challenges the gentlemen: "Destroy my desires, erase my ideals, show me something better and I'll follow you" (E: 35). Unfortunately, there is no building that he would not feel compelled to stick his tongue out at. Finally, he uses ritual religious language when he declares that he will not bow down [tak ved' klaniat'sia ne budu] (PSS 5:120). What disturbs him is that even though he must reconcile himself to his earthly disappointment, he still yearns for something else:

> Why then was I made with such desires? Is it possible that I was made that way only to come to the conclusion that the making of me was simply a swindle? Could that be the whole purpose? I don't believe it. (E: 35)

The concluding remark, "Ia ne veriu" (PSS 5:121) [I don't believe it], closes the door on the opening remark aimed at the gentlemen: "Vy verite v khrustal'noe zdanie . . ." (PSS 5:120) [You believe in the crystal edifice]. A close reading of Chapter X confirms that the ideal that the Underground Man yearns for is religious. Despite the direct reference to faith in Christ and God which was censored, the text still yields enough clues to suggest, at least, a yearning for something higher.

Culpability and the Image of Human Being in "Underground"

If *Underground* can be taken as an integral "saying" about human freedom, then the question remains whether this saying reveals a philosophical conception of man. Philosophical anthropology indicates that culpability is an essential consequence of human freedom. If freedom is central to man's definition, then the consequences of that freedom ought also be present.

One of the prevalent themes in Part One of *Underground* is human culpability. It is a central occupation not only in terms of the philosophical ideas, but also in terms of the form of the narrative. The confessional narrative is based upon a confession of a misdeed. At the same time, the Underground Man is addressing in his philosophical reflections questions concerning the origin of guilt, its meaning and its relation to human life.

We have noted that Bakhtin observes how the Underground Man's discourse is always aimed at another consciousness. In this way he is dependent on the other's will and predetermined by it: "His own thought is developed and structured as the thought of someone personally insulted by the world order, personally humiliated by its blind necessity."[32] The discourse with the world as with others is dialogic, says Bakhtin. Hence, like blind Lear shaking his fists in the storm, the Underground Man is demanding an answer from the world as such. Bakhtin finds this "other-seeking" feature of the discourse to be a sign of an all encompassing dialogic whose meaning is open-ended and indeterminate. The poetic form only reinforces the philosophical question of culpability in the narrative.

The question which the narrative "asks" is: for what and to whom is man accountable? Gadamer speaks of the question that a historical text makes to the interpreter in Truth and Method: "For an historical text to be made the object of interpretation means that it asks a question of the interpreter."[33] Underground asks a question concerning the possibility of a meaningful, "true" confession. Taken as a parody of the confession genre, the text indirectly calls into question the possibility of authentic confession. With the Underground Man there are the facts of guilt, blame, and culpability whose origin is unclear. However, since confession is dialogical and requires at least one other consciousness in order to achieve its aim, a solipsistic confession cannot accomplish its goal. The reason why confession is dyadic is that it reflects the structure of guilt. Guilt requires a bearer of the guilt and a party before whom the guilt is demanded. Guilt is the recognition of a debt owing to a party to whom it is entitled on account of a misdeed.

The Underground Man introduces the problem of blame and guilt into his notes as a parody of Chernyshevsky's conception that man is solely analyzable in terms of nature. If this is so, then there can be no support for guilt or blame for any wrongdoing. Concerning the object of the Underground Man's parody, Frank writes:

> . . . The pseudo-scientific terms of the underground man's declaration about "hyperconsciousness" are a parody of Chernyshevsky, and the statement is a paraphrase of Chernyshevsky's assertion, in The Anthropological Principle in Philosophy, that no such capacity as free will exists or can exist, since whatever actions man attributes to his own initiative are really a result of the "laws of nature."[34]

In the rational discourse of Chernyshevsky, there is no room for an Underground Man. His only means of speaking to men of reason about human freedom is by necessity *ir*-rational. Freedom is for Chernyshevsky *nihil*. The "anthropological principle" refers to Chernyshevsky's conception of man as a unitary organism which ought to analyzed as another natural entity:

> Anthropology is a science which, no matter what part of the human vital process it may deal with, always remembers that the process as a whole, and every part of it, takes place in a human organism, that this organism is the material which produces the phenomena under examination, that the quality of the phenomena is conditioned by the properties of the material, and that the laws by which the phenomena arise are only special cases of the operations of the laws of nature.[35]

Dostoevsky's critique of Chernyshevsky's materialist anthropology amounts to a philosophical defense of free man against his subsumption into a narrowly scientistic conception of man as a "phenomenon" of nature. The Underground Man assimilates and imitates Chernyshevsky's teaching and the only way freedom can appear in his discourse is by way of caprice, contradiction, and negation.

The Underground Man realizes the tragic implication of this verdict: If a man were to take his toothache or some other form of suffering as an insult from the hands of nature, he would have no court of appeal, for nature is deaf to man's cries: "Nature doesn't ask your approval; she couldn't care less about your desires and whether you like her laws or not" (E: 12; *PSS*; 5:105). Even so, this odd juxtaposition brings to light the correlation between human culpability and the laws of nature. There is no dialogue between nature and the blame that man feels. If man were to seek in nature an answer for his culpability he could never find an answer. This accords with the idea that philosophical anthropology emerged as a doctrine of man in light of the failure of theodicy to account for the problem of evil, as we have seen in Chapter One. Schelling argues that the philosophy of man assumes the responsibility of articulating the metaphysical origin of evil with recourse to a story about an original Fall. The consequence of the philosophical defence of human freedom is that evil resides in man primordially and ineradicably. Human freedom is henceforth linked with culpability and guilt.

Paul Evdokimov explains that Dostoevsky did not seek to avoid the problem of human evil in his portrayal of man:

> Pour Dostoïevsky, ce n'est pas de la raison que relève le problème du mal. Le mal, de même que la liberté, plonge dans la profondeur non éclairée, irréductible au savoir explicite, à la connaissance analytique, et c'est dans leur coexistence incompatible que réside le tragique de l'homme.[36]

Not only should this evil not be reasoned away, but moreover, it is the gateway which reveals the problem of human freedom. The consequence of freedom and its price is the possibility of real evil and apostasy. Dostoevsky realized this and still defends man's freedom even at the cost of resistance to the "antheap" or Crystal Palace.

There is no ground for the blame that the Underground Man bears. In a parallel manner, he speaks of a slap on the face, and the insult it brings. For a man of honor, insult from another man ought to result in a demand for satisfaction by duel. Hence there is a type of human justice which redresses slaps, insults and other wrongs suffered at the hands of another man. On the other hand, for any of man's complaints which rise from natural causes such as pain from toothache, or poverty and homelessness, nature provides no justification: "More important though, no matter how you look at it, I still come out most to blame for everything, and, what is most painful, to blame without any reason and, so to speak, because of the laws of nature" (E: 9; PSS 5:103).

To establish through science and philosophy that these laws of nature are immutable and that henceforth the question of guilt disappears like a wall, is not a satisfactory answer: "As if such a stone wall really were any solace and really did contain the slightest word of conciliation . . ." (E: 13; PSS: 5:106). The Underground Man raises the question of the theodicy (i.e., of God's omnipotence and human culpability) and yet there is no theodicy, since God is not addressed. The Underground Man is addressing no one; first of all, he mocks the idea that his confession may be read by others, secondly, he makes it clear that even if he were to take the blows and sufferings of nature as an insult, there is no one to blame:

> . . . and, as a consequence, grinding your teeth in silent frustration, to sink sensuously into inertia, dreaming that, as it turns out, there is not even anyone to be mad at; that the object cannot be found, that there has been a switch, doubledealing, a swindle, that it is simple nonsense--no one can tell who or what, but in spite of all these uncertainties and doubledealings, it hurts you just the same, and the less you know the more it hurts! (E: 13; PSS 5:106)

The absence of an interlocutor only underscores the centrality of the Underground Man's guilt. This guilt in its philosophical sense is primordially linked with the Underground Man's freedom. The narrative does not articulate an abstract theory of man's guilt but rather indicates that it is inescapable, and its cause cannot be found in nature. The parody of a theory of man based solely on nature underscores man's ineradicable culpability. It is taken to the extreme, to its absurdity, making explicit the aporia.

"Underground" and Existentialism:

The Rejection of Reason

In the preceding sections I have demonstrated that it is possible to overcome the obstacles which this complex narrative presents in order to establish the image of man and his freedom which the work makes present. In what follows I will review "existentialist" interpretations of Underground which were once influential, but are no longer so. The reason for their obsolescence is that they were unable to treat the artwork as a whole, composed of both poetic and "thought" features which are inextricably enmeshed. Hence they latched too easily upon irrational features of the Underground Man's discourse without giving credit to the ideological background, which as we have seen colors the underground hero's thoughts. The principal error the existentialist interpreters make is to see freedom as antithetical to reason.

Reason at an Extreme

Granted, the arguments of the Underground Man are immoderate both in regard to the object of his polemicizing, i.e., the "gentlemen," and with regard to his depiction of man's freedom as untrammeled caprice. In his polemic, reason is portrayed in an extreme sense which completely undermines man's freedom, and freedom is portrayed in a way that defends against the domination of reason at any cost:

> If you say that all these things--chaos, darkness, curse--can be calculated by the table so that the very possibility of preliminary calculation will stop everything and reason will have the upper hand--then man will purposely make himself insane for the occasion so as

> not to have reason and to have his own way! (E: 30; PSS 5:117)

The Underground Man conceives of man as being at the mercy of the confrontation between a maximum of reason and a maximum of willing. Will is the virtue that saves man against the absorption into "calculation according to the tables." But is man truly saved by the deployment of his will at any cost?

Reason taken in the extreme sense is unreasonable. Ordinarily reason functions within a practicable limit. Likewise, freedom is moderate and operates in accordance with reason. The Underground Man unwittingly allocates to man an excess of freedom at the expense of sober reason. As a result, the Underground Man forfeits the moderate share of freedom that is his by virtue of being human. Hence as a figure or hero, the Underground Man depicts a strong unfreedom and a dubious status as human being.

The question of whose walls are more limiting, Gorianchikov's or the Underground Man's, is difficult to say. As I have shown, Dead House portrays a world that is physically inhibiting; Underground celebrates a freedom that has no limit, but in effect, is no more liberating. One interpretation which highlights freedom above all else in the definition of man is existentialism.

Underground and Existentialism

The existentialist interpretation of Underground maintains that this work ranks as one of the great contributions to existential thought. If one identifies "existentialism" in a loose way, as does the following author then this is tenable: "They [existentialists] stress the dignity of the individual; they remind man of his inalienable freedom and responsibility to be what he is."[37] To be sure, in Underground the dignity of the individual is stressed; man's inalienable freedom is emphasized, and his responsibility to be himself is highlighted. Accordingly, Dostoevsky looks like an existentialist author. The problem with this approach is that in classifying the "thought" of Underground as a statement of existentialist philosophy interpreters have tended to arrive at conclusions and definitive statements that foreclose on the open-ended, ambivalent and highly questionable nature of the image of man that the narrative paints.

For example, in perhaps the finest presentation of the "existentialist" interpretation of Underground, i.e., Irina Kirk's Dostoevskij and Camus: The Themes of Consciousness, Isolation, Freedom and Love (1974),[38] we find the Underground Man prophetically anticipating Sartre's definition of existentialism [l'existence précede l'essence[39]]:

> Closely related to the Underground Man's attempt to live according to his will and caprice is the idea of existence preceding essence. Existentially speaking, human nature is not predetermined by an abstract essence, but is perpetually created by each individual out of his own unique essence.[40]

If one takes a "strict" idea of existentialism as does Kirk, it is not fruitful to consider Dostoevsky an existentialist. Underground treats the human directly and somehow, when one introduces an existentialist terminology such as Kirk does, it falls short of the artwork's presentation of man. It is a long way from the idea of will at work in Underground to the highly dogmatic assertion that existence precedes essence. And a close reading of the text cannot support this thought. However, Kirk is not alone in her appraisal of Dostoevsky's "existentialism." Important works by Camus, Shestov, Berdiaev, and Gide which if not "existentialist" have been loosely affiliated with existential thought have associated Dostoevsky with existentialism.[41]

To wit, Camus has this to say about Dostoevsky: "Ce n'est donc pas un romancier absurde qui nous parle, mais un romancier existentiel."[42] And Shestov likens the Russian novelist as the twin brother of Kierkegaard. He highlights the full extent of Dostoevsky's radical rejection of reason in favor of human possibility. In an essay where he describes Dostoevsky as Kierkegaard's double, Shestov likens the Russian novelist's rejection of reason to be as profound as the father of existentialism. In referring to Underground Shestov writes: "And when Dostoevsky spoke of the 'stone walls,' no one even guessed that this was the true critique of pure reason; all eyes were turned toward speculative philosophy."[43] Granted, Underground criticizes reason, however, it is not a "critique" in the sense that Kant introduced it.[44]

Shestov praises this work because it confirms that reason and knowledge are contrary to man's freedom: "Knowledge has not given man freedom; in spite of what we habitually believe, in spite of what speculative philosophy proclaims, knowledge has made us slaves."[45] To attack reason in the name of human freedom is for Shestov the virtue of existentialism. It is for this reason that he likens Dostoevsky's thought to Kierkegaard's philosophy. However, Shestov's interpretation is too irrational; he simply goes too far on the side of irrationality. While it is true that a close reading which centers on the meaning of freedom indicates that reason cannot defend freedom but can only imprison it, and while it is not via reason that freedom is preserved but rather contra rationem, freedom and reason are both central to the work. It is more accurate to say that Underground reveals that freedom and reason do not fall together harmoniously and that there is even a conflict between man's reason and his freedom. The bantering of the Underground Man fits into an aphoristic and paradoxical tradition in philosophy--one need only think of Kierkegaard, Nietzsche, Maimonides, even Wittgenstein to find that some philosophers choose to go toward their ideas in an indirect rather than a direct manner. The Underground Man is a philosopher of this type. The narrator remarks at the end of his "Notes": "The 'notes' of this paradoxicalist [etogo paradoksalista] do not end here . . ." (E: 125; PSS 5:179). Further, the Underground Man refers to his underground activity as "philosophizing": "Forgive my philosophizing, gentlemen, it is the result of forty years in the Underground" (E: 27; PSS 5:115). Granted, his argumentation and logic is not at all like Kant or Aristotle, still that does not make it un-philosophical.

Since it hinges on the conception of man, and on the meaning of freedom, in contradistinction to the meaning of will, the existentialist interpretation is significant, albeit inaccurate. A close consideration of the text renders the strict existentialist interpretation highly doubtful. Hence, while it is not inaccurate to say that the Underground Man makes a definitive contribution to an existentialist conception of man, nor that Underground is the greatest overture to existentialism ever written,[46] still, we must emphasize that the image of man that the work portrays is not "existentialist" but is, in fact, unique to Dostoevsky. It is this image that I wish to describe in what follows.

The "New Man"

The line that I will pursue below emphasizes the concept of the "new man" that is suggested in Underground. Berdiaev identifies the Underground Man [podpol'nyi chelovek] as the first phase in portraying an image of a "new man." The thought that begins in

Underground carries through in all of Dostoevsky's major works that follow:

> This dialectic of the destiny of mankind which Dostoievsky [sic] began in Letters from the Underworld [sic] is developed throughout his novels and reaches its height in the Legend of the Grand Inquisitor.[47]

That the essential being of man is central to Dostoevsky's work and that it is linked with the conception of freedom has often been cited. For example, Berdiaev writes: "For Dostoievsky the theme of man and his destiny is on the first place the theme of freedom."[48] Berdiaev has discovered a significant truth. The horizon for the interpretation of man is the theme of freedom, and freedom reveals man.

Ivanov, in discussing the role of tragedy in Dostoevsky's artistic conventions writes:

> For man, when empirically considered, appears to be, if not entirely without freedom, yet certainly not absolutely free. But this is not so; for if it were, then man could not be man--that is to say, he would not be the only one of God's creatures to experience life tragically.[49]

Both authors identify the centrality of freedom within man's essential make-up. And yet, freedom though an essential ingredient for man is not a "thing," an "element" or a "simple."

The Underground Man gives no abstract or theoretical presentation of man--no clear, univocal definition. He praises man, and blames him. He attempts to define man as an ungrateful biped. He denies that he is a man, says that he is a mouse, a loafer, a babbler, and so on. The Underground Man mocks and ridicules all that he sees. In particular, he mocks the philosophical conception of man which would lead to a scientistic denial of man's freedom. It should be clear that Chernyshevsky's materialist theories are very far from Dostoevsky's conception of man. Chernyshevsky's anthropology is not philosophical for the very simple reason that he bases his discussion upon the findings of hard sciences such as physics and chemistry. Chernyshevsky's definition of man is that he is a phenomenon that can be described in purely materialistic terms. Philosophical anthropology bases its consideration of man on man alone. Other sciences might assist in defining man but man is not dissolvable into any other scientific discourse. The Underground Man presents a conception of man that can be interpreted as a contribution to philosophical anthropology.

An Objection

It will be objected that Dostoevsky's artwork cannot amount to a philosophical defense of anything, since it is art and incommensurable with anthropological "theory." For example, Kirpotin allows that the philosophical attempt to formulate a new image of man is one of the objects of the Underground Man's contempt and ridicule. For Kirpotin, Dostoevsky in Underground is not concerned with the construction of a philosophical conception of man: "In the 40s [1840s] problems of "anthropological" and social philosophy troubled Dostoevsky--now [early 1860s] they are clothed in flesh and in blood."[50]

According to this author, Dostoevsky is not attempting to define man according to a philosophical theory. Instead, he is critiquing an image of man that is defective. Indirectly, by saying what man is not, however, the Underground Man sketches as more "human" man. The contribution to a philosophical understanding of man lies in the meaning of this epithet, "more human."

On the other hand, Kirpotin asserts that the presentation of a literary type [tip], i.e., the Underground Man, cannot count as an exhaustive refutation to Chernyshevsky's optimistic and sociological theory:

> Maybe the theory is mistaken, maybe it is insufficient, but it leans on researches of the foundation and general laws of society or even humanity, the literary type by the very nature of art cannot express an anthropological "formula" for all men, the literary type ranks with other types.[51]

On one level this is simply a case of apples and oranges which are not commensurate. On the other hand, Kirpotin observes that the presentation of literary type, while not being able to refute a theory might nonetheless, ". . . bring an important part of truth about man before the mistakes of the general, 'theoretical' programs."[52] It is this "truth" about man which the Underground Man presents that makes a contribution to a philosophical understanding of man.[53]

Perhaps the Underground Man does not exist but people like him do exist. Commenting on Dostoevsky's footnote on the first page of Underground (PSS 5:99) Jackson writes: "We have here a very simple and precise explanation of the literary social type to reality: he does not really exist, but people like him exist, though they do not turn up so vividly."[54] It is this resemblance to other men that makes the Underground Man not only a successful literary type, but also an example of a social type who reveals something essential about being human.

Conclusion

Underground helps to elucidate human freedom in a special sense. As we have seen in the survey of philosophical conceptions of man, human freedom was traditionally taken to mean freedom to act. Such a viewpoint presupposes an ideal conception of man, as a finished being. But man is not, as Heidegger makes clear, a being that possesses itself like a rock or a stream. Man's being is a project that must be completed. Human freedom is a freedom to be. The conception that man is an unfinished being created by God who must complete himself is Pico della Mirandola's. The Underground Man presents this image of man. Granted, it is his own self-assertion which says I am a mouse, a test-tube man, a future man, but not a man. Interestingly enough, by figuring himself as *un*-human, the Underground Man's confession underscores a question, what is man? It presents an apophatic approach toward man's essential being. Despite the Underground Man's ambivalent posturing, and despite its narrative complexity, *Underground* can be taken as a defence of human freedom in an essential, philosophical sense. Taking into account the literary and poetic structure of the work allows us to see how the Underground Man defends the conception of human being in terms of an essential freedom to be.

The Underground Man defends this image of man by negating those materialist discourses which would render man unfree as a child of nature or a chemical phenomenon. The legitimation of the human being as a human being is first of all a saying "no" to all of the theories, and philosophies which attempt to speak for man. At the same time, there is the danger in any attempt to speak univocally for man. Such a positive way of defining man threatens to usurp him. The reason for this is that in any dogma, science or teaching, man is already spoken for. A thought needs to latch onto something concrete, even if incorrect, in order to achieve a provisional insight. This is the nature of thinking. With regard to abstract conceptions the matter affords more difficulty:

> *Homo anthropologicus* rarely becomes visible, because the philosophical question about the first principles of a field of being is rarely asked. The view of the whole is

> concealed by more special, more concrete varieties of human existence which are based on it. . . .[55]

Hence, in order to speak of the essence of man, one must enter into and go beyond a discourse which predicates man as human animal, or a living being with language, or a child of God, and so on.

On the other hand, through the work the question of the human essence as freedom is revealed and suggested when its being is confronted with its radical negation in a scientific-materialistic discourse:

> When they prove to you that actually a drop of your own fat must be dearer to you than a hundred thousand of your fellow men, and that in the end this conclusion will solve all the so-called virtues and duties and other ravings and prejudices, you've got to take it as it is, there's nothing else to do, because two times two is mathematics. Go argue with that. (E: 12; PSS 5:105)

This parody of utilitarian ethics entails a very strict logical argumentation. The Underground Man recognizes that a "hedonistic calculus" such as Bentham's utilitarian theory proposes entails a deterministic view of man's character. This theory is legitimated with mathematics and is hence indubitable. And yet, the Underground Man does in fact argue with "two times two equals four." To merely accept the laws of nature and mathematics and then formulate "the so-called virtues and duties, and other ravings and prejudices" of man in the same terms is to deprive the human being a mature, individual essence. This viewpoint robs man of his identity, and he is re-absorbed into maternal Nature and is commensurate with her being.

Underground appeared at a time when man threatened to be subsumed in a humanitarian and optimist-socialist anthropology. It is on this epochal horizon where man threatens to be dissolved into ciphers, statistical figures, and mathematical formulas which speak in terms of man's best advantage that the essential meaning of being human appears as a problem. A man who "desires according to tables" is in fact not really desiring at all. And without desires he is no longer a man. The Underground Man observes, "He would immediately change from a man to an organ cog" (E: 26; PSS 5:114). The end of man is suggested and imaginatively dramatized. Frank calls this tendency an ideological eschatology. It is, according to Frank:

> [T]he imaginative dramatization of the absolute limits of an idea, and by the intuitive realization of the concrete human behavior appropriate to existing in such "fantastic" (though perfectly verisimilar) situations.[56]

It is to be sure apocalyptic art, or an art which speaks for man in the face of his dissolution or annihilation (a-nihil-ation).

Part I of Underground is a rhetorical defence of human freedom. Part II enacts the problem with freedom that the Underground Man faces. His failure with Liza amounts to a failure to engage in "living life" [zhivaia zhizn']. Jackson makes clear how the action of Part II makes explicit the Underground Man's pathetic unfreedom. Even so, the juxtaposition of his rhetorical defence of freedom only serves to emphasize what he is lacking. Man is not obliged to fulfill his authentic being. He has the capacity to incubate, to be stillborn. But the possibility of real life presents itself to him.

Dostoevsky had discovered that a "maximum" of thought destroys man. Idealism and the attempt to bring about the kingdom of heaven on earth crushes man. The maximum of happiness sought for equals the maximum of tears achieved. Only realism can save man from the onslaught of idealism. But what is "realism" and where is it to gain a foothold? Realism for Dostoevsky is revealed in Dead House as a thirst for life. Thirst is crucial. Thirst for life, whatever the cost, keeps man alive. In Underground this thirst is found in the Underground Man's veto to every type of social utopia and crystal palace, and in his statement that he thirsts for something else. He rejects 2x2=4 as death, but states: "Evidently we have reached the point where we almost consider "living life" [zhivaia zhizn'] as a chore, almost a job, and we all inwardly agree that living according to the book is better" (E: 124; PSS 5:178). But precisely what this zhivaia zhizn' is we do not know. Despite the paradoxicality of its narrative, one idea that clearly emerges from this work is an unprecedented, all-out attack upon idealism in any variety, literary or political. Lev Shestov has identified this work as the most significant work for revealing Dostoevsky's anti-Idealistic thought. Idealistic man is ashamed of his body and would rather produce test-tube babies than real living men.

The Underground Man who wrote his cynical treatise in the early 1860s indicates how things have soured with the humane portrayal of man. One reads Underground to discover the 1840s idealist who has become empoisoned and can only destroy ideals with caustic spittle. He is a master of negation who fell short of "living life." His failure to engage with Liza results in an obsession with rhetoric, confession, and the defence of a freedom that he has not actualized.

Notes

1. Fyodor Dostoevsky, Notes from the Underground, trans. Serge Shishkoff (New York: Thomas Y. Crowell, Inc., 1969). This English translation will be referred to throughout the chapter and is identified as "E" followed by the page number. The Russian text consulted is drawn from Dostoevsky's collected works, Polnoe sobranie sochinenii, volume 5. References to this work will be identified as PSS 5 followed by the page number.

2. Gary Saul Morson, Narrative Freedom: The Shadows of Time (New Haven and London, Yale University Press, 1994), Chapter Four.

3. August Boeckh, On Interpretation and Criticism, trans. John Paul Pritchard (Norman: University of Oklahoma Press, 1968), 61.

4. Mikhail Bakhtin, Problems of Dostoevsky's Poetics, trans. Caryl Emerson (Minneapolis: University of Minnesota Press, 1989), 229.

5. Ibid., 232.

6. Ibid., 230.

7. Ibid., 237.

8. An epithet combines a noun with an adjective such as "zloi" and "chelovek." There are three types of epithets: a) redundant--the example is "cold snow"; b) congruent--the example is "white snow"; and c) incongruent--the example is "hot snow" (Thomas Beebee, February 1996).

9. V. Dal', Tolkovyi slovar' zhivogo velikorusskogo iazyka (Sankt-Peterburg: Bodwina de Kurtene, 1903), t. I, 683.

10. Concerning the difficulty of translating zloi, one translator has this to say: "It [zlov, zlost'] has been usually translated as 'spiteful.' I feel that 'spite' connotes pettiness and revenge. The word 'zloi' (having zloj: 'evil' as its root) is a much broader term" (Shishkoff, p. xxv). The Academy of Sciences dictionary gives the following definitions for "zlo": "1. Vse durnoe (bad, evil, nasty), plokhoe (bad, poor), vrednoe (harmful, injurious) . . . 2. Beda (misfortune, calamity), neschast'e (accident), nepriiatnost' (unpleasantness, nuisance, annoyance, trouble) . . . 3. Zloe chuvstvo (bad feeling), gnev (anger, rage, wrath), dosada (vexation, disappointment, spite) . . ." (Slovar' Russkogo Iazyka, Tom I, [1981], 611-12). It is clear that "zlo" has a broad range of meanings. The definitions given for "zlost'" are: "Zloe, razdrazhennovrazhdebnoe chuvstvo (irritating and hostile feeling); zloba (malice, spite)" (ibid., 614).

11. Bakhtin, Problems, 233.

12. For a discussion of Bentham's utilitarian ethic see W. Windelband's, A History of Philosophy, trans. James Tufts (New York: The Macmillan Co., 1919), 662-65.

13. Berdiaev, Dostoievsky, 68.

14. Joseph Frank, Dostoevsky: The Stir of Liberation, 1860-1865 (Princeton: Princeton University Press, 1986), 347.

15. Joseph Frank, "Nihilism and Notes from the Underground," in Notes from the Underground, trans. Shishkoff (New York: Thomas Crowell, Inc., 1969), 152.

16. Nicholas Chernyshevsky, The Anthropological Principle in Philosophy in Russian Philosophy Volume II, ed. Edie et al. (Chicago: Quadrangle Books, 1965), 29-60.

17. Frank, Stir, 324.

18. Robert Louis Jackson, "Aristotelian Movement and Design in Part Two of Notes from the Underground," Chapter VI in The Art of Dostoevsky: Deliriums and Nocturnes (Princeton: Princeton University Press, 1981), 172-73.

19. Ibid.

20. Aristotle, On Poetry and Style, trans. Grube (Indianapolis: Bobbs-Merrill, 1958).

21. Jackson, "Aristotelian," 172.

22. Ibid., 186.

23. Ibid.

24. Robert Louis Jackson, Dostoevsky's Underground Man in Russian Literature ('S-Gravenhage: Mouton and Co., 1958), 15.

25. Voltaire, Candide in Three Philosophical Voyages (New York: Laurel Language Library, 1964).

26. Robert Louis Jackson, Dostoevsky's Quest for Form (New Haven and London: Yale University Press, 1966), 91.

27. Michel Foucault, Madness and Civilization: A History of Insanity in the Age of Reason, trans. Richard Howard (London and New York: Tavistock/Routledge, 1989), xi.

28. Plato, Protagoras 345d. Other philosophical subtexts include: Immanuel Kant, Analytic of the Beautiful, from the Critique of Judgement, With Excerpts from Anthropology from a Pragmatic Viewpoint, Second Book, trans. Walter Cerf (Indianapolis: Bobbs-Merrill, 1963); Jean-Jacques Rousseau, A Discourse on Inequality, trans. Maurice Cranston (Harmondsworth, Middlesex, England; New York, Penguin Books, 1984); Aristotle, Metaphysics, trans. Christopher Kirwan (Oxford: Clarendon Press, 1971); The Dialogues of Plato, trans. M. A. Jowett (Oxford: Clarendon Press, 1964). The narrative seems to have as subtext both Kant's philosophy ("the sublime and the beautiful"), Rousseau ("l'homme de la nature et de la vérité"), Socrates ("and it is known that not a single man can knowingly act against his own advantage" (Shishkoff, 19), and Aristotle's

Metaphysics Book E ("Where are the primary causes to sustain me, where are the foundations?" (Shishkoff, 17).

29. Carol Flath, "Fear of Faith: The Hidden Religious Message of Notes from the Underground," Slavic and East European Journal 37, no. 4 (Winter 1993): 524.

30. Ibid., 524-25.

31. Olga Meerson, "Old Testament Lamentation in the Underground Man's Monologue: A Refutation of the Existentialist Reading of the Notes from the Underground," Slavic and East European Journal 36, no. 3 (Fall 1992): 317.

32. Bakhtin, Problems, 236.

33. Hans-Georg Gadamer, Truth and Method (New York: Crossroad, 1975), 333.

34. Frank, Stir, 319.

35. Chernyshevsky, Anthropological, 60.

36. Paul Evdokimov, Dostoïevsky et le problème du mal (Paris: Desclée de Brouwer, 1978), 377.

37. Jesse Mann and Gerald Kreyche (eds.), Reflections on Man (New York: Harcourt, Brace and World, 1966), 557.

38. Irena Kirk, Dostoevskij and Camus: The Themes of Consciousness, Isolation, Freedom and Love (München: Wilhelm Fink Verlag, 1974).

39. Jean-Paul Sartre, L'existentialisme est un humanisme (Paris: Gallimard, 1946).

40. Kirk, Dostoevskij, 69.

41. Camus' two "philosophical" works, Le mythe de Sisyphe (1942) and L'Homme revolté (1951) both explicitly treat Dostoevsky's work in light of an "absurd reasoning." Literary works of Camus that also highlight Dostoevskian themes are: The Stranger (New York: Village Books, 1946); Caligula (New York: Vintage Books, 1962); and The Fall (New York: Alfred A. Knopf, 1961). See also Camus' theatre adaptation of Dostoevsky's Devils.

Shestov has discussed Dostoevsky in many of his works. The most significant are: La philosophie de la tragedie: Dostoievski et Nietzsche reprinted as Dostoevsky, Tolstoy and Nietzsche, trans. Bernard Martin (Athens, Ohio: Ohio University Press, 1969); Sur la balance de Job (Paris: Flammarion, 1971); Kierkegaard and Existential Philosophy, trans. Bernard Martin (Athens, Ohio: Ohio University Press, 1969) and the article "Kierkegaard and Dostoevsky," in Russian Philosophy Volume III, Edie et al. (Chicago: Quadrangle Books, 1965), 227-47.

In addition to Berdiaev's monumental study of Dostoevsky's work: Dostoievsky: An Interpretation, trans. Donald Attwater (New York: Sheed and Ward and Co., 1934), see also The Russian Idea, trans. R. M. French (London: Lindisfarne Press, 1992).

Gide delivered his ideas about Dostoevsky's literary work in a volume entitled Dostoevsky (New York: New Directions, 1961). He, like Camus, also reflected some themes from Dostoevsky which lend themselves to his artwork; for example, Les caves du Vatican [Lafcadio's Adventures (New York: Vintage Books, 1960)]; and Les faux monnayeurs [The Counterfeiters (New York: Alfred A. Knopf, Inc., 1951). Also see Madeleine: Et nunc manet in te (New York: Alfred A. Knopf, 1952) and Numquid et tu? Journal, 1942-1949 (Paris: Gallimard, 1950).

42. Albert Camus, Le mythe de Sisyphe (Paris: Gallimard, 1942), 150.

43. Lev Shestov, "Kierkegaard and Dostoevsky," in Russian Philosophy Volume III, ed. Edie et al. (Chicago: Quadrangle Books, 1965), 246.

44. Kant's definition of critique means to ask after the conditions of the possibility of a thing being rationalizable.

45. Shestov, "Kierkegaard," 245.

46. In addition to Kaufmann's incorporation of Dostoevsky's Notes from the Underground into his existentialist compendium, Existentialism from Dostoevsky to Sartre (New York: Meridian Book, 1975), a number of other additional chroniclers of existentialism have included Dostoevsky and his work into their consideration: Ernst Breisach, Introduction to Modern Existentialism (New York: Grove Press, Inc., 1962), 58-68; William Hubben, Dostoevsky, Kierkegaard, Nietzsche and Kafka: Four Prophets of Our Destiny (New York: Collier Books, 1952); and Paul Roubiczek, Existentialism: For and Against (Cambridge: Cambridge University Press, 1964). Whether these authors are for or against existentialism, they all see Dostoevsky's thought as a major source for existentialist thought.

47. Berdiaev, Dostoievsky, 51.

48. Ibid., 67.

49. Vyacheslav Ivanov, Freedom and The Tragic Life: A Study in Dostoevsky (New York: The Noonday Press, 1960), 15-16.

50. Valeri Kirpotin, Dostoevskii v shestidesiatye gody (Moskva: Khudozhestvennaia Literatura, 1966), 5.

51. Ibid., 471.

52. Ibid., 472.

53. Concerning the conception of literary type [tip] and its significance in Dostoevsky's aesthetics see Jackson's Dostoevsky's Quest for Form (1966), Chapter 7, "The Problem of Type."

54. Jackson, Quest, 94.

55. Landmann, Fundamental, 2.

56. Frank, Stir, 248.

CHAPTER 4

CRIME AND PUNISHMENT (1866)

In this chapter we will explore the artistic techniques Dostoevsky employed in Crime and Punishment [Prestuplenie i nakazanie], which portray an image of a free man. Dostoevsky constructed the narrative in such a manner that his hero's freedom is portrayed as a "second skin," something that he cannot shake off. From beginning until end, the hero is fixated upon the question of his freedom to act, and the meaning of its consequences. There are many theories which account for Raskolnikov's crime by referring to motives. While some of them are plausible, none of them truly succeeds in accounting for an act which is essentially free. This is true not only for Raskolnikov's actions, but for other characters' actions in the novel as well. What unites all of the characters is their suffering, and yet, suffering in each case is very unique and reveals individuality. What unites individuals with regard to suffering is a freedom that is irrevocable.

For sake of brevity and clarity we will turn directly to those aspects of the narrative which bear directly upon this theme. Section one considers the meaning of Raskolnikov's crime and explores the problem of its motive. Several theories which attempt to account for the crime are presented. Since an implicit image of man as either free or unfree is related to the account which justifies the motive cause of a criminal act, an analysis of theories which attempt to explain Raskolnikov's motives will assist in the discovery of

Dostoevsky's conception of man. The theories which fail to account for Raskolnikov's motives still teach us something about man's essential freedom. Section two makes suggestions based upon the "how" of the artwork emphasizing some narrative techniques in Crime which have a bearing on the image of man in the novel. Finally, in section three, the presentation and meaning of suffering and victimhood in the novel is discussed. Punishment is often sought after for its own sake as a means of taking suffering onto oneself. Suffering is embodied in many ways in Crime. Marmeladov and his family are considered as the primary example. I suggest in conclusion that an exploration of the meaning of suffering in Crime is fundamental to its presentation of a human being who is free in an ineradicable way.

Raskolnikov's Crime: Its Meaning and the Image of Man

As a result of the narrative technique which defers the meaning of Raskolnikov's crime throughout the novel, certain considerations become prominent. First of all, what is the meaning of this deferment? Does it serve any other function than to draw the reader into a state of suspense? Secondly, does this technique draw the hero into perpetual ambiguity as it does the Underground Man? Finally, how does this narrative technique influence the presentation of the essential meaning of crime and human freedom?

The narrative technique which Dostoevsky employs in Crime, the narrated monologue, is tailor-fitted to Raskolnikov's indecision. As he walks out onto the hot July streets in Petersburg, giving his landlady the slip, the young hero laughs at himself for fearing his "creditoress," when in fact he is contemplating a far more serious matter: "I plan to attempt a thing like this, yet I allow that kind of rubbish to scare me!" [Na kakoe delo khochu pokusit'sia i v to zhe vremia kakikh pustiakov boius'!] (E: 33; PSS 6:6).[1] This "thing" which Dostoevsky emphasizes, this "matter" [na kakoe delo] that the hero is planning to do, is not stated. These words and expressions substitute for the murder of the old pawnbroker. However, he notes that people fear making a new step [novyi shag], of uttering their own new word [novoe sobstvennoe slovo]. Raskolnikov's thought stops abruptly (signified with three dots . . .) and then he states in a self-referential way: ". . . perhaps I am babbling too much." [. . . A vprochem, ia slishkom mnogo boltaiu (PSS 6:6).] Others fear their own new word, but what about our hero? Raskolnikov wants to take the new step, to say the new word, but he is indecisive. "Dreaming in my corner is all I ever do recently," he muses. Finally he asks, "Am I really capable of this? Is this a serious matter? Of course it isn't" [Razve ia sposoben na eto? Razve eto ser'ezno? Sovsem ne ser'ezno] (E: 34 [italics mine] PSS 6:6). The referent of the word "this" [eto] like the ambiguous na kakoe delo, signifies an as yet unstated substantive act. The ex-student is aware of the axiom that man lets "everything" slip past his nose because of cowardice. But this is not his fate. From the moment the narrator underlines his hero's indecision and the question of his resolve, his ability to act is raised. The meaning, then, of this as yet undetermined act, this new step, and this new word, begs for an answer. In short, its meaning is deferred.

The meaning of the crime is suspended throughout the novel. In the beginning of the narrative, the murder of the old pawnbroker is substituted with several expressions: vse, mechta,[2] kakoe delo. Raskolnikov cannot directly articulate what he is brooding over. It is not crystallized in his mind. There is a suspense which keeps the reader guessing at its meaning. But this deferment of meaning has a greater significance in that it underscores the problematic, philosophic meaning of crime and how it is intimately related to the personal will which enacts it. The deferment of the meaning of Raskolnikov's crime is a narrative technique which allows the criminal act to become nearly identical with the hero's "consciousness." From the outset of the novel until the epilogue, the hero is so engaged with his obsession that the reader meets a hero who is synonymous with his crime. Moreover, by use of this technique, the crime's motives become clearly delineated even if they remain unsolved. By suspending the meaning of the crime, and yet allowing manifold explanations for it to arise, the text enmeshes the reader into this task of giving an account for the murder. Finally, the deferment creates suspense--a standard technique of the detective novel.

As observed in the analysis of "deferment of meaning" in _Underground_, the narrative reveals freedom in the manner in which the objective, semantic meaning of the Underground Man's discourse is postponed. This rhetorical device works chiefly in two ways: 1) as Bakhtin points out, the anticipated response of the other holds the meaning of the Underground Man's monologue at bay; 2) the meaning of _svoboda_ and _volia_ achieves signification in consideration of the meaning of subsidiary terms such as _zloi_, _vygoda_, _kapriz_, _khoten'e_, and their derivatives. In _Crime_, on the other hand, the meaning of freedom is depicted primarily through the narrative description of the action of an embodied hero. The emphasis upon acting out one's will distinguishes Raskolnikov's indecision from the Underground Man's perpetual ambivalence. This means that the criminal act of murdering the pawnbroker actually begins a process of moving toward "real life."

Roger B. Anderson finds in Raskolnikov an archetypal hero. _Crime_ can be read as a myth of a hero on a journey. The murderous act allows him to move into a "liminal condition" from which he is able to redefine himself:

> Formulaic departures, like the act of murder, function to dissociate the individual from the known. They shift responsibility for understanding from older, static rules to the dynamic process of a basic reorganization of the unformed self.[3]

The question of Raskolnikov's discovery of self, indeed, hinges upon a murderous act. It is essential to his presentation in the novel so much so that it is difficult to imagine Raskolnikov apart from his crime. Murder can be seen as a "happy mistake," which ultimately leads to the hero's rebirth. Although it is questionable whether, in fact, Raskolnikov enacts this mythic journey, toward "reorganization of the unformed self," it is clear that _zhivaia zhizn'_ and "real life" are definite options for him, while the Underground Man remains entirely self- enclosed, never having established contact with "living life."

The deferment of meaning of Raskolnikov's crime, which coincides with the presentation of the hero, has a final and more philosophical significance when we consider that the deferment of the meaning of the crime is central to a question which the novel puts before the reader. The novel puts the question to the reader: what is crime and what is punishment? It does so in the fundamental meaning of human freedom. It is within this narrative matrix that the philosophical question is unfolded. Deferring the meaning of the crime amounts to the same thing as deferring the motive for the crime, for even after the crime is enacted, no clear motive emerges. The act does not in itself give meaning for the act.

Motives

The epilogue of _Crime_ recounts the legal proceedings of Raskolnikov's court case. The narrator relates that Raskolnikov sought to incriminate himself by saying that the reason he killed the pawnbroker and her sister was for money. Psychologists concluded that he was "under the influence of some dangerous monomania involving murder and robbery for murder and robbery's sake, without ulterior motive or thought of gain" (E: 614; _PSS_ 6:411). The reason for this conclusion is that Raskolnikov apparently had never looked inside the stolen purse, hence he had never known what it contained. Exploring the motives for Raskolnikov's crime places us in the middle of a thorny debate. Literary critics have placed a great deal of emphasis upon this matter in their studies of _Crime_.

Certain Utilitarian thinkers would prefer to see the crime as the result of environmental influence and poverty. Another account finds in Raskolnikov a representative of the Romanticist idea which separates the world into ordinary and extraordinary people. Neither theory fully accounts for the crime. The failure of these and allied theories to provide a convincing motive for Raskolnikov's act leads one to consider the hero's freedom as providing an ambiguous motive. Neither the result of external influence as the environmental theorists would claim, nor the result of a titanic, Napoleonic will, Raskolnikov's crime is the act of a human being perplexed by his choice and unable to evade his free will. Despite their flaws, a consideration of the rejected theories will assist in clarifying the ultimate meaning of Raskolnikov's freedom.

The Environmental Theory

The central question raised by radical ideologists in the 1860s addressed the environment and its effect upon man. The formulation of the relation between man and the environment was at the core of this argument. Does the environment weaken man's responsibility for his actions? Does a man made poor by society possess the right to commit a crime to ameliorate his position? Do the people who are oppressed in filth and squalor possess the right to rise up, take arms and end their oppression? To these and other questions, an 1860s radical such as V. A. Zaitsev answered unequivocally, "yes." For Dostoevsky, the matter required more thought.

In an article from the 1873 issue of his Diary of a Writer, which discusses the "acquittal mania" in the courts and the tendency to absolve citizens of their responsibility for their crimes, Dostoevsky writes:

> Making man responsible, Christianity eo ipso also recognizes his freedom. However, making man dependent on any error in the social organization, the environmental doctrine reduces man to absolute impersonality, to a total emancipation from all personal duty, from all independence; reduces him to a state of the most miserable slavery that can be conceived.[4]

Paradoxically, the "environmental doctrine" which absolves man from responsibility for his actions also deprives him of his freedom.

In addition to the influence of environment upon crime, another ideological theme "in the air" concerned the raznochinets or radical intellectual of the 1860s. The choice of Raskolnikov as a hero falls in line with what Frank calls, "the dominant literary trend of the time." Frank cites several examples of literary works which explicitly address the image of man, and the future man: "All of these revolved around one fundamental fulcrum--the image of the new man."[5] There is Turgenev with his artistic creation, Bazarov, the radical hero of Fathers and Sons (1862).[6] There is Pisemsky's The Unruly Sea, and Strakhov's note in one of the final issues of Epokha that Russian literature was preoccupied with "new people," not to mention Chernyshevsky's What is to be Done? (1863).

Chernyshevsky's rational egoism, which formed the hub of the Underground Man's polemic, merged into the radical ideology of the 1860s. This fascinated Dostoevsky. The intelligentsia of the 1860s attempted to base morality upon a Utilitarian foundation.[7] This is for the most part in line with Chernyshevsky's doctrine; however, the left-wing periodical, The Russian Word, moved Utilitarian morality in a much more radical direction. In this way, Russian nihilism, which was made famous by Bazarov, was brought into contact with socialism. "Socialism is thus equated with Nihilism, and both are seen as advocating something like total destruction, the creation of a tabula rasa."[8] A literary critic cum radico-ideologist whose interpretation of Crime moved along these lines was Dmitri Pisarev (1840-1868).

Pisarev has been associated with the "Belinsky School" of literary criticism, and he saw Dostoevsky as an ideological opponent. His treatment of Crime reflects this biased stance:

> Pisarev, therefore, attempted to turn Dostoevskij's [sic] Prestuplenie i nakazanie inside out, to reinterpret the content of the work so that it served as substantiation of the ideas of Pisarev rather than those of the author.[9]

Pisarev maintained that poverty is the main compelling motive for Raskolnikov's crime. This is not to say that he condoned the murder. Pisarev did not find Raskolnikov's crime to be justifiable because he is not a "thinking realist": "Raskol'nikov's theory has nothing in common with those ideas which constitute the philosophy of the enlightened people of today."[10] Pisarev's realism springs from the conviction that literary art ought to mirror insofar as possible the external conditions of life which can account for the action of the hero. An account for Raskolnikov's deed cannot be rendered so simply. It is no surprise that Pisarev cannot find common ground between

Raskolnikov's crime and "the philosophy of the enlightened people today."

Frank emphasizes that it was Pisarev's criticism of Bazarov in Fathers and Sons which established the Nihilist hero as the "hero of our time." Pisarev interpreted Bazarov as an exalted individual who stands tall above the masses. He claims that the titanic stance of the young hero, as well as his ideas, inspired Dostoevsky to create Raskolnikov. In reference to Bazarov, Pisarev commented that he possessed a "Satanic pride." In noting that this remark inspired Dostoevsky, Frank writes: "Dostoevsky --and most emphatically not by chance--will employ exactly the same phrase in his notes to describe the aspect of Raskolnikov's personality that comes to the fore after the murder."[11] Raskolnikov sees himself as a member of a new race of exalted individuals capable of "saving" mankind. This thinking falls in line with some Romanticist ideas as we shall see below. It is in this messianic monomania that his Satanic pride is revealed.

Utilitarianism

Perhaps it is possible to find a defense for Raskolnikov's crime in a utilitarian ethic. It is possible to follow Raskolnikov's idea up to a certain point if it is viewed from a strict utilitarian or socialist point of view. And in this sense Raskolnikov is merely going farther in this thought-experiment than anyone else dares. Logically, socialist, and in particular utilitarian, strands of thought advance the modus operandi that the ends justify the means, and hence, to the extent that Raskolnikov's article on crime advances this idea, it is an example of the "new thought of the younger generation," albeit radical. And Pulkheria Raskolnikova has a right to be proud of her son.

The polemic with Chernyshevsky, which figures centrally in Part One of Underground, surfaces in Crime in the character of Lebeziatnikov, and underlies at least one of the poles of influence which forms Raskolnikov's "idea." The relationship between Luzhin and Lebeziatnikov is rather complex. Piotr Luzhin is proud that he was once the tutor of Lebeziatnikov, a man he conceives to be "one of the foremost young progressives, who even played a significant role in certain curious and legendary circles" (E: 427; PSS 6:278). He realizes upon meeting him that Andrei Lebeziatnikov is insignificant and merely latches onto any new ideas. Still, Luzhin finds it in his own best interest to learn whether these new ideas will help or hinder his own agenda. Thus, Luzhin parrots ideas that he has newly learned from his former pupil. For example, at the first encounter with Raskolnikov, Luzhin describes how a man attempting to love his neighbor cuts his caftan in two, actually depriving two people of a coat: "If you love only yourself, you will conduct your enterprises in a proper manner and your caftan will remain whole" (E: 193; PSS 6:116). This statement echoes the doctrine of rational egoism which advocated the pursuit of individual egoistic needs as a means of benefiting society. Gorianchikov derogatorily refers to this way of thinking when he considers Nastasia Ivanovna's gift of Bibles to the prisoners in Dead House: "Some people say (I have heard this and read it) that the most elevated love of one's own neighbour is at one and the same time the greatest egoism. What egoism there could be in this I cannot for the life of me imagine" [Um v chet tut-to byl egoizm-- nikak ne poimu] (E: 112; PSS 4:68). It is a despicable idea that the gift of a Bible is egoism and it is unimaginable to Gorianchikov. There is irony in the parenthetical remark: "(I have heard this and read it)." The knowledge that comes from reading [po knizhke; knizhno] is of an inferior and doubtful variety. But this knowledge is the kind that Luzhin bandies about. Raskolnikov sees through Luzhin and accuses him of speaking in cliches, and of parroting the newest ideas that he has learned since coming to St. Petersburg.

There are three characters with three different relations to "new ideas": "Andrei Semyonovich [Lebeziatnikov] really was rather stupid. He adhered to the cause of progress and 'our younger generations' as a kind of enthusiastic pastime" (E: 429; PSS 6:279). Lebeziatnikov is a shabby exponent of the "environmental theory." Concerning the question of charity and almsgiving, he argues against splitting one's coat to help warm another's body. Luzhin, on the other hand, was only interested in his personal gain: "If he were to be quite honest, none of these theories, ideas and systems (with which Andrei Semyonovich positively assailed him) was of the slightest interest to him. He had his own, personal motive" (E: 428; PSS 6:279). Then there is Raskolnikov's relation to these ideas. This is more difficult to surmise. However, he is a type of fanatic who is willing to kill or be killed for an idea: "But a thousand times before he had been ready to give up his existence for an idea, for a hope, even for an imagining" (E: 622-23; PSS 6:417). The degree to which he identified all of his vital energy to his "idea" is unlimited, he held nothing back. This is an aspect of the dynamism of his relationship to the idea--absolute commitment. Luzhin is only out for himself, while Lebeziatnikov is a half-educated petty tyrant.

Although both Luzhin and Lebeziatnikov are representatives of ideas "in the air," the ideology which they possess could in no wise account for Raskolnikov's idea. Raskolnikov is not a man of the

1860s. He is a special type of character. His ideology is more akin to the powerful wind that blows over human history in men like Caesar, Mohammed, and Napoleon. On the superficial level of current affairs, Raskolnikov's crime fits in with the ideas of the 1860s, and in fact it was big news in the summer of 1865. The idea of murdering Alena Ivanovna came to Raskolnikov while eavesdropping on the officer and student at the drink shop ["_traktir_"]. Hence, it is the kind one might overhear in a little tavern in St. Petersburg in 1865. Nonetheless, the significance of Raskolnikov's reception of this idea transcends the "topical." It is apocalyptic and superhistorical.

For men like Luzhin and Lebeziatnikov, whose relationship to ideas is unfaithful or weak, ideology makes sense and is simply a tool which can be used to win influence (for Luzhin), or female affection (Lebeziatnikov desires Sonia; Svidrigailov desires Dunia). As for Raskolnikov, even though his idea contains ideological remnants, it cannot be understood aside from the obsessional and energetic intensity with which he maintains it. Raskolnikov's "idea" is significant both in terms of its content, as well as its obsessive character.

A Lebeziatnikov-styled nihilist might have lionized Raskolnikov as the murderer of the pawnbroker because he had removed a harmful louse from society. The "new radical utilitarian" might justify the murder of an old, useless woman who was a leech in that way. However, there is more to Raskolnikov's idea than the radical utilitarian can account for. This leads to another possible motive for the crime; namely, Raskolnikov's Napoleonic idea which might be defended by certain Romanticist notions of extraordinary individuals.

Romanticism and Raskolnikov's "Napoleonic Idea"

The Napoleonic Theory, which asserts that certain individuals are above the moral law and can therefore eliminate less worthy people, is stated clearly in the text in Raskolnikov's scholarly article. Porfiry Petrovich refers to Raskolnikov's article from the Periodical Leader [Periodicheskyi rechi] whose thesis established that a certain type of illness accompanied the enactment of a crime. Porfiry underscores the Napoleonic Theory when he paraphrases the conclusion of Raskolnikov's article: "There may exist in the world certain persons who are able . . . or rather, who are not only able, but have a perfect right to commit all sorts of atrocities and crimes, and that it's as if the law did not apply to them" (E: 311; PSS 6:199). Raskolnikov espouses this elitist idea, but his problem remains--is he one of the elect?

Raskolnikov's idea emerges polyphonically from the narrative. First of all, in his interior monologue, then in the quandary he finds himself in attempting to justify his crime. Now, in response to Porfiry's paraphrase of the article which he had not realized had been published, he says:

> It's only my central idea that I place my faith in. That idea consists in the notion that, by law of their nature, human beings in general may be divided into two categories: a lower one (that of the ordinary), that is to say the raw material which serves exclusively to bring into being more like itself, and another group of people who possess a gift or a talent for saying something new, in their own milieu (E: 313; PSS 6:200).

This talent for saying something new echoes the opening pages of the novel and the hero's personal and idiosyncratic monologue. However, when stated in public, Raskolnikov's credo resembles certain ideas espoused by Friedrich Schiller.[12]

For Schiller, certain individuals possess a moral genius and an innate sense of ethical value. These individuals are above the law. Referring to Schiller's conception of moral genius, Windelband writes: "The moral genius also is 'exemplary,' he does not subject himself to traditional rules and maxims, he lives himself out and thereby gives himself the laws of his morality."[13] The resemblance between Rakolnikov's idea and this Romanticist theory of exemplarity is striking. Does Dostoevsky want to portray Raskolnikov's murder as some sort of exemplary, genius act? This idea is at the core of Raskolnikov's article, "On Crime," which appeared in the Periodical Leader that alarms Porfiry Petrovich, and startles Razumikhin. It is mind-boggling that Raskolnikov could justify murder by conscience [po sovesti]. Where his article steers off course entirely is the above-stated emphasis upon "conscience." This idea arrives out of the blue; it cannot be deduced from utilitarian or socialist ideology. The Romantic idea of a Schoene Seele emerges here, but in a monstrously distorted form. That some individuals possess an ethical genius is one thing, but to say that some chosen individuals possess a genius for murder or whatever else they like, is astonishing. Such a thought can only be called "demonic."

Raskolnikov's relation to Schillerism is ambivalent. He vehemently accuses Luzhin of being a Schillerean Schoene Seele: "That's the way it always is with these Schillerean Schoene Seele [. . . i etikh shchillerovskikh prekrasnikh dush]--right up until the last possible moment they'll deck a man out in peacock feathers, hoping for the good and refusing to believe in the bad . . ." (E: 76; PSS 6:37). When Svidrigailov called Rodion "A Schiller, a Russian Schiller, a Schiller, no less!" (E: 556; PSS 6:371), it is not exactly a compliment. This is why Svidrigailov chastises

Raskolnikov, saying, "you wince at my eavesdropping but justify killing old women" (ibid.). Raskolnikov is a genius of the idea and in this respect he is, like Svidrigailov calls him, a "Schiller." "You Schiller," Svidrigailov accuses him. Just like he had earlier called the lecher on the street, "you Svidrigailov." Raskolnikov does not deserve this title--his crime is neither beautiful nor noble.

Whereas Raskolnikov's relation to the Napoleonic Idea is tentative, Svidrigailov is the Napoleonic champion, the strong man who conquers the world through his will. Recall that Svidrigailov is Raskolnikov's lower double. Svidrigailov tells him that they are like two berries from the same field. Both have "stepped across" and exist in a realm beyond the ordinary characters. Also both characters are locked up within themselves. Svidrigailov presents a picture of who Raskolnikov might become. He is a polarity or potential for the hero.

In the notebooks of _Crime_, the character who would become Svidrigailov is named Aristov, a reference to a prisoner Dostoevsky saw in the Siberian prison camp. This is A-v whom Gorianchikov refers to many times throughout his narrative as the Major's spy and a man despised universally by the prisoners. Likewise, Svidrigailov is despised but unlike A-v, who was a political prisoner, Svidrigailov is a murderer and a lecher. Svidrigailov is an example of a man under the sway of self will [_volia_]. There is no limit to the exercise of his will, no external will that might limit him. He is enclosed in the tautology of self will. Svidrigailov is the embodiment of nihilism, when we consider that he has no need for anyone else. Need of others in its deepest sense reveals a need for God. Devoid of neediness, Svidrigailov has no God, and is incapable of prayer. Suicide is the logical conclusion for this character and the fruition of his labor.

It is crucial to observe in the early drafts of the novel that Dostoevsky chose suicide as Raskolnikov's end. The fact that Svidrigailov, and not Raskolnikov, takes this course in the finished novel points toward the hero's potential to choose a "higher" path. Taking Svidrigailov as the Napoleonic champion within the novel, we see why Raskolnikov's idea fails to justify his action or to provide a motive for his crime. Raskolnikov is like Svidrigailov in many ways but ultimately, his movement is toward life, and not death.

Narrative Technique in "Crime"

Attention to the form of the narrative highlights the extent to which the content of a philosophical conception of man in Crime is inseparable from the "how" of its presentation. A close reading of the text taking into consideration the narration, the narrative sources, the description of the hero, the plot, and the key terms will make clear how the narrative form presents a philosophical image of man based upon freedom.

Sources

In addition to Underground, the finished Crime its origin principally in two sources.[14] The first is Dostoevsky's experience in prison which is recorded in Dead House, whose theme is the value of criminal punishment in light of the rich diversity of human character which includes ruthless, bloodthirsty criminality as well as saintliness. The second source is a novel Dostoevsky was planning entitled "The Drunkards." The plot of this novel appears in a June 8, 1865, letter to A. A. Kraevsky, the editor of Fatherland Notes:

> My novel is called "The Drunkards" and it will be connected with the current problem of drunkenness. Not only is the problem examined, but all of its ramifications are represented, most of all depictions of families, the bringing up of children under these circumstances, and so on [italics mine].[15]

Although "The Drunkards" never appeared, it serves putatively as the Marmeladov subplot in Crime. This novel which failed to emerge evidently treated alcoholism as a social problem in St. Petersburg. It is difficult to surmise what would have become of it, since Dostoevsky continuously reworked his novels on major points of the plot, as a cursory survey of his notebooks makes clear. Even so, Marmeladov plays a major role in Crime, and we will return to him in our discussion of suffering at the end of this chapter.

Third Person Narration

The contrast between Underground and Crime helps to make clear the degree of narrative innovation in the latter. The first thing we notice as we move from Underground to Crime is the change from a first to a third person narration. From the claustrophobic, autobiographical, self-mutterings of the Underground Man, we come to meet a sober and direct third-person narrative voice. Early drafts of the novel as found in the Notebooks indicate a first-person narration.[16] The shift to third person was the technical breakthrough which made possible the narrator's shared observation bolstering Raskolnikov's internal monologue to present a subjective, interior monologue like that of the Underground Man, while at the same time providing a narrative description of the hero which is "objective" giving a weight, a distance, and an added significance to his "consciousness" such as the Underground hero never enjoyed. The narrative shift allows the reader to enjoy a specific relationship to the "consciousness" of the hero. It also allows the hero to be depicted in a more objective manner than the Underground Man; the hero is outside the indeterminacy of the Underground man's word with a loophole. This changes the way Raskolnikov enters into relation with other characters, uncovering a philosophical insight concerning the relation of self to other.

That this point of view was a matter of special importance to Dostoevsky we learn from his notebooks: "Dostoevsky learned, to judge by the finished Crime and Punishment, that he wanted to dramatize more than the self could consciously be aware of."[17] The notebooks for Crime indicate that he experimented with several narrative points of view before fixing on the mixed variety: "the first person as diary and as memory, and the third-person, which in a kind of limited omniscience constitutes the narrative manner of the finished version."[18]

Rosenshield comments upon this narrative innovation:

> The narrator of Crime and Punishment, however, is not invisible; nor does he stay with Raskolnikov from beginning to end. Dostoevsky must have changed his mind about his original plan some time before he submitted the first part to the publisher, because in the final version of the novel, the narrator is significantly personalized, if not dramatized, and often leaves his hero both to give background material and to transcribe scenes at which Raskolnikov was not present.[19]

A study of the notebooks indicates just how far the narrative evolved until its publication. Concerning the narrator, Rosenshield observes, "No other aspect of Crime and Punishment caused Dostoevsky so many problems."[20] The third person narrator allows Dostoevsky the freedom to "miniaturize" the insights won from the Underground Man's narrative technique while also conveying a sober, realistic account of St. Petersburg in the light of day.

As we have seen, other people do not really exist for the Underground Man except as creations of his rhetoric. For example, the Underground Man's narrative makes "the Gentlemen" appear in a merely projective, rhetorical way. Even the account of flesh and blood character like Liza might be falsified owing to the manner in which the Underground Man narrates his confession. This accords with Bakhtin's analysis of the Underground Man's discourse strategy indicating how he retained the final meaning of his discourse in a perpetuum mobile.[21] As we have seen, this narrative strategy translates freedom in such a way that the form of the narrative embodies its thought or meaning as Gary Morson would say, "isomorphically."[22]

The narrative form of Crime translates freedom and its "saying" about man in another manner. The field of the hero's play is enlarged through doubling; or in Bakhtin's terms, the multi-voicing of the polyphonic novel accounts for how others come into contact with the hero's internal monologue. The young hero is, like the Underground Man, alienated, self-enclosed, and too cerebral. Upon receiving his mother's fateful letter and reading about a Mr. Svidrigailov, who was tormenting his sister, Raskolnikov obsessively repeats certain ideas found in the letter in his internal monologue as he walks along the street. Spying a plump, thirty year-old man eying a young drunken girl with evil intent, Raskolnikov accosts him: "Hey, you! Svidrigailov! What do you want here?" (E: 81; PSS 6:40). Raskolnikov incorporates Svidrigailov into his internal monologue and attempts to draw him into dialogue by accosting this lecherous man. This narrative technique foreshadows Svidrigailov's entrance in the novel, and initiates a link between the hero and his double.

The narrative describes the hero as an attractive 24 year-old, hyperconscious--even obsessive--but not insane. The hero of the novel is introduced on the first page as "molodoi chelovek," whose name we will learn from his own utterance at the pawnbroker's three pages later: "My name's Raskolnikov, I'm a student, I came to see you about a month ago" (E: 37; PSS 6:8). The name Raskolnikov is introduced for the first time several pages into the novel when the hero names himself. This postponement in giving the hero a name further emphasizes the third person narration. In describing his hero, the narrator uses the word "he" until Raskolnikov identifies himself. This reinforces the reliability of the narration. Whereas the Underground Man's unreliable narration painted an unattractive figure, whose name was never given, Crime depicts a more realistic hero.

Onomastics

Attention to onomastics is significant in the novel. It is clear from the text that the name of the hero, "Raskolnikov," suggests both the group of religious dissenters from the Orthodox Church in the mid-seventeenth century, the raskol'niki, as well as an inner moral split.[23] But our hero is not a Raskolnik in this sense. Ironically, Porfiry Petrovich tells Rodion Raskolnikov that the "Raskolnikov" is Mikolai: "And did you know that he's a Raskolnik [on iz raskol'nikov]--or rather, not so, much a Raskolnik as simply a sectarian . . . " (E: 526; PSS 6:347). Mikolka is not a "Raskolnikov" but simply a sectarian. On the other hand, Raskolnikov's name suggests a split not in terms of a religious dissension, but more generally, a split from people and humanity.

This is not the psychological splitting of the hero in The Double into Goliadkin Senior and Goliadkin Junior, but rather is a moral split.[24] The Russian word "raskol'nik" has as its cognate the word "raskol" whose primary meaning implies a splitting [kolot': "to break, chop, split"], and whose anterior meaning is related to religious dissenters and schismatics.[25]

Raskolnikov's Isolation

In a monologue reminiscent of the Underground Man, Raskolnikov's first words appear to capture his thought ("consciousness") in mid-flight: "Hm . . . yes . . . Everything ["vse"] lies in a man's hands, and if he lets it all slip past his nose its purely out of cowardice . . . that's an axiom" (E: 33-34; PSS 6:6). The statement of this "axiom" finds its place in Underground:

> As far as I in particular am concerned, I only carried out in my life to the extreme what you didn't dare carry out even halfway, and, to top it all, you took your cowardice for common sense, deceiving yourselves, and you were comforted by it. (E: 124; PSS 5:178)

The germ of Raskolnikov's "idea" is suggested, but what is the referent of this word, "everything" [vse]? This ambiguity is not a defect in the narrative, but is a technique which engages the reader's interest in Raskolnikov's thinking process. The voice of the Underground Man makes a brief appearance in Raskolnikov's first brief monologue: "But I'm rambling. [A vprochem, ia slishkom mnogo boltaiu.] That's why I never do anything--because I ramble on to myself like that. Or perhaps it's the other way around: I ramble because I never do anything" (E: 34; PSS 6:6).

In a similar manner, at the conclusion of chapter six in Part One of his notes, the Underground Man discusses his inaction:

> Ah, gentlemen, perhaps the only reason I consider myself an intelligent man is that all my life I have neither

> started nor finished anything. All right, all right, so I am a babbler [boltun], a harmless, annoying babbler just like all of us. (E: 18; PSS 5:109)

The reader of Dostoevsky's Underground is well aware of the degree of inactivity which the Underground Man is capable, however, with Raskolnikov, the problematic issue of action is underscored. He must "come together" not only with his word but with his step, i.e., his action.

Just as Dostoevsky takes great care in the manner in which the hero appears in Crime, he also takes great care in the manner in which others appear in the hero's consciousness. Attention to how the narrator introduces others into the hero's field is meaningful and reflects specifically how he sees others. One can find here a metalinguistic parallel between the meaning of criminal action in human life and in particular, murder, with the manner in which self and others are narrated. The extent to which the self, if alienated and enclosed to an extreme degree, can admit the right of another to truly exist is fundamental to an understanding of crime. The question of how much Raskolnikov is willing to admit the existence of individual others, is particularly meaningful both in terms of narration and in terms of the meaning of murderous crime.

Raskolnikov is alienated from others from the start, and his brooding upon crime enhances his alienation. In order to hear and understand others requires that he make a breakthrough to real life. Viacheslav Ivanov describes this breakthrough to the other person as a transcension of the subject: "It is a transcension of the subject. In this state of mind we recognize the other Ego not as our object, but as another subject."[26] Such a "penetration" [proniknovenie], to use Dostoevsky's word, which recognizes the other as "Thou art," Ivanov tells us simultaneously establishes that God indeed lives.

The crime of murder is of course antithetical to this movement. A close look at the meaning of crime [prestuplenie] underlines this point.

The Meaning of Prestuplenie

As we have seen, Raskolnikov's name suggests an inner split as well as heresy. This underscores the central problem of the hero, which is "getting back" into the human race. Being cut off from the world, having transgressed an ultimate boundary, Raskolnikov needs a bridge back to the moral world. The word for crime in Russian, "prestuplenie," is derived from the verb "perestupit'" meaning "to step over" or "to overstep."[27] The meaning of perestupit' is central not only to this work's title but to the dramatic action of the hero, Svidrigailov and also Sonia. To wit, Svidrigailov tells Raskolnikov that he has transgressed and hence, shares a similar fate of being cut-off. Raskolnikov tells Sonia: "You've also stepped across . . . found it in yourself to step across [perestupit']" (E: 389; PSS 6:252). In this novel, these three characters in particular occupy a space beyond the realm of ordinary ethical life. Raskolnikov attempts to live without others, and his crime puts him on another threshold from Razumikhin, Dunia, and his mother. Sonia and Svidrigailov are doubles who offer the hero two different versions of whom he might become. The movement in his consciousness finds embodiment in these doubles. They provide the hero with an external locus for his choice. The significance of "stepping across" is that it refers to the state of being in relation to the world and others which transcends mere thought, rambling, or babbling. Further, a primordial act of "stepping across" makes crime possible. From the very beginning of the novel, Raskolnikov is caught up in a philosophical predicament. He is ambivalent and indecisive. He wants to say some new word, to make a deed in order to assert himself. The form of his internal dialogue indicates in several ways that he has already set himself somehow outside humanity.

Novelistic Space

Another narrative feature which reveals the meaning of human freedom in Crime is place and novelistic space. The Underground Man called St. Petersburg the most artificial city on earth. Remember that the city was built upon swampland on Peter the Great's decree. Pushkin's eternal poem, "The Bronze Horseman," immortalizes the origin of this city of canals. Raskolnikov, as city dweller is deracinated, cut off from his provincial roots. For this reason, nature symbolism is highlighted by way of contrast to the bleak, urban setting.

In narrative terms, time and space are the fabric within which the novelistic universe coheres.[28] The description of temporality and spatiality reveals how freedom is enacted in the work. Accordingly, an interpretation of this freedom reveals the human being insofar as he is free. As Dead House makes clear, freedom is often portrayed concretely in terms of getting away from here to there, or from now to then, that is, in terms of the spatial dimension or temporal dimension that the narrative sketches. Cramped spaces are equated with unfreedom: for example, Raskolnikov speaks of his imprisonment as one arshin of space. An "arshin" is a Russian unit of measure equivalent to 28 inches or 71 cm. Gorianchikov remarks concerning his prison bed: "I had three boards of plank board to sleep on: that was all the space I had that was mine" (E: 29; PSS 4:10). Concerning the role of space within the novel to reveal human happiness, for example, in an imaginary voyage, Bourneuf and Ouellet remark:

> En ces romans, où l'espace joue le rôle primordial, se cristallisent de vieux rêves de l'humanité: voler dans les espaces intersidéraux comme Icare, découvrir sur notre planète un Eden caché ou l'homme pourra retrouver dans la nature sa félicité perdue.[29]

Hence, there is a perpetual reaching beyond the given horizon toward some sort of promise of happiness: "[L]e voyage qui ouvre l'espace aux hommes apparaît comme une promesse de bonheur."[30] The entire action of the novel is set in St. Petersburg, and only in the epilogue does the distant land of Siberia appear. Paradoxically the "lost horizon" that the structure of the narrative promises for Raskolnikov is the Siberian prison camp. His journey is in the contrary motion from Gorianchikov's. Siberia carries a different meaning, and yet both "heroes" discover a vision of freedom looking out over the river Irtysh to the steppes. In the epilogue of <u>Crime</u>, Raskolnikov looks across the river Irtysh, as did Gorianchikov, and notices the nomadic herdsmen who have lived there since the time of Abraham: "Over there is freedom . . ." (E: 628; <u>PSS</u> 6:421). But he also calls prison "freedom": "Now in prison, in freedom . . ." (E: 623; <u>PSS</u> 6:417). He also calls life before prison "freedom." He observes how much prisoners love life: "It seemed to him that in prison it [life] was loved and valued and treasured more than in freedom" (E: 624; <u>PSS</u> 6:418). The expression "in freedom" [<u>na svobode</u>], is associated with place, either in prison or outside of prison.

Freedom is depicted or enacted symbolically within the structure of the novel in a number of ways. The environment mirrors what is humanly lower (filth, poverty, degradation) and higher (the great cathedral with its gleaming dome, St. Petersburg's splendor). Concerning Dostoevsky's depiction of St. Petersburg, Berdiaev writes:

> . . . the town and its particular atmosphere, the lodging-houses with their monstrous appointments, the dirty, smelly shops, the external plots of the novels, are so many _signs and symbols of the inner spiritual world of men_, a reflection of its tragedy [italics mine].[31]

The environment of the city is a locus that reveals man's spirit in its height and depth. The material conditions and descriptions of Petersburg are patently ugly--there is filth, destitution, and only rarely a breakthrough or higher vision, such as Raskolnikov sees looking down from Nikolaevsky onto the Neva River; just before he cuts himself off from everyone and everything, standing on the same spot where he has stood one hundred times before and admiring the panorama with its cathedral dome (presumably St. Isaac's) gleaming (_PSS_ 6:90).

Crime reveals a dual, two-tiered novelistic construction. On the one hand there is an almost photo-realistic description of St. Petersburg in the sweltering month of July 1865. The air scorches, dust makes one thirsty, the streets and alleys stink. Out of this milieu emerges Raskolnikov with his obsessional internal monologue which forms the core of this tragedy. Yet, the mystery of Raskolnikov's tragic murder cannot be resolved within the mechanics of this milieu. The spaces in which Raskolnikov moves symbolize and externalize his trauma. For example, the cramped space of his tiny flat which the narrator reports: "resembled a closet more than a place of habitation" [pokhodila bolee na shkaf, chem na kvartiru] (E: 33; _PSS_ 6:5), mirrors the hero's self-enclosed consciousness.

An example of technical use of space and habitation is found in the fact that Sonia's room at Kapernaumov's tenement is adjacent to Svidrigailov's (cf. Part Four; Chapter Four). There is an empty room between which allows him to eavesdrop on Raskolnikov's confession to Sonia. The narrative space allows a depiction of how these three characters are related in a unique, moral sense that is not shared by any other character. Also, the act of eavesdropping is an intimate participation in the hero's privacy. The thought which he has kept hidden within himself, and found only Sonia capable of hearing, Svidrigailov interlopes upon. That the narrator chose to depict Sonia's and Svidrigailov's spaces in this way exercises a significant influence upon plot and characterization, but more importantly. in a key moment establishes the triadic relationship with Raskolnikov and his higher and lower doubles.

Space and the Dream

Raskolnikov's motion though space is described minutely in detail throughout the novel. To cite one locus where place takes on a great deal of significance is the dream about the mare in Part One, Chapter Five. Raskolnikov's first dream occurred on Petrovsky Island. In the dream Raskolnikov was a little boy with his father outside a tavern in the country. The young Raskolnikov witnesses a drunk peasant named Mikolka beating and then killing an old mare. When he awakens, immediately following his dream about Mikolka, he wonders whether he will really kill the old woman (PSS 6:50). The dream may say a number of things. Raskolnikov's dream establishes an identity between the dreamer and the horse, the horse and the old pawnbroker. This dream reveals all at once as though on a tableau that Raskolnikov is innocent like the horse being beaten, yet the horse stands for the old pawnbroker whom he will murder, hence identifying him with Mikolka, the cruel man in his dream. Part of the artistic power of the dream is its ability to usher in such "double logic" which allows multiple identifications to be drawn from the same dream image. The narrator has already established that in a dream, the dreamer may accomplish an integral vision of nature, that even a mature artist like Pushkin or Turgenev would be incapable of producing.

It is worthwhile to note that upon arriving at his flat following the murder, Raskolnikov takes off his coat and shivers like a horse that has been driven too hard ["Razdevshis' i ves' drozha, kak zagnannaia loshad'. . ." (PSS 6:90)]. This use of simile is not the only literary convention which establishes the parallel between Raskolnikov and the horse of his dream. He falls into a sleep and in another example of "situation rhyme" repeats his dream.[32] This time it is the landlady instead of the mare who is being beaten: "Suddenly Raskolnikov began to tremble like a leaf . . ." [Vdrug Raskolnikov zatrepetal kak list . . .] (E: 157; PSS 6:91). This statement echoes Rakolnikov's physical reaction to the first dream.

Suffering and Individual Freedom

Raskolnikov's "Monomania"

Raskolnikov is closer to Svidrigailov than Lebeziatnikov. Even after he takes his suffering upon himself, the hero is still under the sway of the "Napoleonic theory." By taking on his own suffering, he can still prove that he is elect. In the epilogue we see Raskolnikov as something of an ascetic. However, the motive for this sacrifice is just the next step for the strong man who wants to prove that he can endure everything including prison. This is substantiated when Raskolnikov attempted to further incriminate himself at the trial (E: 614; PSS 6:411). "In prison we are told by the narrator that "he felt no remorse for his crime" (E: 623; PSS

6:417). That there are criminals in prison who feel no remorse for their crime comes as no surprise to the reader of Dead House. We see in Raskolnikov's first months in prison a picture of a criminal not unfamiliar to Gorianchikov. However, the figure at the end of the epilogue is new.

Raskolnikov wants to see if he is among the elect throughout history, that is the core of his monomania. One could add to this core any number of particular arguments and reasonings, and propose a course of heroic action. Raskolnikov hit upon murder. His delusion is the idea that he personally can do whatever he wants. This delusion precedes any moral reasoning, dialectic, or ethical maxim. It is the "hidden idea" (which gives the power) that generates his action. He distorts the meaning of Schiller's aesthetic humanism and must admit that his murder was not aesthetic, to say the least. Schiller's romantic conception of the moral genius becomes confused when it is put at the service of socialist and utilitarian ideology. The moral justification is just a cover up, the idea of helping his mother and sister is an ineffectual, well-meaning sentiment. The reason why confession itself does not liberate his healing is because he remains attached to this dark, all possessing idea. Even after several seasons in prison, he still has not recanted this "inner" idea. It is only after his dream of the Trichinae from Asia, which lead men to destroy one another in toto, that he is healed (E: 626; PSS 6:419-20).

As James Rice describes in his book Dostoevsky and the Healing Art, "monomania" was a complex which psychiatrists were trying to classify in the middle of the nineteenth century. The term first appeared in 1823 in Esquirol's book which emphasizes that this is a mental illness which tends to fixate upon one idea [l'idée fixe].[33]

To become so thoroughly wrapped up in an idea so as not to be able to take any distance from it--this is what Raskolnikov seeks. The novel begins with a presentation of the hero as an indecisive character. He sets out from his apartment indecisively [nereshimost' (PSS 6:5)]. His internal monologue is a continuous struggle to achieve some sort of decision toward a definite course of action. Not only is the idea of murder significant but also his relation to it. Insofar as Raskolnikov becomes one with his idea, he escapes the vagaries and uncertainty of his human condition, but in doing so his intellect entirely subdues the principal living element within him.

Following his nightmare with the beating of the horse, Raskolnikov decides to put the thought of murder behind him. This is Raskolnikov's monomania, or l'idée fixe, which has matured from a scholarly essay, written months before the actual crime, into the experimental phase. We meet the hero in the beginning of the novel, when the idea has grown and is ready to hatch from his mind: "A strange idea had popped up in his head, like a chicken broken from an egg [kak iz iaytsa tsyplenok], and he was finding it very absorbing" (E: 99; PSS 6:53). He experiences relief: "It was as though the abscess on his heart, which had been gathering to a head all month had suddenly burst. Freedom, freedom! Now he was free from that sorcery, that witchcraft, that fascination, that infatuation!" (E: 95-96; PSS 6:50). Certainly Sonia's love plays a part in this liberation and healing process, but only insofar as it is a catalyst. The central mechanism of Raskolnikov's delusion must be defused before he can return Sonia's love, rejoin the human race, pick up the Gospel and read.

Raskolnikov is in conflict with the ugliness of the world that surrounds him; he cannot find the truth of his being in this corrupted world. Furthermore, he loves his mother and wants to save her. The corrupted world is his outer shell which he cannot shake off. If one can find a pure impulse in Raskolnikov's idea, it is this: to throw over the present corrupted world in order to achieve truth and beauty. The beauty that is revealed within his soul yearns to polish and restore the streets of Petersburg and hence, he finds himself maximally in conflict. None of the teachings of the journalists, the critics, priests, or socialists make any sense because they are all attempting to escape from the same conflict. Each group wants to do the job in its own way in order to renew the face of the world. So he adopts his "black catechism."

Raskolnikov would begin his purge with the elimination of one old louse. Yet, as he finds out in his prophetic dream in Siberia, the end of that would be that the people of the world will be infected with a plague which will cause them to devour and kill one another, like Hieronymous Bosch's "City of Earthly Delights." Raskolnikov finally sees that a worldwide Trichinae plague is not desirable at any cost, as it will permanently cancel the brotherhood of man. The nightmare reveals the core idea which has obsessed Raskolnikov for so long. The shadow side of his messianic idea is the destruction of the world. It is apocalyptic. The dream symbolizes that he has come to psychic terms with the negativity of his Napoleonic idea. Now he can renounce its tyrannic hold. In renouncing this idea he says "yes" to the world.

Just as the nomadic Kirghiz herdsmen live upon the boundless steppe where time seems to have stopped, the Siberian prison stands in a timeless periphery to Raskolnikov's St. Petersburg. According to Svidrigailov, Raskolnikov had two options: suicide (death); or Siberia (life). Raskolnikov chooses Siberia and there discovers life. To be able to see the tribesmen across the river Irtysh is to see a way of life that continues on untouched by the influence of Napoleon, and revolution, outside of history. Surely to realize the meaning of this must surpass the monomania which possessed Raskolnikov, for he was possessed most primarily with the power and inescapability of human history.

"Downtrodden Folk"

The novel certainly allows and even invites ideological criticism which posits an image of man as a utilitarian or socialist being. In either case, as we have seen, man's freedom is called into question. There is also a depiction of man that is deeper, even mystical, which concerns a knowledge and perception of man that is not limited to the sensual material presentation. Alongside of this polemical interest, we find in Dostoevsky a mystical concern with the human soul and the truth of being human. This aspect was recognized by Nikolai Dobroliubov, who found in Dostoevsky's early works the question of the meaning of man's split personality in relation to his social and natural environment, and the power of the unconscious, which exerts its influence upon the personality "behind the scenes." Dostoevsky gives to the human personality an ultimate value. In speaking of Makar Devushkin, hero of Poor Folk, and of other less fortunate little folk, in his critical article "Downtrodden People" which appeared in Sovremmenik in 1861 Dobroliubov writes:

> And for these people, who possess some amount of initiative, it is a good thing to look into the state of affairs, to know that a large part of these downtrodden people, whom they have perhaps considered done for and morally dead, still harbor within them a living soul, strong and deep, although in hiding even from them-selves, and an eternal consciousness of their human right to life and happiness, a consciousness not to be put to rout by any amount of sufferings.[34]

Thus, no matter how accurately the outer poverty of such "downtrodden" men is analyzed, the inner essence of such men remains a mystery.

Perhaps the best drawn "downtrodden" man in Crime is titular counselor Marmeladov. The problem of alcoholism is presented in the novel primarily in the figure of Marmeladov whose name suggests marmalade, hence, sweetness to an excess. He figures largely in the opening books of the novel and from the moment he appears, his alcohol problem is central to his character and the plight of his family. Although he is not the central figure in the novel, in many way Raskolnikov's chance meeting with Marmeladov in the drink shop leads to the intermeshing of the hero with the drunkard's family.

The narrator employs a strategy of direct, parallel symbolism to identify Marmeladov and Raskolnikov. When Marmeladov is run down on the street under a carriage, Raskolnikov recognizes him, and identifies him: "He's a retired civil servant, a titular councillor--his name's Marmeladov!" [--eto chinovnik, otstavnoi, tituliarnyi sovetnik, Marmeladov!] (E: 223; PSS 6:136). He shows his money to the police and proffers his address. He:

> . . . gave them his [Raskolnikov's] address, and with all his might, as though it were his own father [. . . kak budto delo shlo o rodnom ottse . . .] who lay there, set about persuading them to carry the unconscious Marmeladov up to his lodgings [italics mine]. (E: 228; PSS 6:138).

In her hysterical speech Katerina Ivanovna emphasizes (though incorrectly) that Semyon Zakkarovich knew Raskolnikov as a boy: ". . . but now (she pointed to Raskolnikov) we are being helped by a certain magnanimous young man who is possessed of means and connections, and whom Semyon Zakharovich knew as a boy . . ." (E: 228; PSS 6:141). The text reveals that Raskolnikov, in some sense, adopts Marmeladov as a stepfather, and that Katerina adopts

Raskolnikov as a son. The parallel symbolism points to this. In linking Raskolnikov with Marmeladov, the narrative brings Marmeladov's idea that suffering purifies into the orbit of the hero.

Certain other parallels established earlier in the narrative forge the link in Raskolnikov's relationship to Marmeladov. The symbolism centers chiefly upon the horse and the horse-whip (knout). For example, when Raskolnikov mindlessly walks into the path of an oncoming carriage on the Nikolaevsky Bridge, two things are significant. First of all, Raskolnikov is sketched in imagery that identifies him with a horse. Second, the shouts of the passersby are meaningful and link Raskolnikov with the drunkard, Marmeladov. The driver of the carriage beats Raskolnikov's back with his knout in order to prevent him from going beneath the horses' hooves. Raskolnikov is angered and begins to gnash and grind his teeth. A pedestrian shouts, "That's an old one: they pretend to be drunk and fall under the wheels on purpose; then you're responsible for them" (E: 155; PSS 6:89). This shout, though circumstantial, foreshadows Marmeladov's end and forges another link between Raskolnikov and the old drunkard. When we consider Marmeladov's death, it is in fact this Raskolnikov who takes responsibility for him.

Another symbol which draws a parallel relation between the titular counselor and the ex-student is the wheel. The policeman tells the doctor about Marmeladov's accident: "The policeman told him that the patient had been caught in the wheel and dragged along, turning round with it for some thirty yards along the roadway" (E: 230; PSS 6:142). This echoes Raskolnikov's superstitious attitude in Part One, Chapter Six: "As though a corner of his clothing had got caught in the flywheel of a machine, and he was being drawn into it" (E: 107; PSS 6:58).

It is significant that Dostoevsky abandoned "The Drunkards" as a project for a novel. However, the central role that Marmeladov plays in Raskolnikov's life makes evident that Dostoevsky did not abandon the projected work entirely. The primary contribution to Crime is the thesis that man craves suffering. By various rhetorical means; through symbolism and parallels, Raskolnikov comes to be inextricably linked with the old drunkard. "The Drunkards" would never be published as a novel, and yet without the influence of Marmeladov and his family, it is difficult to imagine how Raskolnikov might have pulled himself out of his self-absorption.

Conclusion

At the deepest level the theme which gathers together all of the diverse threads in Crime is human suffering--the suffering of victims such as Sonia, the pawnbroker, Katerina Ivanovna, Dunia, Marmeladov, Raskolnikov, and even Svidrigailov. In each case the suffering is unique to the individual. Hence, there is really no one theory which can account for the particular meaning of the suffering. The suffering of the hero is palpable from the outset and does not let up until the very end of the novel. We have the figure of Mikolka who confesses to the crime in order to take suffering upon himself which is part of his religious conviction. On the other hand, suffering is a two-edged sword in Dostoevsky and ought not to be summarily treated as a good which purifies. To wit, there is Sonia who takes to prostitution as a means of assisting her impoverished mother.

Taking alcoholism as an example of human suffering, we note the unique impact it has on each character brought into its orbit. Alcohol did not figure largely with Underground Man (save for his drunken night on the town). We have seen how great a role alcohol played in the life of the prisoners in Dead House. There, Dostoevsky's discovery that man craves and thirsts to express himself at whatever cost was explored in Gorianchikov's depiction of the criminal "spree." Whether or not this was a theme of "The Drunkards," we find in the character of Marmeladov the embodiment of the idea that man craves suffering. The tavern meeting is Marmeladov's great moment upon the stage. It is there that he delivers his keynote speech arguing that man craves for suffering. "Not revelry do I seek, but pure sorrow . . . I drink, for I desire to suffer doubly!" (E: 46; PSS 6:15). Marmeladov's suffering is histrionic. Katerina Ivanovna's is hysterical. On the other hand, his daughter Sonia suffers for the most part for his proclivity for the bottle. And Raskolnikov's chance meeting with Marmeladov draws him into the moral orbit of this tragic family which he never escapes.

A close look at the presentation of suffering in Crime reveals Dostoevsky's conception of man as a being which suffers its freedom. Man is neither good nor evil per se but free to choose either good or evil. Being a victim, choosing to suffer, or to make others suffer, even to murder, is the result of human freedom. Attempts to account for human suffering by reference to environmental theories invariably fail because they undermine the human ability to react freely to an environment. On the other hand, neither is man a Napoleonic champion who can conquer the world in an act of supreme will. Rather, man is in between these two theories. Dostoevsky does not offer a theory of freedom as a rebuttal to the socialists of his day. Instead he offers us Raskolnikov. This is a paradoxical hero who is both free and unfree, and yet, in an essential way is entirely free in the sense that he cannot escape his freedom. Raskolnikov cannot select or dismiss his freedom. He is free to choose or reject the particular act that lies before him. But the injunction that he must choose is essential to him. It is his very nature. Having made the choice to murder the old pawnbroker, Raskolnikov has "taken his fate" upon himself, and wears it like a second skin. The text does not reveal a disengagement between the hero and his act. The murder cannot be put behind. Its consequences follow Raskolnikov wherever he goes. Dostoevsky portrays Raskolnikov as inescapably free. This is the very conception of human freedom which is at the heart of so many twentieth century philosophers.

What is peculiar to Dostoevsky is the manner in which he conveys this truth about man. The concrete depiction of Raskolnikov conveys a philosophical image of man, which is consonant with the view of man found in varying degrees by such twentieth-century philosophers as Scheler, Heidegger, Sartre, and Merleau-Ponty, who emphasized philosophical anthropology in their work. Most of all, Dostoevsky conveyed an image of man through the concrete features of the literary artwork. For example, in narrative technique, the third person narrator, the use of onomastics, the integration of varied narrative sources--through these artistic techniques Dostoevsky was able to present an individual man which speaks about being human. The hero comes across as this hero, this Raskolnikov, and it is in this concrete way that the artwork conveys an image of a free human being.

Notes

1. F. M. Dostoevsky, _Crime and Punishment_, trans. David McDuff (London: Penguin Books, 1991). "E" stands for the English language translation of this text. The Russian text is drawn from the thirty-volume standard edition of Dostoevsky's collected works (_PSS_). The volume number is followed by the page number, hence 6:6 refers to Tome 6, page 6.

2. The term _mechta_ refers to a dream. It refers to Raskolnikov's future crime. The use of words associated with dreaming play a significant role in Dostoevsky's works. As we have seen in Chapter 2 below, the word "dreamer" lost its optimistic, utopian associations, and in _Dead House_ came to stand for the morbid, sullen state of the prisoner's world. This is significant because Komarovich argues that the dreamer (_mechtatel'_) is the hero of the young Dostoevsky's work (Cf. Chapter 2, "Dreaming," above.) Raskolnikov is a dreamer but not a utopic dreamer such as Makar Devushkin in _Bednye liudi_ (_Poor Folk_). The hero of _Crime_ dreams of a murder and not an unattainable achievement of romance.

3. Roger B. Anderson, _Dostoevsky: Myths of Duality_ (Gainesville, Fla: University of Florida Press, 1986), 54.

4. F. M. Dostoevsky, _The Diary of a Writer_, Volume I, "The Milieu," trans. Boris Brasol (New York: Charles Scribner and Sons, 1949), 13.

5. Joseph Frank, "The Genesis of _Crime and Punishment_, in _Russianness: Studies on a Nation's Identity_ (Ann Arbor: Ardis, 1990), 141.

6. Ivan Turgenev, _Fathers and Sons_, ed. and trans. Michael R. Katz (New York: W. W. Norton, 1996).

7. Frank, "Genesis," 131.

8. Ibid., 133.

9. Thelwall Proctor, _Dostoevskij and the Belinskij School of Literary Criticism_ (The Hague: Mouton, 1969), 183.

10. Dmitri Pisarev quoted in Seduro, _Dostoevsky in Russian Literary Criticism, 1846-1956_, 27.

11. Frank, "Genesis," 135.

12. Dostoevsky was presumably brought into contact with Schiller's thought through Belinsky. Amongst the small circle of friends who studied the Romantic literature and the philosophy of Kant, Fichte and Schelling in Moscow in 1830-1840 [including Belinsky], Nikolai Stankevich was considered to be a "beautiful soul" _schoene Seele_: "Stankevich's friends saw him as one of those extraordinary beings--a 'hero' not measurable by the normal scale" (Brown, 21). Cf. Edward J. Brown, _Stankevich and His Moscow Circle 1830-1840_ (Stanford: Stanford University Press, 1966).

13. Windelband, A History of Philosophy, 602.

14. Frank, "Genesis," 124-43.

15. Letter No. 57 to A. A. Kraevsky, June 8, 1865 in Selected Letters of Fyodor Dostoevsky, ed. Frank and Goldstein (New Brunswick and London: Rutgers University Press, 1987), 216.

16. F. M. Dostoevsky, The Notebooks for Crime and Punishment, ed. and trans. Edward Wasiolek (Chicago: University of Chicago Press, 1967).

17. Ibid.

18. Ibid., 9

19. Gary Rosenshield, Crime and Punishment: The Techniques of the Omniscient Author (Lisse: The Peter de Ridder Press, 1978), 14.

20. Ibid.

21. Mikhail Bakhtin, Problems of Dostoevsky's Poetics (Minneapolis: University of Minnesota Press, 1989), 230.

22. Gary Saul Morson, Freedom and Narrative (New Haven and London: Yale University Press, 1994), 11.

23. The Oxford Russian-English Dictionary (Oxford: Clarendon Press, 1992) gives as definition for 'raskol'nik': "1. (rel., hist.) schismatic, dissenter. 2. (polit. fig.) splitter" (678).

24. F. M. Dostoevsky, The Double in The Short Novels of Dostoevsky (New York: Dial Press, 1945).

25. Raskol' means "schism" or "dissent" and is derived from the verb kolot' meaning "to break, chop, split." The Oxford Russian-English Dictionary, 678.

26. Viacheslav Ivanov, Freedom and the Tragic Life: A Study in Dostoevsky (New York: Noonday Press, 1960), 26.

27. The noun prestuplenie is a cognate of the verb perestupit' meaning "to step over" as in, for example, stepping over a threshold (perestupit' porog). The Oxford Russian-English Dictionary, 511.

28. Catteau speaks of the integral symphony (time) and architecture (space) of Dostoevsky's work in a manner that is not merely a metaphor (as is Bakhtin's use of "polyphony"). It is the "metaphysics of the novel" itself where the poetic structure of the novel as well as its significance are integral to and subordinate the artwork as a whole. Cf. Jacques Catteau, La création littéraire chez Dostoïevski (Paris: Institut D'Etudes Slaves, 1978), 563-66.

29. Roland Bourneuf et Real Ouellet, L'univers du roman (Paris: Presses Universitaires de France), 127.

30. Ibid., 126.

31. Nicholas Berdiaev, Dostoevsky: An Interpretation, trans. Donald Attwater (New York: Sheed and Ward and Co., 1934), 41.

32. J. M. Meier, "Situation Rhyme in a Novel of Dostoevsky," in Dutch Contributions to the IVth International Congress of Slavists (The Hague: Mouton, 1958), 115-29. See also Gary Cox, "Treugol'nik muzhskoi zavisimosti i treugol'nik spaseniia v Prestuplenie i Nakazanii Dostoevskogo: k teorii modernistskoi formy," in Dostoevsky and the Twentieth Century: The Ljubljana Papers, ed. Malcolm Jones (Nottingham: Astra Press, 1993).

33. James Rice, Dostoevsky and the Healing Art: An Essay in Literary and Medical History (Ann Arbor: Ardis, 1985), 157.

34. Nikolai Dobroliubov quoted in Seduro, Dostoevsky in Russian Literary Criticism, 1846-1956, 20.

CHAPTER 5

THE BROTHERS KARAMAZOV (1879-1880)

In the following chapter, for sake of brevity, the topic will be limited to the meaning of "karamazovism" and of human freedom in the fifth ("Pro and Contra") and sixth books ("The Russian Monk") of The Brothers Karamazov.[1] This novel offers a unique approach to see how philosophical ideas about human freedom are at work in an artistic system. The goal of this inquiry is to establish what the text says about human freedom and to consider this in light of what philosophers have learned about human freedom based upon their study of Dostoevsky's novel. The first part of the chapter addresses the concrete, poetic considerations of the text. Before attempting to interpret the philosophic meaning of freedom, there are certain difficulties in interpreting this artwork which must be addressed. For example, it is necessary to consider how a philosophical argument can be presented within a literary artwork, and how its meaning can be established within the artistic system. At the risk of being conventional, it is expedient to turn directly to The Grand Inquisitor episode, in which a philosophical theory of human freedom is articulated.

Difficulties of Interpretation

There is a wealth of ideas concerning the novel from the standpoint of literary criticism. I limit myself to a consideration of the major difficulties that bear upon the interpretation of Book

Five (Pro i contra) and Book Six (Russkii inok) in Part Two. Literary critics have identified a number of problems which the novel poses for the interpreter: first of all, its literary form and genre; secondly, the manner in which the text is experienced; thirdly, the context of the passages in question within the novel; and fourthly, the problem in interpreting argumentation within a literary artwork. These literary obstacles make it difficult to interpret the meaning of freedom within these passages. Nonetheless, it is worthwhile to struggle with such difficulty because there is a great deal Brothers can teach us about freedom.

Difficulty of Interpreting "The 'Legend' of the Grand Inquisitor" Based upon Genre

Although Brothers is a penetrating psychological study of parricide which can be read as a detective novel much like Crime, it is also a study of humiliated love and jealousy; a study of saintliness, a family biography, and a lofty consideration of theology. So grand in its scope, Brothers has generated a number of interpretations, some contradictory: "It is frustrating that a single novel can convey views which range from sensualism to asceticism, from atheism to Catholicism to Orthodoxy to Satanism."[2] However, V. E. Vetlovskaia identifies the novel as having a singular genre. She explains that "The philosophic- publicistic dominant of the novel The Brothers Karamazov draws it together within the philosophic-publicistic genres."[3] The "philosophic-publicistic work" [filisofko-publitsisticheskoe proizvedenie], is an expression which does not have an exact equivalent in English. It is a composite of philosophical and "publicist" genres. The latter is a literary genre which deals with social-political issues and current affairs.[4] Both types of non-artistic prose genres, the philosophic and the publicistic, aim at persuading the reader toward the author's point of view. The philosophical genre employs a more strictly logical argumentation than the publicistic. Within an artistic system it must be noted that an argument, even if it is portrayed logically, takes on a different meaning. In an artistic system, an idea might even be more convincing if it is less strictly "logical."[5] In Brothers, the fundamental contradiction or argument that the novel is trying to make is stated in Book Five ("Pro and Contra") and in Book Six ("The Russian Monk") of Part Two.

Nathan Rosen suggests that the best way to read this argument between Ivan and Alyosha's literary subjects is to consider it artistically: "These questions can best be answered by examining 'The Russian Monk' and 'The Grand Inquisitor' from an artistic standpoint rather than as intellectual debating propositions."[6] That is to say that arguments can be won and readers can be persuaded by other means than strict logic. Ivan establishes the terms of the argument which is the center point of the novel. That the novelist allowed the atheist to inaugurate the debate with such a persuasive force was a cause of no small consternation to Dostoevsky and to his conservative religious friends like Pobedenostsev. This placed the burden of the answer in the court of Alyosha. Concerning this response to Ivan's atheistic Inquisitor, Dostoevsky mused in his Notebooks:

> The villains teased me for my uneducated and reactionary faith in God. These blockheads did not even dream of such a powerful negation of God as was put into the Inquisitor and in the preceding chapter, to which the whole novel serves as an answer.[7]

This statement reinforces the idea that the refutation of Ivan's atheism in Brothers was worked out in terms of the entire novel, that is, in terms of the artistic system rather than the logical refutation of an argument. Before turning to considerations of how Ivan's argument is refuted within the artistic system of the novel, there are significant features of the presentation of the argument within the novel that should be addressed.

Boundary Genres

"The Grand Inquisitor," and "The Russian Monk" are examples of what Morson calls "threshold literature." They involve boundary genres which invite contradictory readings: "[T]he author of a threshold work may create an entire text of uncertain status and exploit the resonance between two kinds of reading."[8] In addition to the difficulty of interpreting a literary work within a work whose genres lead to several possible readings, there is an additional difficulty in comparing the "argument" of this poem with Zosima's teachings. In contrasting Ivan Karamazov's poem, "The Grand Inquisitor," with the teachings of the starets Zosima, several points ought to be kept clearly in view: 1) there is no dialectical argument; 2) this is a comparison between a "poem" and a "novella."[9] In terms of the direct presentation of these two "episodes" there is a parallel between the literary creations of Ivan and Alyosha Karamazov. Ivan's poetic genius finds its realization in the spoken poem. (Ivan never wrote the Grand Inquisitor but composed it: "'I didn't write it,' laughed Ivan, 'and I've never written two lines of poetry in my life. But I composed up this poem in prose and I remembered it'" [E: 227]). On the other hand, Alyosha carefully wrote the contents of Chapter Two, which makes up ninety percent of Book Six. It is entitled, "Notes of the Life in God of the Deceased Priest and Monk, the Elder Zosima, Taken from His Own Words by Alexey Fyodorovich Karamazov." Even if Ivan never wrote his "poem," his literary creation reveals a considerable talent. Even though Alyosha's notes are less literary, less imaginative, they are nonetheless the work of a writer. The "episodes" also have in common the fundamental argument within the novel as a whole.

Ivan calls "The 'Legend' of the Grand Inquisitor" a "poem in prose," whereas Alyosha's biographical notes on Zosima in Book Six fall within the genre "zhitie" or life of a saint.[10] Both writings fall within the narrative whole and are hence held within that integral system of meaning. Be that as it may, these two "revelations" have been interpreted independently of the novel proper. Rozanov sees the legend's link with the plot of the novel to be thin: "As is generally known, this is but one episode in his last work, The Brothers Karamazov, but its connection with the plot of that novel is so slight that it can be regarded as a separate work."[11] It is not possible to agree entirely with this assertion. The "Legend" is integral to the meaning of the work as a whole. Its ideation echoes throughout the novel. It picks up on ideas first unfolded in Ivan's meeting with the Elder in Book One. The ideas of the "Legend" are echoed in the nightmare dialogue with the devil. Furthermore, "motifs" which appear in the "Legend" merge, and counterpoint with "motifs" which appear in Alyosha's Life of Zosima. Interpreters have indeed treated the "Legend" as a separate work, going so far as to publish it in an inexpensive pocket edition.[12] Convenient though this may be, a reading of the "Legend" by itself misrepresents Dostoevsky's art. To suggest that the Grand Inquisitor reveals the author's mind on freedom or on any other idea is to emphasize one theme without allowing the contrasting theme to resonate with it in the context of the artistic whole.

Considerations of the difficulty that the reader faces with genre in the interpretation of Ivan's "poem" and of Alyosha's "novella" cannot be dismissed. However, owing to possibilities of interpreting these episodes in light of broader narrative structures, and taking into consideration how ideas and motifs in the novel recur, echo and merge in the experience of the artwork as a whole, it is possible to arrive at an optimal interpretation of the meaning of freedom within this work.

The Experience of the Text

A consideration of the experience of the literary artwork leads us to a consideration of its phenomenology. Hans-Georg Gadamer has addressed the question of how a novel evokes precise "perceptions" from the reader. He has noted how the reader must, to a certain extent, complete the literary artwork. A novel is not in fact an artwork unless there is an understanding reader who reads it. Employing Brothers as an example, speaking of Smerdiakov's fall down Karamazov's stairs in Book 5, Chapter 7: "Smerdyakov went to the cellar for something and fell down from the top of the steps," Gadamer writes:

> I can see the stairs down which Smerdjakov tumbles. Dostoevsky gives us a certain description. As a result, I know exactly what this staircase looks like. I know where it starts, how it gets darker and then turns to the left.[13]

The novel evokes a perception of the fall, albeit different for every reader. The question of the phenomenality of the novel is intriguing and raises important questions about the presentation and representation of the artwork. These are not merely questions of "reader response" or "psychology" but delve into the most fundamental question, what is art? We will not explore this here, but rather look at the experience of Brothers in terms of the interaction of motifs and narrative structures.

Despite the fact that Zosima never was able to come face to face with the Inquisitor to debate him directly, he did meet Ivan Karamazov, and at this meeting several of the central ideas of Ivan's poem were debated. In fact, the crucial ideas of both Ivan's poem and Zosima's teaching had already been presented and on the table since Book One. Furthermore, later in the narrative, many of the Grand Inquisitor's ideas are debated with the Devil during Ivan's nightmare (Part Four, Book Eleven, Chapter Nine). Morson describes Dostoevsky's use of motifs as a principle of unity in a work composed of various generic materials:

> . . . Dostoevsky intended his division of issues into chapters, in each of which articles of various kinds would be grouped together, to serve as an implicit invitation to readers to discover a hierarchy of thematic interrelations: a non-narrative connecting principle.[14]

Such a "non-narrative connecting principle" allows us to speak of a dialogue or "argument" between Zosima and The Grand Inquisitor which is not portrayed face to face in the novel but is enacted throughout the integral work. From specific utterances to literary creations within the text, Dostoevsky employs poetic structure as well as ideation to advance this argument.

Terras indicates the manner in which Dostoevsky's narrative includes dynamic ministructures which interact to advance the story:

> The narrative structure of The Brothers Karamazov is readily broken down into ministructures, or motifs, some of which are dynamic, in the sense that they directly advance the story . . . while others are static. . . .[15]

It is in this sense that motifs present in Ivan's "poema" are brought into dialogue with Zosima's teaching. Belknap's idea of the "structure of inherent relationships" emphasizes the means with which Dostoevsky underlines, reviews and emphasizes certain themes within the plot of Brothers in order that the reader will remember certain characters who have been out of the action for several hundred pages. Certain characters are secondary in significance and their existence need not remain within the reader's memory. For example:

> Few readers worry, "What was happening all this time to Miusov, Grigorij, Kalganov, Maksimov, Paisij, Rakitin, Polenov, Snegirev, Samsonov, Smurov, Herzenstube, Fetjukovic?" or any of the minor figures.[16]

On the other hand the hero, Alyosha, must be kept "present" to the reader through specific reviewing techniques that the narrator employs. Belknap sees the novel as "a folded row of type two miles long and two millionths of a mile wide, one of the most nearly one-dimensional things in art or nature."[17] Unlike a plastic work of art or a painting which is apprehended (though not necessarily understood) all at once, the literary work of art is experienced over a long period of consecutive sittings.

Although this does not influence the present day reader's understanding of the work, the work's original publication was serial and occurred over a period of two years. Hence, the first readers of the novel were held in suspense between installations. That the serial publication influenced the contemporary reader of Brothers, there can be little doubt. As we have noted, the priority of Ivan's "poema" inaugurated the atheist idea. A delay between publications reinforced the power of Ivan's position, however, Dostoevsky was aware of this "effect," and he employed it to advance his own ends.

Dostoevsky employed techniques of recapitulation, foreshadowing and underlining in order to maintain important characters and events in the reader's memory. To cite an example in the text where these effects were clearly at work: on the fifth day after the trial, the narrator refers to Katerina Ivanovna's demand, made at the time of the trial, that the delirious Ivan Karamazov be brought to her house for medical treatment, Belknap indicates the complex temporal relations ensuing:

> The scene at the trial referred to in this passage was separated from the moment being presented by several days in the chronology of the novel, by almost a hundred pages in the reader's experience, and by two months in the original publication dates of the novel.[18]

Considerations of the manner in which the reader experiences Dostoevsky's literary artwork elucidate the meaning that can be derived from the novel's argumentation. It is not fruitful to merely assume that the text argues one way or the other. Be that as it may, a critical consideration of how meaning is derived from an experience with a literary artwork assists in determining its optimal interpretation.

Difficulty in Interpreting the Passages in Light of Context

Ivan's poem must first of all be considered within the context of the book entitled, Pro and Contra, and also in the context of the work itself, Brothers. And yet, pro and contra, or perhaps like two supporting arches, these two literary revelations are at the very center of the architectonic in this enormous literary work--and they center upon the meaning of freedom.

That this book is central to the work Dostoevsky makes clear in the following letter to N. A. Lyubimov: "That is the fifth book, entitled Pro and Contra . . . this fifth book is in my view the culminating point of the novel and must be finished with particular care."[19] It is difficult to ascertain what Dostoevsky meant by "culminating point" when only a few months later he wrote again to Lyubimov stating that the sixth book, "The Russian Monk," is "the culminating point of the novel."[20]

What does the meaning of "pro" and "contra" in the fifth book refer to? Ivan's poem is, according to Dostoevsky, "the synthesis of contemporary Russian anarchism" (no. 660). However, in another letter to Lyubimov he explains:

> . . . [M]y socialist (Ivan Karamazov) is a sincere man, who admits openly that he agrees with the Grand Inquisitor's view of humanity and that Christ's faith (seemingly) raised man much higher than he in fact is.[21]

The Grand Inquisitor's main accusation against Christ is that he demands too much from man--that he places too high a premium upon man's freedom. Christ's view of man is, according to the Grand Inquisitor, as follows:

> Thou didst crave for free love and not the base raptures of the slave before the might that has overawed him forever. But Thou didst think of men too highly therein, for they are slaves, of course, though rebellious by nature. (E: 236; PSS 14:233)

On the other hand, Ivan explains that the Grand Inquisitor is also fond of man:

> But yet all his life he loved humanity, and suddenly his eyes were opened, and he saw that it is no great moral blessedness to attain perfection and freedom, if at the same time one gains the conviction that millions of God's creatures have been created as a mockery, that they will never be capable of using their freedom, that these poor rebels can never turn into giants to complete the tower, that it was not for such geese that the great idealist dreamt his dream of harmony. (E: 242; PSS 14:238)

There are two types of love for man. One elevates him and challenges him to live up to his freedom. The other, recognizing that man almost never acts freely, attempts to help man to achieve a "realistic" happiness. Who is more "the great idealist" [. . . velikii idealist . . . (PSS 14:238)], the greater lover of mankind--Christ or The Grand Inquisitor? It is difficult to decide this. Upon hearing Ivan recite this poem, Alyosha is uncertain whether its author wishes to praise Christ or the Grand Inquisitor. The meaning of "pro" and "contra" is not clearly definable within the literary text. Its function is more to signal that there is a conflict of views which suggests that there is an argument.

Difficulty in the Interpretation of the Meaning of the Argumentation

There is a difference between an argument and its refutation when it appears in an artistic system. Arguments which are not strictly logical can be employed in an artistic work quite persuasively. On the other hand, the artwork allows the presentation of character, figure and type as refutation. Concerning the use of argumentation in a literary artwork, V. E. Vetlovskaia writes:

> In this connection let us repeat that the artistic system of a work significantly broadens the limits of authorial argumentation by permitting the use of arguments that would be impossible outside an artistic system.[22]

The use of an artistic system makes possible communication of arguments and ideas which otherwise could not be used in a non-artistic system.

Elsewhere, concerning Dostoevsky's use of the literary artform in order to argue with more scientific conceptions of man, Kirpotin has written that he uses an artistic figure to answer to Chernyshevsky's sociological conception:

> In answer to the optimistic sociology of Chernyshevsky and his friends Dostoevsky created a figure, presented a literary type [tip]. The refutation of the theory with a figure cannot count as exhaustive evidence.[23]

The presentation of a character in a novel such as Zosima in Brothers is not commensurate to an argument, since it cannot be falsified or proven. Owing to its peculiarity and individuality, Kirpotin points out, the character in a novel cannot provide an anthropological formula for all people. It would require a gallery of "types" to answer to this kind of question.[24] Hence, there are limitations in refuting an argument with an artistic figure. The problem is only compounded when we face more complex character types such as the Grand Inquisitor, who is a wheel within a wheel, being Ivan's literary creation, or the Devil, who may or may not be a figment of his fevered imagination. Zosima's artistic image is no less intricate, whose literary presentation demands specific attention. On the other hand, the type conveys an important truth about man in answer to the mistakenness of general, theoretical ideation. For example, Ivan's abstract love for mankind coupled with his indifference to the murder of his own father.

Philosophical Interpretations

Having considered several poetic features of the novel in our interpretation, it is necessary to consider the philosophical interpretations which have treated the meaning of freedom in this work. That the conception of human freedom with its concurrent image of man is at the core of Ivan's poema has been discussed by many interpreters of Brothers, in particular the interpretations of Gide, Camus, Berdiaev, Shestov, and others.[25] Sartre refers to the leitmotif which recurs throughout the novel, "all things are permitted" [vse pozvoleno] as the starting point of existentialism: "'Si Dieu n'existait pas, tout serait permis.' C'est le point de départ de l'existentialisme."[26] The emphasis on Ivan's atheistic rebellion is acute in both Sartre and Camus. Camus devotes a chapter of L'Homme revolté entitled "Le réfus du salut" to the consideration of Ivan Karamazov's moral rebellion.[27] Shestov finds in the Grand Inquisitor what was begun in the Underground Man, that is, a complete "critique of reason," or in other words, a complete disavowal of reason as a means of salvation. Berdiaev, on the other hand, agrees that the Grand Inquisitor is a figure of the Underground Man but instead of despairing of reason, as Shestov does, Berdiaev interprets the "Legend" as a defense of human freedom against totalitarian control. Rozanov declares that Dostoevsky is on the side of the Grand Inquisitor.[28] D. H. Lawrence writes that the Grand Inquisitor is correct.[29] This is not to mention the numerous literary studies of Brothers which invariably emphasize the philosophical significance of the "Legend".[30]

Berdiaev's Interpretation

Berdiaev interprets Dostoevsky's philosophy of freedom in a "theological" manner. In this respect he differs from the other interpretations cited above. He indicates that man's freedom is dependent upon a belief in God. Brothers gives witness to man's broad range of moral possibility to be with or without God. Ultimately, Ivan Karamazov's philosophy that all is permitted is his own destruction:

> The fates of Raskolnikov and Stavroguin and Kirilov and Ivan Karamazov testify to the truth of this: freedom wrongly directed was the downfall of them all. That does not mean, however, that they ought to have been put under compulsion or submitted to external law and regulation. Their loss is an enlightening lesson for us, and their tragedy a hymn to freedom.[31]

Although man is free to either reject or accept God's existence, Berdiaev argues that if man employs his freedom to satisfy his human wants only, and does not strive for an ideal, then man begins to lose his freedom:

> And if there is no content and object in freedom, if there is no bond between human freedom and divine freedom, then freedom does not exist either. If all things are allowable to man, then freedom becomes its own slave, and the man who is his own slave is lost.[32]

Berdiaev's interpretation takes Zosima's teaching about individualism and the destruction of freedom into his account. The "existentialist" interpreters of Brothers have failed to give equal emphasis to the teaching of Zosima. Despite this neglect by serious philosophers, some of whom were quite gifted literary critics such as Sartre and Camus, the figure of Alyosha's spiritual elder is one of the center points of the artistic system in the work.

Berdiaev argues that when man loses his freedom he ceases to be man. Christianity is the religion that teaches that man is essentially free. Man cannot accede to his freedom without experiencing deformity of his nature and ultimately self-destruction. The difference between the Grand Inquisitor's concern for man (a patronizing pity) and Christ's concern for man (respect for man's freedom of belief) hinges upon the role of freedom in human life. The Grand Inquisitor places the value of human happiness higher than that of freedom, in such a way that the sacrifice of human freedom for happiness and unity looks like a bargain, one that mankind will gladly buy. Christ, on the other hand, establishes human freedom as the ultimate value in the cosmos. As such, it is worth any cost, including suffering. In fact, suffering is central and necessary to the realization of freedom.

Berdiaev describes "Inquisitor" as the summit of Dostoevsky's philosophy of freedom: "Dostoievsky's dialectic of freedom reaches its climax in the 'Legend' of the Grand Inquisitor, in which all the problems are concentrated and all their threads picked up and joined."[33] And:

> The "Legend" of the Grand Inquisitor is the high point of Dostoievsky's work and the crown of his dialectic. It is in it that his constructive views on religion must be sought; all the tangles are unravelled and the radical problem, that of human freedom, is solved.[34]

Even though Christ is silent, Berdiaev finds that Dostoevsky's religious belief is eloquently conveyed in the "Legend." Berdiaev sees Dostoevsky as agreeing with the Grand Inquisitor's critique and analysis of human freedom. It is difficult to argue with the ideas conveyed in Ivan's poem, because the Grand Inquisitor's position is ambivalent. He pities mankind, who is too weak to bear the burden of freedom, and he offers the alternative solution of living life happily but without freedom. To disagree with this position would amount to saying, "Man is free and bears his freedom well." Note that the Grand Inquisitor does not deny that man is free; however, he indicates that man is willing to sacrifice his freedom in order to be happy and secure in the world. To realize that this is not the case requires very little study of human life and interaction. Such an attitude is based upon a patronizing contempt for man. The ambivalence within the Inquisitor's position lies in the old cardinal's pity for man. The crux of the argument is really the question of the value to be assigned to respect for man:

> I swear, man is weaker and baser by nature than Thou hast believed him! . . . By showing him so much respect, Thou didst, as it were, cease to feel for him, for Thou didst ask far too much from him--Thou who hast loved him more than Thyself! (E: 236-37; PSS 14:233)

The Inquisitor is turning tables on Jesus and selling his own version of love for mankind, the "correcting" of Jesus' work. He is a pragmatist who wants Jesus to know that his ideal is too high and has not worked. Hence the real crux of the argument is the meaning and value of love and respect for man. Jesus thinks too highly of man, and this is not caring for him. The Grand Inquisitor feels quite confident that he can prove and demonstrate his concern for mankind. He usurps Jesus' ministry in the name of mankind. However, in order to achieve this he is willing to yield man's most precious attribute, namely his freedom.

Zosima vs. The Inquisitor on the Meaning of Freedom

One method to determine the meaning of freedom in the text is to consider the "debate" between Zosima's conception of man and Ivan Karamazov's. There is certainly no way to present the case that this is a dialectical argument. There is no way to arrive at a logical conclusion between the two positions on freedom. On the other hand, the narrative brings a consideration of the meaning of being human to an intersection in Alyosha. He must bring the teaching which informs his life into contact with the summation of Ivan's teaching. In fact, if there is any comparison, it is between two alternative ways of life--the way of life of a holy monk and a diabolical cardinal. Before turning to a comparison of Zosima and Ivan as figures, let us consider the role that freedom plays in their teachings.

The value, meaning and significance of freedom, is played out in Zosima's teaching between two concepts: isolation and unification. The Grand Inquisitor also treats these concepts, although in an almost diametrically opposite manner. In fact, both Zosima and Ivan's Inquisitor agree that man ought to be unified:

> . . . all that man seeks on earth--that is, someone to worship, someone to keep his conscience, and some means of uniting all in one unanimous and harmonious anthill, for the craving for universal unity is the third and last anguish of men. Mankind as a whole has always strived to organize a universal state. (E: 238; PSS 14:134-35)

While Zosima agrees that man seeks unity, he teaches that the only route is spiritual dignity:

> Equality is to be found only in the spiritual dignity of man, and that will only be understood among us. If we were brothers, there would be fraternity, but before that, they will never agree about the division of wealth. (E: 295; PSS 14:286-87)

The upshot of the Grand Inquisitor's speech hinges upon the meaning and centrality of freedom in human life and upon freedom's relation to happiness. Seen in this light, Zosima's teaching does indeed seem like a point-by-point refutation of the Inquisitor's speech.

In one word, the Grand Inquisitor recognizes the great burden that freedom places upon man and proposes a means of lifting the burden of freedom off of the back of man: "Oh, we shall persuade them that they will only become free when they renounce their freedom to us and submit to us" (E: 239; PSS 14:235). Such a proposal hinges upon a peculiar notion of freedom. Freedom is a burden. Man has a negative relation to his freedom. In this way the Inquisitor is able to accuse Christ of not loving man enough: "By showing him so much respect, Thou didst, as it were, cease to feel for him, for Thou didst ask far too much from him--Thou who hast loved him more than Thyself!" (E: 237; PSS 14:233). Paradoxically, in recognizing man's weakness, the Grand Inquisitor, like a benevolent despot, claims to love man more than Christ. It is out of this love that he would enslave man and ensure his happiness.

The meaning of this freedom is unclear. Can it be the true freedom which is such a burden to man? Zosima also teaches that freedom is a burden, but this is freedom as it is interpreted by the world:

> Interpreting freedom as the multiplication and rapid satisfaction of desires, men distort their own nature, for many senseless and foolish desires and habits and ridiculous fancies are fostered in them. (E: 292-93; PSS 14:284)

Hence there is an illusory freedom which is self-contradictory and does not lead to the truth. Such an apparent freedom is pursued by the world, but only to its own self-destruction:

> The world has proclaimed the reign of freedom, especially of late, but what do we see in this freedom of theirs?

> Nothing but slavery and self-destruction! For the world says: "You have desires and so satisfy them, for you have the same rights as the most rich and powerful. Don't be afraid of satisfying them and even multiplying your desires." That is the modern doctrine of the world. In that they see freedom. And what follows from this right of multiplication of desires? In the rich, isolation and spiritual suicide; in the poor, envy and murder; for they have been given rights, but have not been shown the means of satisfying their wants. . . . (E: 292; PSS 14:284)

The argument concerns the nature of man and is centered upon man's freedom. There is an ambivalence in man's relation to freedom. Freedom leads to slavery for both Zosima and the Grand Inquisitor. However, the meaning of freedom is quite different for the monk and the cardinal.

For Zosima, the worldly conception of freedom leads to enslavement. Zosima distinguishes between two types of freedom: the freedom interpreted in a worldly fashion; and true, real freedom. He learned about the latter from the Mysterious Visitor. This man, who visited Zosima in his youth, warned of a coming period of isolation:

> . . . the isolation that prevails everywhere, above all in our age--it has not fully developed, it has not reached its limit yet. For everyone strives to keep his individuality as apart as possible, wishes to secure the greatest possible fullness of life for himself; but meantime all his efforts result not in attaining fulness of life but self-destruction, for instead of self-realization he ends by arriving at complete isolation. (E: 283; PSS 14:275)

The freedom that is sought for in the world is contradictory; striving for it men end up in slavery:

> And its no wonder that instead of gaining freedom they have sunk into slavery, and instead of serving the cause of brotherly love and the union of humanity have fallen, on the contrary, into separation and isolation, as my mysterious visitor and teacher said to me in my youth. (E: 293; PSS 14:285)

The latter, "true" freedom he refers to in the following way: "The monastic way is very different. Obedience, fasting and prayer are laughed at, yet only through them lies the way to real, true freedom"

(E: 293). Earlier in the narrative, the narrator spoke of this freedom:

> This novitiate, this terrible school of abnegation is undertaken voluntarily, in the hope of self-conquest, of self-mastery, in order, after a life of obedience, to attain perfect freedom, that is, from self; to escape the lot of those who have lived their whole life without finding their true selves in themselves. (E: 21; PSS 14:26)

Both the Grand Inquisitor and Zosima advocate a communion among men. The former seeks to unify mankind in a manner which violates freedom. Zosima, on the other hand, proposes a freedom which unifies man without making them slaves. It is interesting to note that both the Grand Inquisitor and Zosima would seem to advocate the surrender of human will in order to achieve the unity of mankind. Zosima, insofar as he is a starets, states:

> An elder [starets] was one who took your soul, your will, into his soul and his will. When you choose an elder, you renounce your own will and yield it to him in complete submission, complete self-abnegation. (E: 21; PSS 14:26)

Since the Grand Inquisitor was one of those who possessed the terrible knowledge that God does not exist, he is obliged to shepherd men in the manner that comforts them.

Zosima develops further the ideas that he heard from the Mysterious Visitor who warned of impending isolation amongst men. This isolation must come about as a fact: "Until you have become really, in actual fact, a brother to everyone, brotherhood will not come to pass" (E: 282; PSS 14:275). This must come about according to psychological and spiritual laws--the laws which science does not believe because science knows only what is sensibly revealed. Science often rudely denies the higher half of the makeup of mankind--the spiritual.

Is Zosima a humanitarian, perhaps even a socialist? Is it possible to see Zosima as a mechtatel' or dreamer of socialist utopia? Komarovich finds Zosima's idea of earthly paradise to contain the residue of the young Dostoevsky's socialist ideal. This early Soviet critic argues that Dostoevsky continued to promote the vision of mirovaia garmoniia ("worldwide harmony") long after he had accomplished a complete criticism of social-utopism in Underground. The ideal of "worldwide harmony" perpetuates Dostoevsky's optimistic belief in man albeit in a form that is nationalistic, stripped bare of any French socialist content.[35]

Karamazovism

Is Zosima's teaching Dostoevsky's final word about freedom? There are good reasons for doubting this. If it is, then Ivan Karamazov's argument is not given an honest hearing. Moreover, the "Legend" indeed has something of authentic value to teach. What is needed is a method of bringing Zosima's ideas about freedom into confrontation with Ivan's ideas. In order to do this it is necessary to establish a meaning of the word "freedom" based upon a close reading of the Russian text. The optimal starting point for an interpretation of the concept of freedom, in light of a close reading of Brothers, is to interpret the meaning of "karamazovskii," a term Dostoevsky coins to describe the Karamazovs. The title of the novel takes on added significance when we consider that Dostoevsky uses the name Karamazov in an adjectival sense with a specialized meaning. In discussing themes of the novel which give a "pattern-building force," Terras describes the theme of "Karamazovism" as follows:

> . . . "Karamazovism" (karamazovshchina), which Zundelovich defines as an "abandon" (bezuderzh, p. 190), a faculty for going "all the way" in everything; disorder . . ., unbelief (ranging from Ivan's tortured doubts, through the

> complacent Rakitin and the smug Fetiukovich, to precocious Kolia); rupture; joie de vivre (stated explicitly by Father Zosima and by all of the Karamazovs); and finally, resurrection, the theme that emerges triumphant at the end of the novel.[36]

In addition to being integral to the characterization of the Karamazov family, Karamazovism is a central motif in the novel taking on a meaning that is independent of the central family.

Prosecutor Ippolit Kirillovich says about Dmitri Karamazov:

> Because he was of the broad Karamazov character [natury shirokie, karamazovskie]--that's just what I'm leading up to--capable of combining the most incongruous contradictions, and simultaneously contemplating both abysses, the abyss above us and the abyss below us, the abyss of the lowest and foulest degradation. (E: 664-65; PSS 15:129)

The breadth of the Karamazov nature refers to two extremes, high and low. Dmitri realizes that his own excessive moral breadth. In an ironic utterance which parallels the Grand Inquisitor's poem, Dmitri proposes that man is too broad and should be narrowed:

> I can't endure the thought that a man of lofty mind and heart begins with the ideal of the Madonna and ends with the ideal of Sodom . . . Man is too broad, indeed. [. . . shirok chelovek, slishkom dazhe shirok, ia by suzil.] I'd have him narrower. (E: 97; PSS 14:100)

Dmitri's observation that man is too broad, that there is a dimension of man's being which pertains to latitude, is of central feature of the "Karamazov" nature. This breadth associated with the Karamazov nature allows Dmitri an awareness of the full range from what is sacred to what is base and perverse. The adjective shirokii refers to what is broad and wide in the physical sense such as a broad road, but also to the "unrestrained" which gets more at the moral sense of the Karamazov nature.

Without taking Dmitri's statement at face value, we observe in this assertion: 1) a critique of God's creation (parallel to Ivan's "rebellion"); and 2) a consideration of man in the totality of his moral being. Of course, man cannot revise his nature or character. Or can he? The question of the moral reformation of man is a prevailing theme in Dead House and all of Dostoevsky's works following.[37]

Dmitri who asks, "Why is such a man alive?" is capable of killing his father and possesses a motive, yet he chooses not to. In this instance, "all is permitted" refers to a more primordial freedom. Whereas Dmitri interprets the Karamazov nature in terms of a breadth of awareness of what is good and noble, and what is evil and base that is humanly difficult to bear; Ivan speaks of the Karamazov strength in a discussion with Alyosha at the Metropolis Tavern as a base strength: "Karamazov strength--the strength of the Karamazov baseness" [Karamazovskaia . . . sila nizosti karamazovskoi] (E: 243; PSS 14:240). Alyosha asks Ivan what he means by this and whether the Karamazov way [po-karamazovski] means that "everything is lawful" [vse pozvoleno] (PSS 14:240). It is important to note that Alyosha in his question gives the interpretation "all is lawful" as a meaning for "po-karamazovski." Ivan answers:

> "Ah, you've caught up yesterday's phrase, which so offended Miusov--and which brother Dmitri pounced upon so naively and paraphrased!" he smiled queerly. "Yes, if you like, 'everything is lawful' since the word has been said. I won't deny it. And Mitenka's version isn't bad. . . ." The formula, "all is lawful," I won't renounce. . . . (E: 244; PSS 14:240)

The reference to "yesterday's phrase" points to the sixth chapter in Book Two where the action takes place in the presence of Father Zosima. In a discussion about Ivan's article about ecclesiastical courts, it is mentioned that mankind without belief in immortality would be incapable of love (PSS 14:64-65). Dmitri interrupts Miusov and paraphrases Miusov's words. This is "Mitenka's version" referred to by Ivan above:

> "If I've heard aright: crime must not only be permitted but even recognized as the inevitable and the most rational outcome of his position for every atheist!" (E: 60)
>
> [. . . chtoby ne oslyshat'sia: "Zlodeistvo ne tol'ko dolzhno byt' dozvoleno, no dazhe prizano samym neobkhodimym i samym umnym vykhodom iz polozheniia vsiakogo bezbozhnika!"] (PSS 14:65)

When the elder asks Ivan to confirm this interpretation he says: "There is no virtue if there is no immortality" (E: 60). There are hence three "versions" of this thought: 1) All is lawful (Alyosha's); 2) Mitenka's version stated above; and 3) Ivan's dogmatic assertion that there is no virtue without immortality.

Philosophical Reflection

The meaning of the brothers' three versions center upon the dimension of man that is ineradicably free. Ivan's "Legend" intermeshes an ideological debate concerning human freedom whose problematic originates in his published article on ecclesiastical courts. The fateful discussion in which the central polemic is presented occurs in Chapter VI of Book Two, "Why is such a man alive?" All of the Karamazov brothers were present with their father, and Zosima was present as well. That the ideas discussed there are central to the novel and especially to the "Legend," indicates that far from being separable from the corpus of the novel as Rozanov and Belknap suggest, the "Legend" is integrally woven into the fabric of the novel.

Furthermore, the integrity of this philosophic argument within the artwork is highlighted poetically according to its genre as Vetlovskaia suggests. The interweaving of the philosophical discourse within Brothers is very clearly Dostoevsky's aim. Now I would like to highlight some of the main features of the philosophical thought which pertains to the conception of man and his freedom.

The philosophical significance of the "Legend" moves well beyond the ideological polemic with Chernyshevsky on the rational-utilitarian conception of man.[38] Ivan is a socialist, but he is a unique type of socialist. The Grand Inquisitor is not merely the manifestation of the socialist program in its totality, but the Grand Inquisitor is a unique creation, a "suffering Inquisitor" who loved mankind. Meanwhile, Christ is made out to be passive, silent and ineffectual. The Inquisitor comes to be more "christlike" than Christ! Ivan's Grand Inquisitor positions Christ as an idealist, perhaps even a Romantic. But all of this contradiction relies upon Ivan's fundamental unbelief. "Behold, I am with you until the end of the age" are Christ's words to his disciples. Hence there is no need for a return to Seville, Spain, in the sixteenth century when Christ already lives forever. Ivan's poem is literary trickery, a sign of his impending madness. Ivan is masterfully persuasive, but the substance of what he is arguing is flawed. If anything, the Grand Inquisitor is a litmus test of belief and unbelief. The unbeliever should be swayed by Ivan's rhetoric. The net effect of the argument is to demonstrate not that Ivan is wise, but rather, that literary examples are so powerfully persuasive that they can plant seeds of doubt even in the heart of a believer.

Ivan, like Raskolnikov, is the author of a published intellectual article. Prior to going abroad on his 2000 rubles, he published an article in one of the "more important journals." The narrator relates that "The article dealt with a subject which was being debated everywhere at the time--the position of the ecclesiastical courts" [_v tserkovnom sude_] (E: 11; _PSS_ 14:16). This article was brought to the attention of Zosima and read by him, much like Raskolnikov's article on conscience was read by Porfiry Petrovich.[39] This parallel between Ivan Karamazov and Raskolnikov suggests that like the content of Raskolnikov's obsession, which was first mentioned in a scholarly article, the content of Ivan's obsession is also revealed in a scholarly article. At the first meeting between Zosima and Ivan--"The Unfortunate Gathering"--Ivan says that he wrote the article responding to an opponent who stated three propositions: 1) that no social organization should dispose of the civic rights of its citizens; 2) that criminal and civic jurisdiction ought not belong to the church; and 3) that the church is a kingdom not of this world. Ivan's answer to this opponent is that the state should be subsumed in the church. "Ultramontanism!" cries one of the young priests. In fact these ideas are at the heart of Ivan's poem, "The Grand Inquisitor." It is probable that he composed the poem in proximity to the submission of this article because he tells Alyosha that he had composed it, but not written it down, about a year earlier.

Three clues suggest that Ivan's relationship to the idea in his article is not entirely whole-hearted. First of all the narrator in referring to the publication of the article writes ironically, ". . . a strange article . . . on a subject of which he might have been supposed to know nothing, as he was a student of natural science" (E: 11; PSS 14:16). Indeed, what should a natural scientist know about ecclesiastical courts? The second clue relates to Father Paissy's almost prophetic saying concerning Ivan's atheism:

> For even those who have renounced Christianity and attack it, in their inmost being still follow the Christian ideal, for hitherto neither subtlety nor the ardour of their hearts has been able to create a higher ideal of man and of virtue than the ideal given by Christ of old. (E: 156; PSS 14:156)

Ivan's underlying attack of Christianity is still aiming from a Christian arsenal. He still demands a purity, and justice which is higher than the world. Ivan's critique remains fundamentally incoherent to anyone without a particular attachment to the Christian ideal.

In consideration of the radicality of Ivan's rebellion, accusing God of allowing the suffering of innocents, it is time to open up the concentrated philosophical bitterness of his "idea." Ivan was raising the age old question of theodicy, of how a good God allows bad things to happen to good people.[40] One traditional answer proposed that God is absolutely good and out of a number of possible worlds he created the best of all possible worlds, hence God is not in any way culpable for the evil in this world since he did the best job he could have done and kept to a minimum whatever evil was necessary to get the job done. A version of this idea is found in Liebniz' Theodicea. The other option is to deny that there is any actuality to evil, and to deny that there is any reality to freedom. Determinism, which teaches fate in many guises; whether naturalistic, economic, socialistic, or psychological, adds up to a denial of man's free choice. Since nature is a deterministic system, no one really chooses to do evil and hence no one can be held responsible for moral conduct either. Those are the two main choices to resolve this dilemma; some type of theodicy or a retreat to determinism. Naturally there are some who will not follow either path but refuse to cease their questioning. Ivan is of this variety. He is addressing his thought to the very root of the problem, i.e., toward God. He finds no answer and hence seeks willful rebellion. Reminiscent of the Underground Man, Ivan is choosing to stick his tongue out at God's world, to surrender his ticket. He is leaving the realm of reasonability and entering the realm of conscious refusal.

Concerning the problem of evil Schelling wrote in 1809:

> But the question why God did not prefer to forgo self-revelation altogether, since he necessarily foresaw that evil would result, at least attendantly, indeed does not deserve a reply. For this would amount to saying in order that there be no opposition to love, love itself should not be, i.e., the absolutely positive should be sacrificed for what has existence only as an opposite, and the eternal should be sacrificed for the merely temporal.[41]

The question why God did not forgo the Creation is like asking why am I here? It presumes a counterfactual argument, what would the world be like if I did not exist? While interesting to mull around, the question leads nowhere. One must assume one's standpoint. Ivan is not a philosopher like Schelling. He is not making the type of argument which would be counterfactual. He has found the last stage of his intellect and he is rebelling against the world in which he finds himself. That Dostoevsky was aware of the potency of Ivan's argument, he wrote a letter which revealed trepidation for the monster that he unleashed.[42] But even so, Ivan does not emerge victorious.

The third clue which suggests a hole in Ivan's idea is the state of his madness.[43] The very fact of his mental demise casts serious doubts on his rebellion. Since the content of his idea is linked to the onset of his madness, suggests that Father Paissy was correct in his prophecy that Ivan could not wholly evade the ideal which Christ revealed. Ivan's argument only reveals the limitations of his intellect. After considering his fruitless way, the question remains how could he resolve this dilemma. What is it that Ivan lacks? For the answer look to the figure of Zosima.

Zosima is not teaching "church" in any orthodox sense (in fact, Orthodox theologians protested Dostoevsky's portrayal of the Starets).[44] Vetlovskaia writes:

> [I]n having the elder Zosima call for the immediate abolishment of suffering (first and foremost the suffering of children), Dostoevsky affirms his own disagreement with the theological point of view that excludes the necessity of changing the world.[45]

We have noted that Ivan's ideas have something in common with Zosima's. Zosima teaches that love not only for man, but for all of creation is possible and indeed necessary. Hence, the upshot of the argument pro and contra with the Grand Inquisitor is not so much whether God exists, or even whether man is free, but rather what is the meaning of man's freedom and how does he bear it? Love takes on a total significance. Not merely as an emotion but as an all-encompassing framework which makes possible human freedom, understanding of human life and of the creation. This is the way of life that Zosima embodied. Ivan's poem relies upon the conviction that man is incapable of loving his neighbor, that love for mankind can only be achieved at a distance. The commandment to "love one another" is asking too much of man if man is not by nature capable of loving his neighbor.

We have noted how the meaning of freedom taken in the sense of Ivan's motif: "all is permitted," contrasts with the meaning of freedom in Zosima's teaching. Despite the fact that Zosima's teaching can be read as a point by point refutation of the idea that "all is permitted," philosophical interpreters of Brothers have tended to emphasize not Zosima's conception of freedom but Ivan's. As we have noted, it is Ivan's conception of freedom which, according to Sartre, is the starting point of existentialism. But this interpretation is less than optimal. "All is permitted" leads to a realm in which freedom loses its human significance while the Grand Inquisitor would usher in a world of non-humans who have surrendered their greatest asset. There is yet another meaning of freedom that the work gives.

The Fundamental Meaning of Freedom

A close reading of the text paying particular attention to the meaning of "karamazovism" uncovers a more primordial conception of freedom which underlies both Ivan's and Zosima's discourse. Accordingly, when we consider Smerdiakov's freedom to enact Ivan's teaching that all is permitted in murdering Fyodor Karamazov, freedom is understood in the sense that makes possible an individual choice to either murder or not to murder. Smerdiakov justifies his action to Ivan by reminding him of his teaching: ". . . if there's no everlasting God, there's no such thing as virtue, and there's no need of it. You were right there" (E: 599; PSS 15:67). Smerdiakov interprets Ivan's dogma "all is permitted" as universal license to do anything whatsoever, because it means that God does not exist. Likewise, when we consider Alyosha's relationship of obedience to the elder as an enactment of Zosima's teaching that the path to true freedom lies in the renunciation of self and selfish desire, we discover a freedom which makes possible a choice of a more saintly life. When Alyosha gives a final "speech at the stone" to the Ilyushechka circle of boys, he admonishes the boys to be good: "'I say this in case we become bad,' Alyosha went on, 'but there's no reason why we should become bad, is there, boys?'" (E: 734; PSS 15:196). Alyosha comprehends a freedom to go either way and advocates the right way to go. And in doing so, he concretely acts out his master's teaching.

The presentation of freedom in both cases (Smerdiakov and Alyosha) presupposes a more primordial freedom, a freedom to be this or that kind of human being. The human being is inherently a moral agent. He is responsible for all he is, not just for his action. Smerdiakov is responsible for all mankind in the sense that he has shown the world what being human can be, concretely and not just in idea. Smerdiakov is a "nihilizing" character bringing destruction not only to himself, but also to his father. The half brother's capacity to bring to nought presupposes an even more basic freedom to bring himself forward into humanity as Smerdiakov, despite his eventual suicide.

"Karamazovism" refers to a breadth of nature that the Karamazov brothers possess. As such, karamazovism encompasses both Ivan's "all is permitted" as well as Alyosha's seraphic humility. The breadth that Mitya Karamazov finds within his soul, which alarms him, makes possible that he is capable of housing the range of moral possibility that extends from the purest image of the virgin Madonna to the most perverse image of Sodom: "Yes, man is broad, too broad, indeed. I'd have him narrower" (E: 97; PSS 15:100). This breadth of nature implies a more primordial sense of freedom. In order to be holy or corrupt, a man must first of all be free to be this or that type of human being. This freedom is of a different order than the ability to choose to act in a particular manner and underlies any such choice.

Dmitri discovers his moral breadth via his hatred for his father. Seeing the old man's profile in his window, Mitya loathed him: "'I don't know, I don't know,' he had said then. 'Perhaps I shall not kill him, perhaps I shall.'" Dostoevsky inserts a line of dots to demarcate the text and then writes: "'God was watching over me then,' Mitya himself said afterwards" (E: 370; PSS 14:355). The fact that he stated his intention to see his father dead, the fact that he possessed a motive to kill him, and the fact that he found an opportune moment are accessory to the fact that he chose not to murder. Even if he lacked a conscious understanding of his choice, and attributed it to divine intervention, or to any other determining motive, he still possessed a moral choice whether to kill or not. This profound possibility is his nature.

Existential anthropology understands that our freedom to make choices, even choices between good and evil, presupposes a much more radical conception of freedom. Freedom is identified with man's ability to transcend the natural environment in the direction of various cultural worlds. Contemporary philosophical anthropology establishes that man possesses a flexible nature and not a determinate nature strictly guided by instincts. Freedom in its essential sense is dependent upon man's lack of a determinate nature. Man makes himself, but in order to make himself he must first of all possess a primordial freedom of self-definition.

The figures of Zosima and the Grand Inquisitor or the brothers Alyosha and Ivan present two differing conceptions of human freedom. Some interpreters have placed a greater emphasis on Ivan's "all is permitted" as a fundamental conception of freedom (Camus and Sartre, for example).[46] However, there is a more primordial, underlying conception of freedom which Ivan's sense of freedom implies. Sartre addresses this sense of freedom in saying that every individual step and action engages all of humanity. This is so because in acting I always choose to create a certain image of man. Consequently, I am responsible for my action in a total way:

> Notre responsabilité est beaucoup plus grande que nous ne pourrions le supposer, car elle engage l'humanité entière.[47]

This idea echoes Zosima's teaching that each human being is responsible for humanity.

Ivan's "all is permitted" is a very limited sense of freedom which is refuted by Zosima's teaching ". . . [W]hat do you see in this freedom of theirs? Nothing but slavery and self- destruction!" (E: 292; PSS 14:284). However, the sense of freedom disclosed in karamazovism underlies both Ivan's "all is permitted" as well as Zosima's "responsibility for all." This finding is in accordance with the contemporary philosophical anthropology, which sees the human being as a being without a determinate nature who must make himself to be, as a project. Each human being must concretize the humanity of man in a finite form.[48] Sartre argues this while maintaining that human freedom entails atheism:

> L'existentialisme n'est pas autre chose qu'un effort pour tirer toutes les conséquences d'une position athée cohérente.[49]

To truly understand the sense of freedom that Zosima presents renders Sartre's atheistic project unnecessary. Human freedom does not entail atheistic consequences. A fundamental conception of human freedom transcends the antinomy between theism and atheism.

Sartre defines authenticity in such a way that one cannot act freely without willing other men's freedom. Considered in this light, the Grand Inquisitor is the artistic embodiment of inauthenticity. The cardinal's patronizing contempt for man is enlarged as he demands the surrender of freedom. The human being surrenders his or her freedom gladly in an act of "bad faith," as an attempt to escape the anguish and responsibility that freedom entails:

> Si nous avons défini la situation de l'homme comme un choix libre, sans excuses et sans secours, tout homme qui se réfugie derrière l'excuse de ses passions, tout homme qui invente un déterminisme est un homme de mauvaise foi.[50]

Accordingly, religion, for Sartre as well as for Ivan Karamazov, is in bad faith. However, this conclusion is not in harmony with Zosima's teaching.

Zosima teaches authenticity as well as responsibility. He teaches human freedom and is fully aware of the anguish it brings. At the same time, Zosima teaches humility and love for all men based upon the Gospel. There is no revelation that Ivan Karamazov posses that Zosima does not comprehend. Karamazovism, rather than Ivan Karamazov's "all is permitted" encompasses Zosima's teaching about universal human responsibility as well as the Grand Inquisitor's description of human bad faith. Hence, it is to karamazovism that the philosopher ought to look to learn something essential about man. Sartre comprehends a great deal of this teaching but unnecessarily links atheism with human freedom. Essential freedom does not entail this link, either logically or morally. The French existentialist argues that man ought to respect his neighbor's freedom even if God does not exist. This is precisely what Ivan Karamazov found unthinkable. It is here that the two paths diverge.

Conclusion

The Brothers Karamazov offers a profound consideration of the philosophic meaning of freedom. There are two principal presentations of freedom in the work: Zosima, the Christian monk, who teaches that man without Christ cannot be free; and Ivan Karamazov, the intellectual atheist, ". . . a humanist who has lost his love of mankind, a seeker of Truth who no longer believes that there is a truth, a God-seeker who has lost his faith in God." Ivan is a rebel who ". . . has nothing more to lose, hence he is entirely free."[51] Ivanov identifies Ivan's Luciferian freedom with Raskolnikov's:

> The Luciferian force impels man, like the Goethean hero who calls himself a "superman" and in Heaven is named "the thrall of God," to strive by his own efforts "continually towards the same existence."[52]

Such absolute power invariably ends in total stagnation for a human being because human freedom is dependent upon God's will. Berdiaev's insightful study of Dostoevsky's literary work describes this paradox: "If all things are allowable to man, then freedom becomes its own slave, and the man who is his own slave is lost."[53] Human freedom depends upon divine freedom in order to be a true freedom. Zosima is aware of this and teaches the same.

Zosima's "love" reveals a hidden dimension which is a real possibility for man. Love is the key to understanding the problem of human freedom, not in an intellectual way, but love is a way of knowing that manifests a world that is present but hidden. We might say Zosima's epistemology is based upon a "thinking" from the heart and an understanding of the world with eyes that see with love.[54] This, then, is the humanly possible path of freedom and not the path designated by the Karamazov slogan "vse pozvoleno" ("all is permitted"). It is the poetic function of the art work which allows Dostoevsky to reveal both Ivan Karamazov's philosophy of freedom together with Zosima's without being merged into any "higher, monologic voice" as Bakhtin indicates.

At the conclusion we want to know what Dostoevsky's philosophical conception of freedom teaches us about man. We note this striking feature; his depiction of human freedom is inseparable from his depiction of man. Freedom reveals man's being. Dostoevsky nowhere introduces a "new type of man," nor does he attempt to refashion human existence. His depiction of his characters' ability to choose their own destiny reveals a more basic sense of freedom. It is this particular sense of freedom which was unique and which influenced the twentieth-century interpretation of man.

That Dostoevsky nowhere gives a definitive image of man might be taken as a sign of nihilism or atheism, this seems to be the line that Nietzsche took, that man is merely "on the way" and does not properly exist.[55] No, in remaining neutral in its saying about God, either pro or contra, the work allows us to see the human ground from which both a profound affirmation and a profound denial of God arises. This ground is man's essential freedom, this is what is characteristically human. The presentation of this sense of freedom is at the same time a radical defense of man as man and a severe critique of scientism or any other "reductionistic" anthropology.

Dostoevsky the artist reveals man in a way that neither science nor theology can accomplish. Brothers shows how two opposing conceptions of freedom (Ivan vs. Zosima) reveal a common human capacity for being either for or against the Grand Inquisitor. Ivan has become aware of his unlimited capacity for freedom. Despite its nihilistic consequence it is a definitive revelation concerning human potential for non-being. It is a revelation of the philosophical conception of human freedom. Zosima, on the other hand, reveals a primarily theological interpretation of the meaning of freedom. Somehow the reader must make sense, as does Alyosha, of both senses of freedom. This is the focal point of the novel's revelation about human freedom.

Notes

1. F. M. Dostoevsky, *The Brothers Karamazov*, Norton Critical Edition, ed. Ralph Matlaw; trans. Constance Garnett (New York: W. W. Norton and Co., 1976). "E" stands for the English language translation of this text. The Russian text consulted is drawn from the standard edition of Dostoevsky's works (*PSS*), volumes 14 and 15. Hereafter "*Brothers*" refers to the above Norton Critical Edition.

2. Robert Belknap, *The Structure of "The Brothers Karamazov"* (Evanston, Ill.: Northwestern University Press, 1967), 6.

3. "Filosofsko-publitsisticheskaia dominanta romana 'Brat'ia Karamazovy' sblizhaet ego s filosofko-publitsistecheskimi zhanrami." V. E. Vetlovskaia, *Poetika romana "Brat'ia Karamazovy"* (Leningrad: Izdatel'stvo 'Nauka', 1977), 8.

4. For "*publitsistika*" the Academy dictionary gives this definition: "Literary genre--social-political literature on contemporary, topical themes" [Literaturnyi zhanr--obshchestvenno-politicheskaia literatura na sovremennye aktual'nye temy]. *Slovar' Russkogo Iazyka ANSSSR* (Moskva: Izdatel'stvo 'Russkkii Iazyk,' 1983), 555.

5. "Mozhno dazhe skazat', kak eto ni stranno na pervyi vzgliad, chto v khudozhestvennoi sisteme mysl' tem bolee ubeditel'na, chem menee ona 'logichna'" (Vetlovskaia, 8).

6. Nathan Rosen, "Style and Structure in *The Brothers Karamazov*," in Norton Critical Edition of *The Brothers Karamazov*, 843-44.

7. From Dostoevsky's *Notebooks* translated by Ralph Matlaw. In Norton Critical Edition, *The Brothers Karamazov*, 769.

8. Gary Saul Morson, *The Boundaries of Genre: Dostoevsky's "Diary of a Writer" and the Traditions of Literary Utopia* (Evanston, Ill.: Northwestern University Press, 1981), 48.

9. Victor Terras, "Narrative Structure in *The Brothers Karamazov*," in *Critical Essays on Dostoevsky*, ed. Robin Feuer Miller (Boston: G. K. Hall and Co., 1986), 217. Terras calls the sixth book a "novella."

10. Rosen writes: "'The Russian Monk' is indeed a saint's life (*zhitie*), that is, it is not a reliable factual biography, but a sort of dramatized sermon, the most popular genre in old Russian literature" ("Style and Structure," 845). The attempt to depict moral perfection, as does Dostoevsky with Zosima, is very difficult and the limitations of a realistic novel render the task even more challenging. Cf., Sven Linner, "Portrait of a Saint: Moral Ideal and/or Psychological Truth," in *Critical Essays on Dostoevsky*, ed. R. F. Miller (Boston, Mass.: G. K. Hall and Co., 1986), 194-204.

11. Vasily Rozanov, *Dostoevsky and the "Legend" of the Grand Inquisitor*, trans. Spencer Roberts (Ithaca and London: Cornell University Press, 1972), 7.

12. "The Grand Inquisitor" has been published separately from The Brothers Karamazov. See, for example, Fyodor Dostoevsky, The Grand Inquisitor (New York: Fredrick Ungar Publishing Co., 1956).

13. Hans-Georg Gadamer, The Relevance of the Beautiful and Other Essays (Cambridge: Cambridge University Press, 1986), 27.

14. Morson, Boundaries, 31.

15. Terras, "Narrative Structure," 217.

16. Belknap, Structure, 54.

17. Ibid., 50.

18. Ibid., 52.

19. Letter no. 660 to N. A. Lyubimov, Staraya Russa, May 10, 1879. Printed in The Brothers Karamazov, Norton Critical Edition, 757.

20. Letter no. 685 to N. A. Lyubimov, Ems, Germany, August 7, 1879. Printed in Norton, 760.

21. Letter no. 664 to N. A. Lyubimov, Staraya Russa, June 11, 1879. Printed in Norton, 759.

22. V. E. Vetlovskaia, "Rhetoric and Poetics: The Affirmation and Refutation of Opinions in Dostoevsky's The Brothers Karamazov" in Critical Essays on Dostoevsky, ed. Robin Feuer Miller, (Boston: G. K. Hall and Co., 1986), 229.

23. Valery Kirpotin, Dostoevskii v shestidesiatye gody (Moskva: Khudozhestvennaia Literatura, 1966), 471. The Russian word 'tip' which means "type, model" (Oxford Russian-English Dictionary, 804) is difficult to translate into English. To translate tip as 'type' does not convey the manifold associations and significance of this expression in Dostoevsky's aesthetic theory. Perhaps it is best to translate "tip" as "literary type." Jackson devotes a chapter to "The Problem of Type" in Dostoevsky's Quest for Form (New Haven and London: Yale University Press, 1966), 92-123.

24. Kirpotin, ibid.

25. I have in mind the following works: André Gide, Dostoevsky; Albert Camus, Le mythe de Sisyphe: Essai sur l'absurde and L'homme revolté; Nicholas Berdiaev, Dostoevsky: An Interpretation, trans. Donald Attwater; Lev Shestov, Dostoevsky, Tolstoy and Nietzsche, trans. Bernard Martin. See also, "Kierkegaard and Dostoevsky," in Russian Philosophy, Volume III, and In Job's Balances, trans. Camilla Coventry and C. A. Macartney.

26. Jean-Paul Sartre, L'existentialisme est un humanisme, 36.

27. Albert Camus, "La refus du salut," in L'homme revolté, 75-82.

28. Concerning Rozanov's Dostoevsky and the Legend of the Grand Inquisitor, Seduro writes, "Rozanov's reflections on the "Legend" as a criticism of Roman Catholicism took the form of a passionate defense of Russian Orthodoxy, which had preserved the evangelical spirit of faith long since lost by the west." Vladimir Seduro, Dostoevsky in Russian Literary Criticism, 1846-1956 (New York: Columbia University Press, 1957), 50.

29. D. H. Lawrence, "The Grand Inquisitor," in The Norton Critical Edition of The Brothers Karamazov, 829-836.

30. For other studies emphasizing "The Legend of the Grand Inquisitor," see, O velikom inkvizitore: Dostoevskii i posleduiushchie (Moskva: Molodaia Gvardiia, 1991). This volume includes Dostoevsky's "Legend" and important critical essays by K. M. Leontiev, V. S. Soloviev, V. V. Rozanov, S. N. Bulgakov, N. A. Berdiaev, and S. L. Frank.

31. Berdiaev, An Interpretation, 77.

32. Ibid., 76.

33. Ibid., 88.

34. Ibid., 188.

35. V. L. Komarovich, "Mirovaia garmoniia," in O Dostoevskom: Stat'i, introd. Donald Fanger (Providence, R.I.: Brown University Press, 1966), 117-49. "Nakonets, sozdavaia samyi polnyi natsional'nyi obraz svoi, 'russkogo inoka,' Dostoevskii i ego nadelil svoim gumanicheskim idealom: o 'zemnoi radosti' propoveduet i Zosima, a o Paissi prorochestvenno ukazyvaet vdal', gde dolzhno nechto sovershit'sia, kak utverzhdenie zemnogo schast'ia chelovechestva: 'sie i budi, budi!'" (p. 148).

36. Terras, "Narrative Structure," 216.

37. For a detailed historical description of the manner in which Dostoevsky's narrative dovetailed with the reform movement and the liberation of serfs see, Joseph Frank, Dostoevsky: The Stir of Liberation, 1860-1865 (Princeton: Princeton University Press, 1986), 213-32. See also, "Leaving Prison," Part Two, Chapter 10, in The House of the Dead, trans. McDuff (London: Penguin, 1985), 352-57. That moral reformation and drawing out the image of man go hand in hand I have emphasized in Chapters 2, 3 and 4 above.

38. Two of the central documents which present Chernyshevsky's rational-utilitarian conception of man are the 'scientific' essay, "The Anthropological Principle in Philosophy," in Russian Philosophy, Volume II, ed. Edie et al. (Chicago: Quadrangle Books, 1964), 29-60. Chernyshevsky wrote a novel based upon the rational-utilitarian ideas of this essay entitled Chto delat'? [What is to be Done?] (Moskva: Moskovskii Rabochii, 1976).

39. Porfiry Petrovich refers to Rodion Raskolnikov's article "On Crime" which was published in the Periodical Leader. Cf. Crime and Punishment, trans. McDuff (London: Penguin Books, 1991), 330.

40. For a consideration of 'theodicy' see W. Windelband's A History of Philosophy (New York: Macmillan, 1919), 489-99. For the best representative of this type of writing see, Leibniz's Theodicy, ed. and trans. C. Huggard (London: Routledge and Kegan Paul, 1951). Voltaire's Candide, (London: Penguin Books, 1981) is a pointed refutation of Leibniz's idea about the "best of all possible worlds."

41. Friedrich Wilhelm Joseph von Schelling, Philosophical Investigations into the Essence of Human Freedom and Related Matters, trans. Priscilla Hayden-Roy. In Philosophy of German Idealism, Vol. 23, The German Library, ed. Ernst Baylor. (New York: Continuum Press, 1987), 273.

42. Letter no. 694, to K. P. Pobedonostsev, Ems, Germany August 24, 1879. Printed in Norton, 761-62.

43. Henri de Lubac, The Drama of Atheist Humanism (San Fransisco: Ignatius Press, 1995), 316.

44. For a book which examines Starets Amvrosy as the prototype for Zosima see, John B. Dunlop, Staretz Amvrosy: Model for Dostoevsky's Staretz Zossima (Belmont, Mass.: Nordland Publishing Co., 1972). For a book written by an Orthodox prelate which analyzes Dostoevsky's works see, Mitropolit'' Antonii, "Oproverzhenie Dostoevskim'' vozrazhenii protiv'' Evangeliia," str. 230-33 in F. M. Dostoevskii kak'' propovednik'' vozrozhdeniia (Montreal: Monastery Press, 1965).

45. V. E. Vetlovskaia, "Rhetoric and Poetics," 233.

46. See the discussion in Chapter 1 above.

47. Sartre, L'existentialisme, 32.

48. "The essence of man . . . lies in the fact that he has no choice but to force himself to know, to build a science, good or bad, in order to resolve the problem of his own being and toward this end the problem of what are the things among which he must inexorably have that being." Jose Ortega y Gassett, Man and Crisis, trans. Mildred Adams (New York: W. W. Norton and Co., 1958), 21.

49. Sartre, L'existentialisme, 77.

50. Sartre, L'existentialisme, 68.

51. Victor Terras, "The Metaphysics of the Novel-Tragedy: Dostoevsky and Viacheslav Ivanov," in Russianness: Studies of a Nation's Identity In Honor of Rufus Mathewson, 1918-1978 (Ann Arbor: Ardis, 1990), 160.

52. Viacheslav Ivanov, Freedom and The Tragic Life: A Study in Dostoevsky (New York: Noonday Press, 1960), 129.

53. Berdiaev, An Interpretation, 76.

54. Alexander Bulanov, Um i serdtse v russkoi klassike (Saratov: Izdatel'stvo Saratovskogo Universiteta, 1992).

55. For a pointed comparison between Nietzsche and Dostoevsky, see, de Lubac, 277-308.

CONCLUSION

We cannot speak of Dostoevsky's philosophy of human freedom. He was not a systematic philosopher, but a thinker [myslitel'] whose artworks say something significant about man, his freedom and their essential interpenetration. I have indicated that it is precisely this "take" on freedom which resonates with the conclusions of twentieth-century philosophical anthropologists such as Scheler, Heidegger, Sartre, Camus and Merleau-Ponty.

Each artwork was interrogated with tools in harmony with the individual poetic design at work. The works are also interpreted in light of a greater whole. Russian filmmaker Andrei Tarkovsky speaks of how the artistic image substitutes a smaller part, a detail, in order to show what is greater:

> The artistic image is always a metonym, where one thing is substituted for another, the smaller for the greater. To tell of what is living, the artist uses something dead; to speak of the infinite, he shows the finite. Substitution . . . the infinite cannot be made into matter, but it is possible to create an illusion of the infinite: the image.[1]

The metonymic function of an artistic image allows broader "wholes" to be represented by means of particular details of "parts" within a work. Further, the particular meaning of a single artwork can be taken up into a broader "nexus" in the artist's oeuvre. Accordingly we are able to gather some observations concerning Dostoevsky's conception of human being and its relation to freedom.

I have attempted to show in each novel how Dostoevsky depicts human freedom in a manner that is inseparable from his being. In Dead House, Gorianchikov describes how a prisoner overcomes one wall after another and finally arrives to the wall that he alone constructs which he cannot escape. Dostoevsky's work raises the question of whether human freedom is to be described in terms which nature dictates or rather in terms of man dictating his own nature. Gorianchikov's commentary on "terrible monsters" which includes Korenyev, the carnal bandit, A--v [Aristov], the "moral Quasimodo," or Orlov a man described in glowing terms as though he were a negative saint raises the question of a man overcoming his natural instinct with his will or vice-versa. The theme is announced--to what extent can a man overcome his human nature. This theme is played out in Underground where the question of the human "edge" is central to the Underground Man's narrative confession. In Crime and Punishment, Raskolnikov's obsessive "idea" is poised equally between an ambivalent will toward a criminal act and a will to overcome his moral finitude in toto. The duplicity of Raskolnikov's crime underscores the fundamental concern for the essence of the moral act--how it involves the entire person. Finally, Ivan Karamazov's complicity in Fyodor Karamazov's murder raises the same concern for the meaning of moral rebellion to the level of a thorough rejection of God's world.

There are several general observations which confirm Dostoevsky's image of man:

1) The first observation is that man and his freedom are related in an essential way, i.e., man cannot be man without being free. Paradoxically, the manner Dostoevsky chose to reveal this is to portray man in crisis, at the edge of his humanity while striving to surpass it (Raskolnikov, Ivan Karamazov, Orlov) or merely to incubate like the Underground Man or trying to abdicate one's will, to surrender to humility like Zosima. Each

limit case succeeds in sketching and underlining the nature of the problem which addresses the essential freedom of the character. It is specific to the presentation of each of the above-mentioned characters that freedom is a "total" problem addressing the person to the very root. The response demanded from freedom is total and though man may attempt to "trade places" and take someone else's place like Sushilov in _Dead House_, or to trade in human souls like the Grand Inquisitor, freedom is ultimately non-negotiable.

2) The second observation concerns Dostoevsky's obsession with crime, criminality, and the dark side of human nature. There is a tradition of critics who have labelled him negatively: Gorky called him a "_zloi genii_" (evil genius), Bunin referred to him as a "_zlobnyi avtor_" (malicious author), and in one of the earliest and most stinging epithets, Mikhailovsky dubbed Dostoevsky, a "_zhestokii talant_" (cruel talent). However, it is possible to account for this "negativity" in Dostoevsky's work in such a way that illuminates his conception of human freedom positively. The crisis situation, the criminal act, the threshold where man threatens to dissolve--Dostoevsky strategically exploits these episodes in order to better show the problem of human freedom. Man's relation to freedom is primarily problematic, if not negative. The greatest threat to man's freedom, as Dostoevsky's artwork shows, is man himself. The human being is all too eager to sell-out on his/her most precious asset, i.e., the freedom to be human. The meaning of human freedom is the possibility to actualize and make concrete the kind of humanity one chooses.

3) As <u>Crime</u> makes clear, man suffers his freedom. Whether victim or criminal, man is accountable for not only his action but his being. Attempts to discover a motive for the hero's crime fail for a specific reason. For even if it is poverty and the hero's environment which causes such an act, Raskolnikov is responsible in a much more profound manner for not only his action, but also his being. Raskolnikov is responsible not only for the object of his choice, but he is responsible for the very choosing itself. A close reading of the text reveals how Raskolnikov's crime cannot be disengaged from his literary presentation. He takes his fate upon himself, and the consequences follow him wherever he goes. Raskolnikov is inescapably free.

4) Human freedom opens up a space in the world where evil and the denial of God become a possibility; however, true freedom consists in seeing the world through the eyes of faith. Evdokimov explains that Dostoevsky did not seek to avoid the problem of human evil:

> Pour Dostoïevsky, ce n'est pas de la raison que relève le problème du mal. Le mal, de même que la liberté, plonge dans la profondeur non éclairée, irréductible au savoir explicite, à la connaissance analytique, et c'est dans leur coexistence incompatible que réside le tragique de l'homme.[2]

Not only should this evil not be reasoned away, but moreover, it is the gateway which reveals the problem of human freedom. The consequence of freedom and its price is the possibility of real evil and apostasy. Dostoevsky realized this and still defends man's freedom even at the cost of resistance to the "antheap," Crystal Palace, Grand Inquisitor or whatever ecclesiastical power would feign to define the parameters of an individual will, who would seduce the individual into sacrificing their inalienable duty to become ones self.

5) A final observation to be made concerning Dostoevsky and human freedom: Dostoevsky's thought concerning man and his freedom is "totalistic." It constitutes a radical approach. Ivan Karamazov, Raskolnikov, the Underground Man, and "terrible monsters" such as Orlov, present all-encompassing pictures of man. For example, the Underground Man remarks that man must hew a road wherever it may lead. There is no fixed purpose for human existence, and like the prisoners in the Dead House who toil breaking up old boats and pounding alabaster on the banks of the Irtysh, man must create his own meaning. This is a consequence of to total freedom. Man cannot look outside himself to find a "boss" to allocate him meaningful projects. Such presentation of total freedom is made possible by the "artistic system" which the medium of philosophy and the sciences cannot render.

Although there is no direct evidence that Dostoevsky read Schelling's 1809 Treatise, he certainly demonstrates a familiarity with this dilemma between freedom and evil. It is fairly certain that Dostoevsky was familiar with Schelling's thought and that he studied a course in philosophy at boarding school with Professor I. I. Davidov, who was a disciple of Schelling.[3] Further, it should be mentioned that Dostoevsky came into contact with Schelling's philosophical system through his mentor, Belinsky, who in turn was tutored by Stankevich.[4]

Schelling had outlined the philosophical contours of this problem in his 1809 treatise. Concerning the problem of the coexistence of actual evil within the infinite substance he writes:

> . . . for either actual evil is allowed, so that evil is unavoidably placed within infinite substance or within the original will itself, whereby the concept of a supremely perfect being is utterly destroyed; or the reality of evil must somehow be denied, whereby the concept of freedom disappears at the same time.[5]

Schelling admirably summarizes the philosophical consequences of this dilemma. If evil is said to be, then it must reside in coexistence with the "supremely perfect being" which undermines this being's supreme perfection. On the other hand, if evil is denied (à la Leibniz's Theodicy) then human freedom is likewise undermined.

For Berdiaev, Dostoevsky did not think through the implications of his theodicy along the same lines as Schelling. It is characteristic of a German philosopher to frame the problem on another level:

> . . . the Slav or Russian genius differs in its notion of the ultimates of being from the Germanic as it is expressed in the idealist philosophy. The German tends to see the conflict between God and Satan, light and darkness, only on the superficial plane, at the periphery of the spirit; when he goes below he finds God, light: all antinomy disappears. But for the Russian Dostoievsky it is the other way around; evil also has a spiritual nature, and the battle between the divine and hellish elements is carried on deep down in the spirit of man: he finds the antagonism of the two principles in the very essence of being and not in the psychic domain where it may be seen by all.[6]

When considering the essential nature of evil and its coexistence with human freedom, the "Germanic" philosophy would tend to dismiss or explain away the ultimate ground of evil within being. For example, Schelling's "system" finds no original opposition between evil and good: "There is duality where two essences actually oppose each other. Evil, however, is not a being, but a non-essence which is a reality only in opposition, but not in itself."[7] The capacity of Schelling's system to think through and reason concerning the problem of evil in its ontological sense is the provenance and power of philosophy. It is the power of the artist to poetically think through this matter and present an artistic solution which is by no means reducible to a "systematic" philosophical discourse.

Taking The Brothers Karamazov as an example, it is clear that this inability to resolve the problem of the theodicy in a philosophical manner appears to be at the basis of Ivan Karamazov's rebellion. Zosima understood this and warned him concerning the question concerning the coexistence of virtue and immortality. Ivan concluded that there can be no virtue if there is no immortality: "If it can't be decided in the affirmative, it will never be decided in the negative. You know that that is the peculiarity of your heart, and all its suffering is due to it."[8] Zosima correctly identifies this "logic" to be at the center of Ivan's thought. Ivan strives for a purity so pure that he can neither believe in nor live up to.

Dostoevsky's thought does not force that one view of human freedom be taken over the other. He does not give a definitive image of man, but in allowing both views (pro and contra) to be taken, Brothers allows us to see the fundamental ground upon which either an affirmation or a denial of God must be made. This ground is inseparable from human freedom, it is the very foundation of it. Presenting freedom in this manner defends man from a dissolution into an either theological or scientistic anthropology.

Just as the Dostoevsky novel makes possible unfinalizable voices, philosophy is, to that extent, incapable of "saying" what this artwork says poetically. It is for this reason that there is a discrepancy between Schelling's System and Dostoevsky's The Brothers Karamazov--it is an essential difference. For this same reason Dostoevsky has not been fully understood in twentieth-century philosophy, and in particular, existentialist philosophy. The imprint of Dostoevsky's conception of man in the twentieth century is enormous, particularly in the philosophy of freedom and in the manner that Dostoevsky's work frames the insoluble paradox between freedom and necessity. His novels to a great extent formed and left a mark upon this particular set of philosophical problems which had been the staple diet of philosophers since antiquity. But more than any set of definitions or ideas, it was the particular angle that Dostoevsky took, his intensity and the light he cast onto these problems which was to carry over into the existentialist conception of man.

Sartre has written that existentialism begins with Ivan Karamazov's "all is permitted." While it is true that this conception of maximal freedom is distinctive to the existentialist conception of man, Sartre's saying does not comprehend the full extent of Dostoevsky's saying about man. That man is one with his freedom, that freedom is his inalienable duty, that man must become himself, that man strives to overcome himself and exceed his freedom but in doing so invariably loses his freedom, and that man can exceed himself only in the sense that he realizes an ideal human possibility; these are the contributions that Dostoevsky makes to a philosophical conception of man. These revelations are not particular and detailed, but are the essential, underlying ideas which prevail upon those philosophers who attempt to think about man in a foundational way. It is better to say that the Dostoevskian man reveals not only the absence of human nature but also the enormous power which man possesses for achieving the ideal human possibility.

For this reason, Dostoevsky's works will continue to make a significant contribution to any thoughtful discussion about man and his freedom.

BIBLIOGRAPHY

Akademii Nauk SSSR Institut Russkogo Iazyka. Slovar' russkogo iazyka v chetyrekh tomakh. Moskva: Izdatel'stvo Ruskii Iazyk, 1981.

Allain, Louis. Dostoïevski et l'Autre. Bibliothèque russe de l'Institut d'Études Slaves, Tome 70. Lille: Presses Universitaires de Lille, 1984.

Anderson, Roger B. Dostoevsky: Myths of Duality. Gainesville, Fla.: University of Florida Press, 1986.

_____. "Notes from the Underground: The Arrest of Personal Development." Canadian American Slavic Studies 24, no. 4 (1990): 413-30.

Aquinas, St. Thomas. Introduction to St. Thomas Aquinas. Edited by Anton Pegis. New York: The Modern Library, 1948.

Aristotle. Metaphysics. Translated by Christopher Kirwan. Oxford: Clarendon Press, 1971.

_____. On Interpretation; Commentary by St. Thomas Aquinas and Cajetan. Translated by Jean T. Oesterle. Milwaukee, Wis.: Marquette University Press, 1962.

_____. On Poetry and Style. Translated by Grube. Indianapolis: Bobbs-Merrill, 1958.

Augustini, Aurelii. De Vera Religione, Liber Unus. In SanctiAurelii Augustini De Doctrina Christiana et De Vera Religione. Edited by K.-D. Daur. Turnholti: Typographi Brepols Editores Pontifici, 1962.

Bagby, Lewis. "Dostoevsky's Notes from a Dead House: The Poetics of the Introductory Paragraph." The Modern Language Review 81, no. 1 (1986): 139-52.

_____. "On Dostoevsky's Conversion: The Introduction to Notesfrom a Dead House." Symposium 39, no. 1 (Spring 1985): 3-18.

Bakhtin, Mikhail. Problems of Dostoevsky's Poetics. Edited and translated by Caryl Emerson. Minneapolis: University of Minnesota Press, 1989.

Beardsley, Monroe C. Aesthetics: Problems in the Philosophy ofCriticism. New York and Burlingame: Harcourt, Brace and World Inc., 1958.

_____. "Dostoyevsky's Metaphor of the 'Underground.'" In Fyodor Dostoevsky, Notes from the Underground, 229-60. Edited by Robert Durgy. New York: Thomas Crowell, 1969.

Beebe, M. "The Three Motives of Raskolnikov. A Reinterpretation of Crime and Punishment." College English 17 (December 1995): 151-58.

Beebee, Thomas O. The Ideology of Genre: A Comparative Study ofGeneric Instability. University Park, Pa.: The Pennsylvania State University Press, 1994.

Behrendt, Patricia Flanagan. "The Russian Iconic Representation of the Christian Madonna: A Feminine Archetype in Notes from the Underground." In Dostoevski and the Human Condition After a Century, 133-43. Edited by A. Ugrinsky, Frank Lambasa, and Vakuha Ozolins. New York: Greenwood Press, 1986.

Belknap, Robert L. "Memory in The Brothers Karamazov." In Dostoevsky: New Perspectives, 227-42. Edited by Robert L. Jackson. Englewood Cliffs, N.J.: Prentice-Hall, Inc., 1984.

_____. The Structure of The Brothers Karamazov. Evanston, Ill.: Northwestern University Press, 1989.

_____. "The Unrepentant Confession." In Russianness: Studies on a Nation's Identity in Honor of Rufus Mathewson, 1918-1978, 113-23. Edited by Robert L. Belknap. Ann Arbor: Ardis, 1990.

Belopolsky, V. N. "Dostoevskii i Shchelling." In Dostoevskii Materialy i Issledovaniia t. VIII, 39-51. Leningrad: Nauka, 1988.

Berdyaev, Nicholas. Dostoievsky: An Interpretation. Translated by Donald Attwater. New York: Sheed and Ward Inc., 1934.

_____. The Russian Idea. London: Lindisfarne Press, 1992.

Bethea, David. "On the Shape of the Apocalypse in Modern Russian Fiction: Towards a Typology." In Russian Literature before 1917, 176-95. Edited by Clayton. Columbus, Ohio: Slavica, 1989.

Bitov, Andrei. "Novyi Robinzon: k 125-letiiu vykhoda v svet 'Zapisok iz mertvogo doma.'" Znamia 12 (December 1987): 221-27.

Blackmur, R. P. "The Brothers Karamazov: The Grand Inquisitor and The Wine of Gladness." In Critical Essays on Dostoevsky, 205-15. Edited by Robin Feuer Miller. Boston: G. K. Hall and Co., 1986.

_____. "The Brothers Karamazov: The Peasants Stand Firm and the Tragedy of the Saint." In The Brothers Karamazov, 870-86. Norton Critical Edition, edited by Ralph Matlaw. New York: Norton and Co., 1976.

Bleicher, Josef. Contemporary Hermeneutics. London and New York: Routledge and Kegan Paul, 1980.

Boeckh, August. On Interpretation and Criticism. Edited and translated by John Paul Pritchard. Norman, Okla.: University of Oklahoma Press, 1968.

Bograd, G. L. et al. Literaturno-Memorial'ni Muzei F. M. Dostoevskogo. Leningrad: Lenizdat, 1981.

Breisach, Ernst. Introduction to Modern Existentialism. New York: Grove Press, Inc. 1962.

Brown, Edward J. Stankevich and His Moscow Circle 1830-1840. Stanford, Calif.: Stanford University Press, 1966.

Bulanov, Aleksandr. Um i serdtse v russkoi klassike. Saratov: Izdatel'stvo Saratovskogo Universiteta, 1992.

Burnett, Leon. "Dostoevsky, Poe and the Discovery of Fantastic Realism." In F. M. Dostoevsky (1821-1881): A Centenary Collection, 58-86. Edited by Leon Burnett. University of Essex, 1981.

Busch, R. L. Humor in the Major Novels of F. M. Dostoevsky. Columbus, Ohio: Slavica, 1987.

Butcher, S. H. Aristotle's Theory of Poetry and Fine Art. New York: Dover Publications Inc., 1951.

Camus, Albert. La Chute. Paris: Gallimard, 1956.

_____. L'Étranger. Edited by Germaine Brée and Carlos Lynes, Jr. Englewood Cliffs, N.J.: Prentice-Hall, Inc., 1955.

_____. L'Homme revolté. Paris: Gallimard, 1951.

_____. Lettres à un ami allemand. Paris: Gallimard, 1942.

_____. Le malentendu suivi de Caligula. Paris: Gallimard, 1958.

_____. The Myth of Sisyphus. Translated by Justin O'Brien. Alfred A. Knopf, 1955.

_____. Le mythe de Sisyphe: Essai sur L'absurde. Paris: Gallimard, 1942.

_____. "The Other Russia," in The New York Herald Tribune, December 19, 1957.

_____. Les possédés, piece en trois parties adaptée du roman deDostoïevski. Paris: Gallimard, 1959.

Carr, Edward Hallett. Dostoevsky (1821-1881): A New Biography. Boston and New York: Houghton Mifflin Company, 1931.

Casañas, M. "L'anthropologie de Dostoïevski et le problème de le fin de l'humanisme d'après Berdiaev." In Études d'Anthropologie Philosophique, 207-20. Edited by G. Florival. Louvain-La Neuve: Editions de l'Institut Superieur de Philosophie, 1984.

Catteau, Jacques. "De la structure de La maison des morts de F. M. Dostoevskij." Revue des etudes slaves 54 (1982): 63-72.

_____. La création littéraire chez Dostoïevski. Paris: Institut D'Études Slaves, 1978.

_____. "The Paradox of the Legend of the Grand Inquisitor in The Brothers Karamazov." In Dostoevsky: New Perspectives, 243-54. Edited by Robert L. Jackson. Englewood Cliffs, N.J.: Prentice-Hall Inc., 1984.

Chances, Ellen. "Pochvennichestvo--Evolution of an Ideology." Modern Fiction Studies (Spring 1974-Winter 1975): 543-51.

_____. "Pochvennichestov: Ideology in Dostoevsky's Periodicals." Mosaic 7, no. 2 (Winter 1974): 77-88.

Chernyshevsky, Nikolai. Chto delat'? iz rasskazov o novykh liudiakh. Moskva: Pravda, 1976.

Chizh, Vladimir. Dostoevskii kak psikhopatolog. Moskva: V Universitetskoi Tipografii, 1885.

Chulkov, Georgi. Kak rabotal Dostoevskii? Moscow, 1939.

Copeau, Jacques. "Sur le Dostoïevski de Suares." In La Nouvelle Revue Française (February 1912): 226-41.

Copleston, Frederick Charles. A History of Philosophy. Westminster, Md.: Newman Press, 1950.

_____. Philosophy in Russia From Herzen to Lenin and Berdyaev. Search Press: University of Notre Dame, 1986.

Cornford, Francis Macdonald. Before and After Socrates. Cambridge, 1976.

_____. From Religion to Philosophy. New York: Harper and Bros., 1957.

Cox, Gary. "Treugol'nik muzhskoi zavisimosti i treugol'nik spaseniia v prestuplenie i nakazanii Dostoevskogo: k teorii modernistskoi formy." In Dostoevsky and the Twentieth Century: The Ljubljana Papers, 175-82. Edited by Malcolm V. Jones. Nottingham: Astra Press, 1993.

_____. Tyrant and Victim in Dostoevsky. Columbus, Ohio: Slavica, 1983.

Dal', Vladimir. Tolkovyi slovar' zhivogo velikorusskogo iazyka, 4 Tom., Moskva: Russkii Iazyk, 1981 (originally published 1882).

Danto, Arthur C. The Philosophical Disenfranchisement of Art. New York: Columbia University Press, 1986.

Darnton, Robert. The Great Cat Massacre and Other Episodes in French Cultural History. New York: Basic Books, Inc., Publishers, 1984.

de Jonge, Alex. Dostoevsky and The Age of Intensity. New York: St. Martin's Press, 1975.

della Mirandola, Giovani Pico. On the Dignity of Man, On Beingand the One and Heptaplus. Translated by Charles Wallis, Paul Miller, and Douglas Carmichael. Indianapolis: The Library of Liberal Arts, 1965.

de Lubac, Henri. Le drâme de l'humanisme athée. Paris: Spes, 1945.

_____. The Drama of Atheist Humanism. Translated by Riley, Nash and Sebane. San Francisco: Ignatius Press, 1995.

Dhavamony, M. "Truth in Art According To Aquinas." Proceedingsof The Fifth International Congress of Aesthetics, 287-91. The Hague: Mouton, 1968.

Dolnikowski, George. This I Remember: From War to Peace. Elgin, Ill.: Brethren Press, 1994.

Dostoevsky, F. M. The Brothers Karamazov. Norton Critical Edition, edited by Ralph Matlaw. New York: Norton and Co., 1976.

_____. Crime and Punishment. Translated by David McDuff. London: Penguin Books, 1991.

_____. Demons. Translated by Richard Pevear and Larissa Volkhonsky. New York: Vintage Classics, 1994.

_____. The Diary of a Writer. Volumes 1 and 2. Edited and translated by Boris Brasol. New York: Charles Scribner's and Sons, 1949.

_____. The House of the Dead. Translated by David McDuff. London: Penguin Books, 1985.

_____. The Idiot. Translated by Constance Garnett. New York: The Modern Library, 1935.

_____. The Notebooks for The Brothers Karamazov. Edited and translated by Edward Wasiolek. Chicago: The University of Chicago Press, 1971.

_____. The Notebooks for Crime and Punishment. Edited and translated by Edward Wasiolek. Chicago: University of Chicago Press, 1967.

_____. Notes from the Underground. Edited by Robert Durgy; translated by S. Shishkoff. New York: Thomas Crowell, 1969.

_____. Polnoe sobranie sochinenii v tridtsati tomakh. Edited by V. G. Bazanov et al. Leningrad: Nauka, 1972-1988.

_____. Poor Folk. Translated with Introduction by Robert Dessaix. Ann Arbor, Mich.: Ardis, 1982.

_____. Selected Letters of Fyodor Dostoevsky. Edited by Joseph Frank and David I. Goldstein; translated by Andrew MacAndrew. New Brunswick: Rutgers University Press, 1987.

_____. The Village of Stephanchikovo and Its Inhabitants, Fromthe Notes of an Unknown. Translated by Ignat Avsey. Ithaca, N.Y.: Cornell University Press, 1987.

Dowler, Wayne. Dostoevsky, Grigor'ev and Native Soil Conservatism. Toronto: University of Toronto Press, 1982.

Dubrovin, M. A Book of English and Russian Proverbs and Sayings. Moscow: Prosveshcheniye, 1993.

Dunlop, John B. Staretz Amvrosy: Model for Dostoevsky's StaretzZossima. Belmont, Mass.: Nordland Publishing Co., 1972.

Edie, Scanlan, Zeldin, and Kline, eds. Russian Philosophy. (3 vols.) Chicago: Quadrangle Books, 1965.

Edwards, Paul, ed. The Encyclopedia of Philosophy. New York: Macmillan, 1967).

Engelberg, Edward. "The Underground Man and Hegel's 'Unhappy Consciousness' and 'The Beautiful Soul.'" In The Unknown Distance: From Consciousness to Conscience, Goethe to Camus, 89-110. Cambridge, Mass.: Harvard University Press, 1972.

Esslin, Martin. The Theatre of the Absurd. Garden City, N.Y.: Anchor Books, 1969.

Evdokimov, Paul. Dostoïevsky et le problème du mal. Paris: Desclée de Brouwer, 1978.

Fabro, Cornelio. God in Exile: Modern Atheism, A Study of theInternal Dynamic of Modern Atheism from its Roots in the Cartesian Cogito to the Present Day. Edited and translated Arthur Gibson. New York: Newman Press, 1968.

Fasmer, M. Etimologicheskii slovar' russkogo iazyka. 4 Tomakh. Moskva: Izdatel'stvo "Progress," 1964.

Flath, Carol A. "Fear of Faith: The Hidden Religious Message of Notes from the Underground." Slavic and East European Journal 37, no. 4 (Winter 1993): 510-29.

Foucault, Michel. Madness and Civilization: A History of Insanity in the Age of Reason. Translated by Richard Howard. London: Tavistock/Routledge (reprint), 1989.

Frank, Joseph. Dostoevsky: The Miraculous Years 1865-1871. Princeton: Princeton University Press, 1995.

_____. Dostoevsky: The Stir of Liberation, 1860-1865. Princeton: Princeton University Press, 1986.

_____. Dostoevsky: The Years of Ordeal 1850-1859. Princeton: Princeton University Press, 1983.

_____. "The Genesis of Crime and Punishment." In Russianness:Studies on a Nation's Identity, pp. 124-43. Ann Arbor: Ardis, 1990.

_____. "The Making of Crime and Punishment." In Critical Reconstructions: The Relationship of Fiction and Life,

168-86. Edited by Robert M. Polhemus and Roger B. Henkle. Stanford: Stanford University Press, 1994.

_____. "Nihilism and Notes from the Underground." In Notes from the Underground, 149-81. Edited by Robert Durgy. New York: Thomas Crowell, 1969.

_____. "The World of Raskolnikov." In Crime and Punishment, 560-71. Norton Critical Edition, edited by George Gibian. New York: Norton, 1975.

Frankl, Viktor. Man's Search for Meaning. New York: Simon and Shuster, 1963.

Freud, Sigmund. "Dostoevsky and Parricide." In Collected Works,XXI. London: 1961.

_____. A General Introduction to Psychoanalysis. Translated by Joan Riviere. Garden City, N.Y.: Garden City Publishing, 1938.

Gadamer, Hans-Georg. Truth and Method. New York: Crossroad, 1982.

Gide, André. Les caves du vatican. New York: Vintage Books, 1960.

_____. Dostoevsky. Translated by Arnold Bennett. New York: New Directions, 1961.

_____. Dostoïevski: Articles et causeries. Paris: Gallimard, 1964.

_____. Les faux monnayeurs. New York: Alfred A. Knopf, Inc., 1951.

_____. Madeleine (Et Nunc Manet In Te). Translated by Justin O'Brien. New York: Alfred Knopf, 1952.

_____. Numquid et tu? Journal, 1942-1949. Paris: Gallimard, 1950.

_____. Oeuvres complètes d'André Gide. Paris: Nouvelle Revue Française, 1932-1939.

_____. Romans: Récits et soties, oeuvres lyriques. Paris: Bibliothèque de la Pléiade, 1958.

Golosovker, Ya. "The Words 'Secret' and 'Mystery.'" In TheBrothers Karamazov, 857-61. Norton Critical Edition, edited by Ralph Matlaw. New York: Norton and Co., 1976.

Green, Garrett. A Kingdom Not of This World: A Quest for a Christian Ethic of Revolution With Reference to the Thought of Dostoyevsky, Berdyaev and Camus. Stanford: Stanford Honors Essays in Humanities Number VIII, 1964.

Grossman, Leonid. "Dostoevsky as Artist." In The Brothers Karamazov, 852-57. Norton Critical Edition, edited by Ralph Matlaw. New York: Norton and Co., 1976.

Guardini, Romano. L'Univers religieux de Dostoïevski. Traduit par H. Engelmann et R. Givord. Paris: Le Seuil, 1947.

Hakim, Albert. Historical Introduction to Philosophy. New York: Macmillan, 1987.

Heidegger, Martin. Basic Writings. Translated by David Farrell Krell. London and Henley: Routledge and Kegan Paul, 1993.

_____. "In Memoriam: Max Scheler (1928)," in The MetaphysicalFoundations of Logic. Translated by Michael Heim. Bloomington, Ind.: Indiana University Press, 1984.

_____. On the Way to Language. Translated by Peter D. Hertz. New York: Harper and Row, 1971.

_____. "The Origin of The Work of Art." In Basic Writings. Translated by David Farrell Krell. London and Henley: Routledge and Kegan Paul, 1993.

Hesse, Hermann. In Sight of Chaos. Translated by Stephen Hudson. Zurich: Verlag Seldwyla, 1923.

Hirsch, E. D. Validity in Interpretation. New Haven: Yale University Press, 1965.

Hospers, John. "Implied Truths in Literature." In PhilosophyLooks at the Arts, 199-214. Edited by J. Margolis. New York: Charles Scribner and Sons, 1962.

Howard, Barbara F. "The Rhetoric of Confession: Dostoevskij's Notes from the Underground and Rousseau's Confessions." Slavic and East European Journal 25, no. 4 (Winter 1981): 16, 32.

Hubben, William. Dostoevsky, Kierkegaard, Nietzsche and Kafka: Four Prophets of Our Destiny. New York: Collier Books, 1952.

Hyde, G. M. "T. S. Eliot's Crime and Punishment." In F. M.Dostoevsky (1821-1881): A Centenary Collection, 87-96. Edited by Leon Burnett. University of Essex, 1981.

Ivanov, Viacheslav. Freedom and the Tragic Life: A Study in Dostoevsky. Translated by Norman Cameron. New York: Farrar, Straus and Cudahy, 1960.

Jackson, Robert Louis. The Art of Dostoevsky: Deliriums and Nocturnes. Princeton: Princeton University Press, 1981.

_____. Dialogues with Dostoevsky: The Overwhelming Questions. Stanford, Calif.: Stanford University Press, 1993.

_____. Dostoevsky's Quest for Form A Study of His Philosophy ofArt. New Haven, Conn.: Yale University Press, 1966.

_____. Dostoevsky's Underground Man in Russian Literature. 'S-Gravenhage: Mouton and Co., 1958.

_____. "Early Shakespeare and the Late Dostoevsky: Two Ivans." In Dostoevskij und die Literatur, 21-29. Edited by Herausgegeben von Hans Rothe. Wien: Bohlau Verlag Koln, 1983.

_____. "The Narrator in Dostoevsky's Notes from the House of the Dead." In Studies in Russian and Polish Literature, 37. Mouton: 'S-Gravenhage, 1962.

Jaroszewski et al. Anthropologie Philosophique de Fedor Dostoievski. Warsaw: Polska Akademii Nauk, 1981.

Jaroszewski, Tadeusz M. "La phénoménologie de la liberté chez Dostoïewski." In Humanitas VII: Anthropologie philosophique de Fëdor Dostoïevski, 7-17. Wroclaw: Polska Akademia Nauk, 1981.

Johnson, Leslie A. The Experience of Time in Crime and Punishment. Columbus, Ohio: Slavica, 1984.

Jones, Malcolm. Dostoevsky After Bakhtin: Readings in Dostoevsky's Fantastic Realism. Cambridge: Cambridge University Press, 1990.

_____. Dostoyevsky: The Novel of Discord. London: Paul Elek, 1976.

Kant, Immanuel. Analytic of the Beautiful, from the Critique ofJudgement, With Excerpts from Anthropology from a Pragmatic Viewpoint, Second Book. Translated by Walter Cerf. Indianapolis: Bobbs-Merrill, 1963.

_____. The Critique of Pure Reason. New York: St. Martin's Press, 1968.

_____. Education. Translated by Annette Churton. Ann Arbor Paperbacks: University of Michigan Press, 1991.

Karlova, T. S. "O strukturnom znachenii obraza 'Mertvogo doma.'" In Dostoevskii: Materialy i issledovaniia, Tom. I, 135-46. Edited by G. Fridlender. Moscow: Nauka, 1974.

Kaufmann, Walter. Existentialism from Dostoevsky to Sartre. New York: Meridian Book, 1975.

Kirk, Irina. Dostoevskij and Camus: The Themes of Consciousness, Isolation, Freedom and Love. München: Wilhelm Fink Verlag, 1974.

Kirpotin, Valeri. Dostoevskii v shestidesiatye gody. Moscow: Izdatel'stvo 'Khudozhestvennaia Literatura', 1966.

_____. Razocharovanie i krushchenie Rodiona Raskolnikova. Moscow: Khudozhestvennaia Literatura, 1986.

Knapp, Shoshana M. "The Dynamics of the Idea of Napoleon in Crime and Punishment." In Dostoevski and The Human Condition After A Century, 31-41. Edited by Ugrinsky, Lambasa and Ozolins. Westport, Conn.: Greenwood Press, 1986.

Kockelmans, Joseph J. Heidegger on Art and Artworks. Dordrecht: Martinus Nijhoff, 1985.

_____. Heidegger's "Being and Time": The Analytic of Dasein asFundamental Ontology. Washington, D.C.: Center for Advanced Research in Phenomenology and University Press of America, 1989.

_____. "Reflections on the 'Foundations' of Psychology and Psychoanalysis." In From Phenomenology to Thought, Errancy and Desire, 527-45. Edited by B. E. Babich. Dordrecht: Kluwer Academic Publishers, 1995.

_____. "Unity and Multiplicity in the Sciences According to Hermeneutic Phenomenology." In Being Human in the Ultimate: Studies in the Thought of John M. Anderson, 259-89. Edited by Georgopoulos and Heim. Atlanta, Ga.: Rodopi, 1995.

Komarovich, V. L. "Iunost' Dostoevskogo." In O Dostoevskom: Stat'i, 73-115. Edited by Donald Fanger. Providence, R.I.: Brown University Press, 1966.

____. "Mirovaia Garmoniia Dostoevskogo." In O Dostoevskom: Stat'i, 117-49. Edited by Donald Fanger. Providence, R.I.: Brown University Press, 1966.

Kovsan, M. L. "'Prestuplenie i Nakazanie': 'Vse' i 'On'." In Dostoevskii: Materialy i Issledovaniia, 72-96. Leningrad: Akademiia Nauk SSSR, 1974.

Kravchenko, Maria. Dostoevsky and the Psychologists. Amsterdam: Verlag Adolf M. Hakkert, 1978.

Kristeller, Paul Oskar. Eight Philosophers of the Late Renaissance. Stanford, Calif.: Stanford University Press, 1964.

Kuvakin, Valerie, ed. A History of Russian Philosophy From theTenth through the Twentieth Centuries, Volume II. Buffalo, N.Y.: Prometheus Books, 1994.

Lambropoulos and Miller, eds. Twentieth Century Literary Theory. Albany, N.Y.: State University of New York Press, 1986.

Landmann, Michael. Fundamental Anthropology. Washington, D.C.: Center for Advanced Research in Phenomenology and University Press of America, 1985.

Lauth, Reinhard. Die Philosophie Dostojewskis. München: Piper, 1950.

_____. Dostoejewski und sein Jahrhundert. Bonn: Bouvier, 1986.

Lavrin, Janko. An Introduction to the Russian Novel. London: Methuen and Co. Ltd., 1942.

Lawrence, D. H. "The Grand Inquisitor." In D. H. Lawrence,Selected Literary Criticism, 233-41. Edited by Anthony Beal. New York: Viking, 1961.

_____. "Preface to Dostoevsky's 'The Grand Inquisitor.'" In Dostoevsky: A Collection of Critical Essays, 90-97. Edited by Rene Wellek. Englewood Cliffs, N.J.: Prentice-Hall Inc., 1962.

Leibniz, Gottfried Wilhelm. Theodicy: Essays on the Goodness ofGod, the Freedom of Man and the Origin of Evil. Edited and translated by C. Huggard. London: Routledge and Kegan Paul, 1951.

Lethcoe, James. "Self-Deception in Dostoevskij's Notes from theUnderground." Slavic and East European Journal 10 (1966): 10-11.

Lindenmeyr, Adele. "Raskolnikov's City and the Napoleonic Plan." In Dostoevsky: New Perspectives, 99-110. Edited by Robert Louis Jackson. Englewood Cliffs, N.J.: Prentice-Hall, Inc., 1984.

Lossky, N. O. Bog i mirovoe zlo. Moscow: Izdatel'stvo Respublika, 1994.

_____. Dostoeyevsky i ego christianskoe miroponimanie. Moskva: Respublik, 1994.

_____. History of Russian Philosophy. New York: International Universities Press, Inc, 1951.

Luijpen, Wm. A. Phenomenology and Atheism. Pittsburgh: Duquesne University Press, 1964.

Madaule, Jacques. Dostoïevski. Paris: Editions Universitaires, 1956.

Mann, Jesse and Gerald Kreyche, eds. Reflections on Man. New York: Harcourt, Brace and World, 1966.

Margolis, J., ed. Philosophy Looks at the Arts. New York: Charles Scribner and Sons, 1962.

Masaryk, Thomas Garrigue. The Spirit of Russia, Volume III. New York: Barnes and Noble Inc., 1967.

Maslow, Vera. "Heidegger and Ortega On Truth In Poetry and Art." In Proceedings of The Fifth International Congress of Aesthetics, 298-302. Mouton, 1968.

Matlaw, Ralph E. "Myth and Symbol." In The Brothers Karamazov, 861-70. Norton Critical Edition, edited by Ralph Matlaw. New York: Norton and Co., 1976.

_____. "Recurrent Imagery in Dostoevskij." Harvard Slavic Studies 3 (1957): 201-24.

_____. "Structure and Integration in Notes from the Underground." In The Crowell Critical Library Edition of Fyodor Dostoevsky's "Notes from the Underground," 181-203. Edited by Robert Durgy; translated by Serge Shishkoff. New York: Thomas Y. Crowell Co., 1969.

McLean, Hugh. "Walls and Wire: Notes on the Prison Theme in Russian Literature." International Journal of Slavic Linguistics and Poetics. Columbus, Ohio, 1982.

Meerson, Olga. "Old Testament Lamentation in the Underground Man's Monologue: A Refutation of the Existentialist Reading of the Notes from the Underground." Slavic and East European Journal 36, no. 3 (Fall 1992): 317-22.

Meier, J. M. "Situation Rhyme in a Novel of Dostoevsky." DutchContributions to the IVth International Contress of Slavists, 115-29. The Hague: Mouton, 1958.

Merleau-Ponty, Maurice. Sense and Non-sense. Translated by Hubert and Patricia Dreyfus. Evanston, Ill.: Northwestern University Press, 1964.

Meyer, Priscilla and Stephen Rudy, eds. Dostoevsky and Gogol. Ann Arbor: Ardis, 1979.

Miller, Robin Feuer, ed. Critical Essays on Dostoevsky, Boston: G. K. Hall and Co., 1986.

_____. The Brothers Karamazov; Worlds of the Novel. New York: Twayne Publishers, 1992.

_____. "Dostoevsky and Rousseau: The Morality of Confession Reconsidered." In Dostoevsky: New Perspectives, edited by Robert Lewis Jackson, 82-98. Englewood Cliffs, N.J.: Prentice-Hall, 1984.

Mirsky, D. S. A History of Russian Literature. Edited by Francis Whitfield. New York: Alfred A. Knopf, 1969.

Mochulsky, Konstantin. "The Brothers Karamazov." In The Brothers Karamazov, 776-93. Norton Critical Edition, edited by Ralph Matlaw. New York: Norton and Co., 1976.

_____. Dostoevskii: zhizn i tvorchestvo. Paris: 1947.

_____. Dostoevsky: His Life and Work. Translated by Michael A. Minihan. Princeton: Princeton University Press, 1967.

_____. "Notes from the Underground." In The Crowell CriticalLibrary Edition of Fyodor Dostoevsky's "Notes from the Underground," 129-49. Edited by Robert Durgy and translated by Serge Shishkoff. New York: Thomas Y. Crowell Co., 1969.

Montaigne, Michel de. Les Essais. Paris: Presses Universitaires de France, 1965.

Morson, Gary Saul. The Boundaries of Genre: Dostoevsky's "Diaryof a Writer" and the Traditions of Literary Utopia. Evanston, Ill.: Northwestern University Press, 1981.

_____. Narrative and Freedom: The Shadows of Time. New Haven: Yale University Press, 1994.

_____. "Verbal Pollution in The Brothers Karamazov." In Critical Essays on Dostoevsky, 234-42. Edited by Robin Feuer Miller. Boston: G. K. Hall and Co., 1986.

Mortimer, R. "Dostoevsky and the Dream." Modern Philology 54, no. 2 (November 1956): 106, 110.

Mounier, Emmanuel. Introduction aux existentialismes. Paris: Editions Denoël, 1947.

Muchnic, Helen. Dostoevsky's English Reputation, 1888-1936. New York: Octagon Books, 1969.

Muller-Lauter, Wolfgang. Dostoevskijs Ideendialektik. Berlin: de Gruter, 1974.

Murav, Harriet. "The Discourse of Iurodstvo and the Discourse of Psychology in Crime and Punishment." In Issues in Russian Literature Before 1917, 162-75. Edited by J. Douglas Clayton. Columbus, Ohio: Slavica, 1989.

_____. "Dostoevskii in Siberia: Remembering the Past." SlavicReview 50, no. 4 (Winter 1991): 858-66.

_____. Holy Foolishness: Dostoevsky's Novels and the Poetics ofCultural Critique. Stanford: Stanford University Press, 1992.

Murdoch, Iris. The Fire and The Sun: Why Plato Banished theArtists. Oxford: Clarendon Press, 1977.

Murry, J. Middleton. Fyodor Dostoevsky: A Critical Study. New York: Russell and Russell, 1924.

Mysliakov, V. A. "Kak Rasskazana 'Istoria' Rodiona Raskolnikova." In Dostoevskii: Materialy i Issledovaniia t.1, 147-63. Leningrad: Akademia Nauk SSSR, 1974.

Nietzsche, Friedrich. Human All too Human: A Book for Free Spirits. Translated by Marion Faber, with Stephen Lehman. Lincoln: University of Nebraska Press, 1984.

_____. Twilight of the Idols. Translated by A. Ludovici. 1911.

Nucho, Fuad. Berdyaev's Philosophy: The Existential Paradox ofFreedom and Necessity. Garden City, N.Y.: Anchor Books, 1966.

Ortega y Gassett, José. The Dehumanization of Art. Garden City, N.J.: Doubleday, 1956.

_____. Man and Crisis. New York: W. W. Norton and Co., 1958.

_____. Meditations on Quixote. New York: W. W. Norton and Co., 1961.

Paris, Bernard I. "Notes from the Underground: A Horneyan Analysis." PMLA 88 (1973): 511-22.

Pascal, Pierre. Dostoïevski. Paris-Bruges: Desclée de Brouwer, 1969.

Peyre, Henri. "The French Face of Dostoevski." In Dostoevskiand The Human Condition After A Century, 115-30. Edited by A. Ugrinsky, Frank Lambasa, and Valija Ozolins. New York: Greenwood Press, 1986.

_____. French Literary Imagination and Dostoevsky and OtherEssays. University, Ala.: University of Alabama Press, 1975.

Plato. The Dialogues of Plato, Vol. I. Translated by M. A. Jowett. Oxford: Clarendon Press, 1964.

Poggioli, Renato. The Phoenix and the Spider. Cambridge, Mass.: Harvard University Press, 1957.

Pribic, Rado. "Notes from the Underground: One Hundred Years After the Author's Death." In Dostoevski and the Human Condition after a Century, 71-77. Edited by A. Ugrinsky, Frank Lambasa, and Valija Ozolins. New York: Greenwood Press, 1986.

Proctor, Thelwall. Dostoevskij and The Belinskij School of Literary Criticism. The Hague: Mouton, 1969.

Pushkin, A. S. The Complete Prose Tales of Aleksandr Sergeyevitch Pushkin. Translated by Gillon R. Aitken. New York: Norton and Co., Inc., 1966.

_____. Polnoe sobranie sochinenii v desiati tomakh, Tom. 7, Khudozhestvennaia Proza. Leningrad: Izdatel'stvo Nauka, 1978.

Rahv, Philip. "Dostoevsky in Crime and Punishment." In Dostoevsky: A Collection of Critical Essays. 16-38. Edited by Rene Wellek. Englewood Cliffs, N.J.: Prentice-Hall Inc., 1962.

Reynus, L. M. Dostoevskii v staroi russe. Leningrad: Lenizdat, 1971.

_____. "Prototypes and Heroes of The Brothers Karamazov." In The Brothers Karamazov, 747-51. Norton Critical Edition, edited by Ralph Matlaw. New York: Norton and Co., 1976.

Rice, James L. Dostoevsky and the Healing Art: An Essay in Literary and Medical History. Ann Arbor: Ardis, 1985.

Rice, Martin P. "Current Research in the English Language on Notes." International Dostoevsky Society Bulletin 5 (1975): 24-34.

Ricoeur, Paul. Interpretation Theory. Fort Worth, Texas: Texas Christian University Press, 1976.

Rosen, Nathan. "Style and Structure in The Brothers Karamazov." In The Brothers Karamazov, 841-51. Norton Critical Edition, edited by Ralph Matlaw. New York: Norton and Co., 1976.

Rosenshield, Gary. "Akul'ka: The Incarnation of the Ideal in Dostoevskij's Notes from the House of the Dead." Slavic and East European Journal 31, no. 1 (Spring 1987): 10-19.

_____. "Artistic Consistency in Notes from the Underground-- Part One." In Studies in Honor of Xenia Gasiorowska, 11-21. Edited by Lauren Leighton. Columbus, Ohio: Slavica, 1982.

_____. Crime and Punishment: The Techniques of the OmniscientAuthor. Lisse: Peter de Ridder Press, 1978.

_____. "The Fate of Dostoevskij's Underground Man: The Case for an Open Ending." Slavic and East European Journal 28, no. 3 (Fall 1984): 324-39.

_____. "Rationalism, Motivation and Time in Dostoevsky's Notes." Dostoevsky Studies 3 (1982): 87-100.

_____. "The Realization of the Collective Self: The Rebirth of Religious Autobiography in Dostoevskii's Zapiski iz mertvogo doma." Slavic Review 50, no. 2 (Summer 1991): 317-27.

Ross, Sir Wm. David. Aristotle. London: Methuen; New York: Barnes and Noble, 1964.

Roubiczek, Paul. Existentialism: For and Against. Cambridge: Cambridge University Press, 1964.

Rousseau, Jean-Jacques. A Discourse on Inequality. Translated by Maurice Cranston. Harmondsworth, Middlesex, England; New York: Penguin Books, 1984.

Rozanov, Vasily. Dostoevsky and the Legend of the Grand Inquisitor. Translated by Spencer Roberts. Ithaca, N.Y.: Cornell University Press, 1972.

Sagarin, Edward. Raskolnikov and Others. New York: St. Martin's Press, 1981.

Sajkovic, Miriam. F. M. Dostoevsky: His Image of Man. Philadelphia: University of Pennsylvania Press, 1962.

Sartre, Jean-Paul. Huis clos. Paris: Gallimard, 1945.

_____. La Nausée. Paris: Gallimard, 1938.

_____. Les mains sales. Paris: Gallimard, 1948.

_____. L'Être et le Néant. Paris: Gallimard, 1932.

_____. L'existentialisme est un humanisme. Paris: Gallimard, 1956.

_____. Literature and Existentialism. New York: Citadel Press, 1964.

_____. Situations I. Paris: Gallimard, 1947.

Sarukhanian, Evgenii. Dostoevski v Peterburge. Leningrad: Lenizdat, 1970.

Scheler, Max. Man's Place in Nature. Boston: Meyerhoff, 1961.

Schelling, Friedrich Wilhelm Joseph von. Philosophical Investigations into the Essence of Human Freedom and Related Matters. Translated by Priscilla Hayden-Roy. In Philosophy of German Idealism, Vol. 23, The German Library, edited by Ernst Baylor. New York: Continuum Press, 1987.

_____. System of Transcendental Idealism. Translated by Peter Heath. Charlottesville: University Press of Virginia, 1978.

Screech, M. A. Montaigne and Melancholy: The Wisdom of the Essays. London: Penguin Books, 1983.

Seduro, Vladimir. Dostoevsky in Russian Literary Criticism,1846-1956. New York: Columbia University Press, 1957.

Seliverstov, Iu. O velikom inkvizitore: Dostoevskii i posleduiushchie. Moskva: Molodaia Gvardia, 1992.

Shanskii, N. M. Etimologicheskii Slovar' Russkogo Iazyka. Tom. I, Moskva: Izdatel'stvo Moskovskogo Universiteta, 1968.

Shein, Louis J. "Kantian Elements in Dostoevsky's Ethics." In Western Philosophical Systems in Russian Literature, 59-69. Los Angeles, Calif.: University of Southern California Press, 1979.

Sherbinin, Julie de. "Transcendence through Art: The Convicts Theatricality in Dostoevskij's Zapiski iz mertvogo doma." Slavic and East European Journal 35, no. 3 (Fall 1991): 339-51.

Shestov, Lev. Dostoevsky, Tolstoy and Nietzsche. Translated by Bernard Martin and Spencer Roberts. Columbus, Ohio: Ohio University Press, 1969.

_____. Kierkegaard and Existential Philosophy. Translated by Bernard Martin. Athens, Ohio: Ohio University Press, 1969.

_____. Sur la Balance de Job: Peregrinations à travers les âmes. Paris: Flammarion, 1971.

Shklovskii, Viktor. Za i protiv: Zametki o Dostoevskom. Moskva: Sovetskii Pisatel', 1957.

Shneidman, N. N. Dostoevsky and Suicide. Oakville, Ontario: Mosaic Press, 1984.

Slochower, Harry. "Incest in The Brothers Karamazov." In TheBrothers Karamazov, 821-29. Norton Critical Edition, edited by Ralph Matlaw. New York: Norton and Co., 1976.

Snodgrass, W. D. "Crime and Punishment: The Tenor of Part One," Hudson Review 13, no. 2 (Summer 1960): 202-53.

Solomon, Robert C. The Big Questions: A Short Introduction toPhilosophy. Dan Diego: Harcourt, Brace, Jovanovich Publishers, 1982.

Soloviev, V. S. "Iz rechei v pamiat' Dostoevskogo." In O velikom inkvizitore: Dostoevski i posleduiuschie, 57-71. Moskva: Molodaia Gvardia, 1991.

Solzhenitsyn, Alexander. One Day in the Life of Ivan Denisovich. Translated by Ralph Parker. New York: Dutton, 1963.

Steiner, G. Tolstoy or Dostoevsky. New York: Alfred A. Knopf, 1959.

Stern, Laurent. "Truth in Literature." In Proceedings of TheFifth International Congress of Aesthetics, 337-40. The Hague: Mouton, 1968.

Sternberg, Meir. "Polylingualism as Reality and Translation as Mimesis." Poetics Today 2, no. 4 (1981): 221-39.

Sutherland, Stewart R. "The Philosophical Dimension: Self and Freedom." In New Essays on Dostoevsky, 169-85. Edited by Malcolm Jones and Garth M. Terry. Cambridge: Cambridge University Press, 1983.

Tarkovsky, Andrey. Sculpting in Time. Translated by Kitty Hunter-Blair. Austin: University of Texas Press, 1994.

Terras, Victor. "The Art of Fiction as a Theme in The Brothers Karamazov." In Dostoevsky: New Perspectives, 193-205. Edited by Robert L. Jackson. Englewood Cliffs, N.J.: Prentice-Hall Inc., 1984.

_____. "The Metaphysics of the Novel-Tragedy: Dostoevsky and Viacheslav Ivanov." In Russianness: Studies on a Nation's Identity, In Honor of Rufus Mathewson, 1918-1978, 153-65. Ann Arbor: Ardis, 1990.

_____. "Narrative Structure in The Brothers Karamazov." In Critical Essays on Dostoevsky, 215-23. Edited by Robin Feuer Miller. Boston: G. K. Hall and Co., 1986.

Thurneyesen, Eduard. Dostoievski où les confins de l'homme. (Trad. de l'allemand). Paris: 1934.

Trace, Arther. Furnace of Doubt: Dostoevsky and The Brothers Karamazov. Peru, Ill.: Sherwood Sugden and Co., 1988.

Troyka, Claudia Moscovici. "Faith and Rebellion: The Tragic Poles of Dostoevsky's Theodicy." In Dostoevsky and the XXth Century: The Ljubljana Papers, 119-36. Edited by Malcolm Jones. Nottingham: Astra Press, 1993.

Tschizhevskij, Dmitry. "Schiller and The Brothers Karamazov." In The Brothers Karamazov, 794-807. Norton Critical Edition, edited by Ralph Matlaw. New York: Norton and Co., 1976.

Turgenev, Ivan Sergeyevich. Fathers and Sons. Edited and translated by Michael R. Katz (New York: W. W. Norton, 1996).

_____. Zapiski okhotnika. Chicago: Russian Language Specialties, 1965.

Ugrinsky, Lambasa et al., eds. Dostoevski and the Human Condition after a Century. New York: Greenwood Press, 1986.

Valevicius, Andrius. Lev Shestov and His Times. New York: Peter Lang, 1993.

Varets, M. I. "Zapiski iz mertvogo doma i epizod v romane Voskresenie (po materialam neopublikovannykh rukopisei)." Filologicheskie Nauki 4 (1981): 62-65.

Vetlovskaia, Valentina. "Alyosha Karamazov and the Hagiographic Hero." In Dostoevsky: New Perspectives, 206-26. Edited by Robert L. Jackson. Englewood Cliffs, N.J.: Prentice-Hall Inc., 1984.

_____. Poetika romana "Brat'ia Karamazovy." Leningrad: Izdatel'stvo 'Nauka,' 1977.

_____. "Rhetoric and Poetics: The Affirmation and Refutation of Opinions in Dostoevsky's The Brothers Karamazov." In Critical Essays on Dostoevsky, 223-33. Edited by Robin Feuer Miller. Boston: G. K. Hall and Co., 1986.

Vivas, Eliseo. "The Two Dimensions of Reality in The Brothers Karamazov." In Dostoevsky: A Collection of Critical Essays, 71-89. Edited by Rene Wellek. Englewood Cliffs, N.J.: Prentice-Hall Inc., 1962.

Vogüé, Eugene Marie Melchior, vicomte de. Le Roman Russe. Paris: Plon-Nourrit et Compagnie, 1924.

Voltaire. Candide. In Three Philosophical Voyages. New York: Laurel Language library, 1964.

Ward, Bruce K. "Dostoevsky and the Problem of Meaning in History." In Dostoevsky and the XXth Century: The Ljubljana Papers, 49-65. Edited by Malcolm Jones. Nottingham: Astra Press, 1993.

Wasiolek, Edward. Dostoevsky: The Major Fiction. Cambridge, Mass.: M.I.T. Press, 1964.

_____. "On the Structure of Crime and Punishment." PMLA 74, no. 1 (March 1959): 131-36.

_____. "Raskolnikov's Motives: Love and Murder." In FyodorDostoevsky's Crime and Punishment. Edited by H. Bloom. New York: Chelsea House, 1988.

Wellek, Rene. "Bakhtin's View of Dostoevsky: 'Polyphony' and 'Carnivalesque'." Dostoevsky Studies 1 (1980): 31-39.

_____, ed. Dostoevsky: A Collection of Critical Essays. Englewood Cliffs, N.J.: Prentice-Hall, Inc, 1962.

_____. A History of Modern Criticism: 1750-1950. Volume 2: TheRomantic Age. New Haven and London: Yale University Press, 1955.

Wernick, Robert. "Declaring an Open Season on the Wisdom of the Ages." Smithsonian, May 1997.

Wheeler, Marcus. The Oxford Russian-English Dictionary. General editor, B. O. Unbegaun. 2nd edition. Oxford: Clarendon Press, 1992.

Windelband, Wilhelm. A History of Philosophy. Translated by James Tufts. New York: The Macmillan Co., 1919.

Zander, L. A. Dostoevsky. SCM Press Ltd.: London, 1948.

Zenkovsky, V. V. "Dostoevsky's Religious and Philosophical Views." In Dostoevsky: A Collection of Critical Essays, 130-45. Edited by Rene Wellek. Englewood Cliffs, N.J.: Prentice-Hall Inc., 1962.

_____. A History of Russian Philosophy. (Vols. I and II.) Translated by George Kline. New York: Columbia University Press, 1953.

Printed in the USA
CPSIA information can be obtained
at www.ICGtesting.com
LVHW090310060923
757301LV00002B/142